AF615427

MAN-COMPUTER PROBLEM SOLVING

MAN-COMPUTER PROBLEM SOLVING

EXPERIMENTAL EVALUATION OF TIME-SHARING AND BATCH PROCESSING

BY
HAROLD SACKMAN

AUERBACH Publishers Inc.

Princeton New York Philadelphia London

Library of Congress Catalog Card Number: 79-124632
Standard Book Number: 87769-050-2

First Printing

Printed in the United States of America

CONTENTS

PART IV: EPILOGUE

LIST OF FIGURES

LIST OF TABLES

PREFACE

THIS book is concerned with the growing experimental evidence on man-computer problem solving, particularly in the competition between time-sharing and batch-processing computer systems. The concept for the book emerged in response to strong and continued demand from the computer world, and from users in related scientific, educational, and technological areas as well, for scientific data on the dynamics of man-computer problem solving and on the associated comparative merits of time-sharing and batch systems.

When time-sharing was first pioneered in the early 1960's, the initial controversy between online and offline systems was a speculative, armchair affair, marked by partisan heat rather than scientific light. This predisciplinary controversy gave way to applied scientific studies as soon as significant experimental data became available. Since investments in computer systems run into billions of dollars, and since the annual gross product of computer goods and services is at the 10 billion dollar level, the interest in comparative experimental findings on man-machine effectiveness between online and offline systems has become intense.

The author—who has worked in this field since the emergence of the first real time command and control systems in the mid-1950's—received many requests for available publications, talks, and specially written papers on different aspects of the comparative cost-effectiveness of online and offline (time-sharing vs. batch) problem solving. Inquiries have come from government agencies, universities, commercial computing centers, engineering and computing groups, large and small business firms, professional and trade journals, and from individuals in the United States and abroad. With the conclusion of his most recent and comprehensive research in this area, a large-scale study at the United States Air Force Academy, it became clear that the dispersed research had reached the point where it should be brought together and integrated into book form for the convenience of all interested parties. The book thus includes all relevant research to date on man-machine cost-effectiveness for man-computer problem solving in time-sharing and batch processing—its early development, method and findings, limitations, and prospects.

The orientation of the book and its organization follow established scientific guidelines. Relevant literature is reviewed, hypotheses are operationally formulated, methodology is carefully described, quantitative procedures are made explicit, empirical results are presented in detail, and interpretations are tied to statistical findings. The more technical aspects are explained for the lay reader as they occur.

The focal audience is the computer world—managers, programmers, systems analysts and users of computers in government, education, scientific, engineering, and business applications. This audience is expected to grow with the steady extension of computers throughout society, and with the imminent rise of mass information utilities. The experimental orientation of this book should make it especially useful to the various scientific disciplines that have some stake in man-computer problem solving and the online/offline controversy. These include the computer and information sciences, engineering and operations research, management science, and, for human creativity and problem-solving in a computerized milieu, the social sciences.

The book is divided into four parts. Part I essentially consists of an introduction to time-sharing and batch processing, the historical background of the scientific study of the human use of computers, and summary accounts of exploratory online/offline studies that preceded the comprehensive studies described in Parts II and III.

Part II covers the collaborative work of the author and M. Gold, based on follow-on analyses of the extensive data from Gold's original doctoral dissertation at Massachusetts Institute of Technology. The original and the follow-on studies represent a breakthrough in the field; they cover numerous performance variables for an open-end problem which permits measurement of the excellence of the solution. The reported study was jointly sponsored by System Development Corporation and Carnegie-Mellon Institute.

Part III is concerned with the largest and most comprehensive online/offline study of man-computer problem solving to date. It was conducted by the author on a sample of 415 cadets at the Air Force Academy. This experiment was performed under the joint auspices of System Development Corporation and the United States Air Force Academy to test the effectiveness of time-sharing and batch processing in teaching introductory computer science, and to gain new insight into leading issues on the dynamics of man-computer problem solving. A wealth of new data and new hypothesis was generated by this recent study, which is described in Part III.

The epilogue, Part IV, was designed to pull together and summarize the various strands of research on man-computer problem solving under online and offline conditions as reported in this book. Special emphasis is placed on the interface between these online/offline studies and the mainstream of the behavioral literature on human problem-solving in such areas as: massed vs. spaced learning, insight vs. trial and error, and the structure of human skills and traits in man-computer communication. The book concludes with a preview of mass computer utilities, and a plea for cooperative interdisciplinary research on experimental community prototypes to meet the challenge of the public interest in the computer-serviced society of the future.

I am deeply indebted to System Development Corporation which has generously provided funds and resources in supporting various studies reported in this book and in the preparation of the manuscript. In particular, I am most grateful to Kenneth W. Yarnold and Lorimer F. McConnell for their administrative support, and to Clark Weissman for his technical support. I owe a major intellectual debt to Dr. Michael M. Gold whose influence is manifest throughout this book, particularly in the collaborative study we performed, as reported in Part II.

The author would like to thank Colonel Roger R. Bate and

Lieutenant Colonel Monti D. Callero for their authorization and support of the reported experiment at the Air Force Academy. I am especially grateful for the steadfast cooperation of instructors and cadets throughout all phases of the pilot study and the main experiment. Special thanks are owed to Captain Duane A. Adams who educated the author in the ways of the Academy, provided extensive administrative and technical support throughout the design and implementation of the study, and contributed to the interpretation of the results. I would like to thank Dr. Lee S. Christie of System Development Corporation for urging me to become involved in this project, and also Dr. Miles S. Rogers there for statistical services.

I owe a continuing debt to Catherine E. Perrone for her endless pursuit of secretarial excellence, not only for all phases of the manuscript, but also for the main studies reported in this book. In closing, I must express my affectionate appreciation to my wife Kathleen, and my children, Jeffry, Sharon, and Amy for their patience and forbearance over the demanding course of work that made this book possible.

PART I

THE EXPERIMENTAL CHALLENGE

1

THE EXPERIMENTAL LAG IN MAN-COMPUTER COMMUNICATION

1.1 INTRODUCTION

MUCH has been written about the enhancement of human intelligence through the aid of computers. Elysian visions have been projected portraying man attended by his computerized robots, living the good life with boundless leisure to pursue his creative bent. A few, such as Wiener (1964), have been alarmed by humanistic neglect in the development of computerized systems, and they have warned us that human responsibilities will grow more difficult and more complex, that the enormity of the challenge for the "human use of human beings" could eventually overwhelm humanity.

Although the enhancement of the human intellect with computers has been the subject of much speculation, remarkably little solid scientific work has been done in man-computer problem-solving. The humanistic lag in the application of computers to social affairs goes hand in hand with the experimental lag in man-computer communication. This chapter outlines the scope and nature of this unfortunate situation. Succeeding chapters review and evaluate the significant studies that have been done to date and spell out leading implications for future scientific work.

Primary emphasis is placed on comparative evaluation of

man-computer effectiveness. In the contemporary context, this comparison is typically between the two generic types of computer systems—time-shared (online) systems and batch-processing (offline) systems. As the subtitle of this book indicates, a central goal is to bring together the key experimental work comparing man-computer problem-solving under online and offline settings. An awareness of the historical background of computer system development, the paucity of experimental studies in man-computer communication, and the leading findings of available studies are needed to appreciate the challenge of the scientific task that lies ahead.

1.2 HISTORICAL ROOTS

The current status of user studies stems from the professional mix that originally developed and used the technology of man-computer communications. The first developers and users were the mathematicians, engineers, and "hard" scientists who pioneered electronic digital computers. The initial World War II applications were laborious and time-consuming mathematical problems, such as computations of ballistic trajectories and analytic problems concerning atomic reactions. Industrial applications were highly specialized, as in digital switching devices for telephone communications, or in process control industries such as petro-chemicals and food processing. Man-computer communication consisted of formulating problems, designing computerized solutions, wiring computers, feeding them with punched-card inputs, and printing outputs such as mathematical tables.

These early man-computer communications—essentially envisioned in much the same form by Babbage a century earlier—were closely tied to the constraints of machine circuitry, and were tightly bound to logical and mathematical symbology. Computer languages were conceived and used by small coteries of specialists, and they were not designed or intended for widespread use. The immediate users were professionally trained in the symbolic tools of their trade, and the small number of computers and computer users made for intimate, person-to-person working relations. The die was cast; the ensuing history of man-computer communications has largely been, and will continue to be, an attempt to move from esoteric symbology toward natural language.

The development of the stored-program computer in the late 1940's made possible the incorporation of instruction sets in computer circuitry and internal storage of operating programs. Commercial electronic computers appeared on the open market in the early 1950's and the first large-scale real-time system was developed for military command and control in air defense (SAGE, for Semi-Automatic Ground Environment). These rapid extensions of computers into military and commercial areas could not be serviced by the small numbers of engineers, scientists, and mathematicians who were able to communicate with computers, and who had other jobs to perform. A division of labor took place, and the professional programmer appeared, in exponentially growing numbers, to translate verbal specifications into workable computer language. The trend in man-computer communication was from part-time specialists, such as engineers and mathematicians, to full-time specialists who were exclusively concerned with the bread-and-butter activities of coding, debugging, and maintaining programs. Thus, the initial tradition of specialization and esoteric computer languages was maintained for another decade.

In response to mounting pressure to provide more programs for more computing applications, programmer indoctrination was typically kept at the bare essentials of mastering machine code and learning debugging fundamentals. Familiarity with users and knowledge of computer program applications was acquired on the job in a haphazard manner, largely in the production of workable machine code. Programmers selected and trained under these conditions had little exposure to and almost no tolerance toward human-engineered programs or user-oriented program products. Such programmers tended to view accommodations for users as costly and disconcerting in the larger and more urgent business of building programs and making them work within limited resources and tight schedules.

The first major breakthrough in interactive man-computer communications occurred in real-time military command and control systems. In SAGE, military operators had consoles equipped with alphanumeric keyboards and verbally tagged dials and switches for composing and sending messages to the central computer. The consoles had two types of cathode ray tube displays, and they were equipped with a light gun in conjunction with switch actions to select and control displayed information. The console had to be designed to permit the average enlisted man to master its operation. Even though a wealth of empirical data was ground out every day in SAGE operations, very little was experimentally systematized and organized for the computer science community—for a variety of reasons, including military security, proprietary industrial information, and an effective lack of appropriately trained human engineers and social scientists who had access to SAGE man-computer communications. (The author has attempted to salvage a substantive portion of the SAGE heritage in an earlier book, 1967.)

Consider, now, the user tradition developed by these historical trends. For two critical, formative decades, the 1940's and the 1950's, comprising the birth and development of electronic digital computers, the social scientists, human engineers, and human factors specialists—the persons professionally trained to work with human subjects under experimental conditions—were only indirectly concerned with man-computer communications, largely with knobs, buttons, and dials rather than at the interactive problem-solving level of the user. In all fairness, there were some exceptions to this rule, but they were too few and too sporadic to make a significant and lasting impact on the mainstream of user development. Since there was, in effect, an applied scientific vacuum surrounding man-computer communication, it is not at all surprising that no significant, cumulative experimental tradition exists for testing and evaluating user performance.

With the advent of the 1960's, the progressive increase in computer speed and storage spurred the development of higher-order, "conversational" computer languages and time-sharing systems. The relatively monolithic computer software culture of the 1950's was transformed into the pluralistic pattern of computer applications today, with the promise of greater diversification in the 1970's.

What does this all add up to? After a human generation of

uninterrupted computer development, we now find a vast gap between the ubiquitous promises made for "user-oriented" computerized systems of every conceivable kind, and the sobering scientific work on user performance that is needed to back up exaggerated claims. In the absence of sustained, responsible criticism from scientific quarters in the computer science literature, and with long standing support from computer system managers, it is the hawker of computerized wares rather than the scientist who talks most and loudest about user performance in the public forum.

The above historical portrait of the user problem in man-computer communication has been sketched on an impressionistic canvas. The problem and its roots are obviously far more complex than this simplified outline indicates. Controversial allegations have been made which have not been proved. The remainder of this chapter looks at the record of man-computer communication in greater detail and from a variety of viewpoints to test these allegations.

1.3 THE CONFRONTATION BETWEEN BATCH PROCESSING AND TIME-SHARING

The batch or offline system is the evolutionary predecessor of time-sharing and is the operational workhorse of most contemporary data processing. In batch processing, jobs are stacked and done one at a time on a waiting-line basis. Programmers typically have only indirect contact with the computer, and in conventional batch systems turnaround time (the interval between submission and completion of a computer job) usually takes hours or days. Proponents of offline systems argue that throughput time (useful computations per unit time) is at a maximum in batch processing with minimum waste of computer resources.

By contrast, in time-sharing the user has direct access to the central computer; he shares the computer facility simultaneously with other users who are a more or less random and changing collection of people at any point in time; typically, but not necessarily, users work on unrelated tasks with different programs; they enter and leave the system independently of one another, and use their terminals for varying and largely unpredictable periods of time. Such use approaches that of a public utility, roughly analogous to the quasi-random pattern of telephone traffic.

According to time-sharing advocates (see, for example, Corbató, Merwin-Daggett, and Daley, 1962, Schwartz, Coffman, and Weissman, 1964; and Shaw, 1964) the user has fast and direct access to the computer when he wants it (provided that guaranteed access is available); for many types of jobs he can get what he wants in minutes rather than hours or days; he may exert continual online control over his program, and he is free to change his mind and do things differently as he interacts with the computer. Time-sharing means expense-sharing among a large number of subscribers with reduced costs for many applications; and time-sharing permits direct man-computer communication in languages that are beginning to approach natural language, at a pace approaching human conversation, and in some applications, at graded difficulty levels appropriate to the skill and experience of the user.

The critics of time-sharing point to higher costs and lower machine efficiency in time-sharing, contrasted with impressive advances in job shop scheduling, mass servicing of users, and faster turnaround in the latest batch systems (for example, see Emerson, 1965; Macdonald, 1965; Patrick, 1963; and Lynch, 1967). Time-sharing advocates respond by emphasizing the compensatory savings in human time for online operations, the convenience to the user, and more rapid program development. The critics counter by insisting that users develop lazy and careless attitudes under time-sharing by going to the computer with poorly designed and untested programs in an effort to trade off computer time for human time.

The online/offline controversy is a gargantuan contest to dominate the multibillion dollar software industry. This competition has major implications for a much larger future industry with the imminent rise of computer utilities for the general public. Here, then, we have pressing and far-reaching confrontation between two generic types of computer systems, a contest in which the human factor increasingly plays the dominant role. Which type of man-computer communication is better? In what respects is it better, by how much, and under what conditions? These are applied scientific questions best solved by system test and evaluation under appropriate experimental controls.

1.4 THE EXPERIMENTAL VACUUM

In the review articles on man-computer performance cited below, innovation and unverified application outrace experimental evaluation on all sides. For example, in a review of man-computer communication, Ruth Davis (1966) pointed out that virtually no experimental work had been done on user effectiveness. She characterized the status of user statistics as inadequate and "primitive," and she urged the specification and development of extensive measures of user performance.

In an analysis of human interactions for time-shared systems, Mitnick (1965) reviewed a variety of psychological factors bearing on user performance. These included language, timing, reinforcement, and training characteristics. He pointed to the lack of experimental work on human behavior in a time-shared setting and the need for extensive experimental validation to determine factors and conditions that contribute most toward enhanced human performance.

Pollack and Gildner (1963) reviewed the literature on user performance with manual input devices for man-computer communication. Their extensive survey, covering large numbers and varieties of switches, pushbuttons, keyboards, and encoders, revealed "inadequate research data establishing performance for various devices and device characteristics, and incomplete specification of operator input tasks in existing systems." There was a vast experimental gap between the literally hundreds of manual input devices surveyed and the very small subset of such devices certified by some form of user validation. They recommended an initial program of research on leading types of task/device couplings, and on newer and more natural modes of manual inputs such as speech and handwriting.

In an extensive review of human factors problems in graphic displays for man-computer communication, Barmack and Sinaiko

(1966) arrived at similar conclusions. Their review covered various types of keyboards, cathode ray tubes, display codes, light pens, switches, and pushbuttons. Innovation studies were rampant; evaluation of user effectiveness was virtually nonexistent.

Barmack and Sinaiko made extensive recommendations for further research on human performance with computer-aided graphics, many of which are pertinent to this review. These are briefly listed.

- For displays, empirical data on representative user populations were recommended—research that would make possible a display designer's handbook.
- New, computer-oriented research was stressed since traditional human engineering data on non-computerized displays was considered inadequate by these authors for the requirements of computer-driven displays.
- Performance measures should include speed and accuracy of typing, block printing, script writing, and effectiveness in pointing to data—in conjunction with measurement of training time and effort to achieve desirable levels of performance.
- Alternative user input methods should be experimentally evaluated for solving standard problems. The results of such tests would indicate which types of problems are optimal for particular types of manual inputs.
- Principles and procedures for developing instructional systems for indoctrinating new users were also recommended, based on cumulative empirical data from user performance.

Various experimental recommendations stemmed from Barmack and Sinaiko's analysis of creative work and its relation to computer-aided innovation. Although in management, educational, and other user communities there is great interest in the potential of computers for enhancing creative effort, virtually no experimental evidence is available to determine whether current systems facilitate or hinder the development of new ideas. Barmack and Sinaiko urged that detailed case histories on the problem-solving process be conducted to assess the extent to which interactive computer-aided graphics furthers the development of significant ideas, particularly in early, formulative stages.

1.5 RELATED BEHAVIORAL RESEARCH

Related behavioral research is briefly reviewed in this concluding section. This research illustrates some aspects of the dynamics of human communication and problem-solving that may have a significant impact on the future design of man-computer networks. Unfortunately, cross-fertilization between the behavioral sciences and the computer sciences is still in its infancy, and the examples cited are, at best, suggestive. I am indebted to Gold's dissertation (1967) for some of the material in this initial survey of related behavioral research.

Although the theoretical and empirical work described below concentrates primarily on intergroup relationships between the parties when both are human, the extension of these findings to the circumstance in which one party is a computer appears reasonable. Whether the member of a group is a person or an interactive computer, the behavior of the other group members might reveal useful similarity. In fact, some of the research into computer-aided instruction reported below indicates that not only can the computer do a better job than the human it replaces, but it also may be more highly regarded by the persons interacting with it.

Leavitt (1958), using Bavelas' communication networks, found that there is reason to believe that "two-way communication is more accurate than one-way. . . ." In related research extending this work, Cohen (1964) found that a group with a centralized communications system took less time and made more correct trials, fewer changes, and fewer final errors than a group with a less centralized communication pattern. In addition, the member of the centralized communication group who was responsible for coordination of communication and interaction had a higher level of satisfaction than either the other members of his group or the members of the other group. In a study measuring physical rather than psychological distance between people, Festinger found a positive relationship between physical distance for persons and sociometric choice (Festinger, Schachter, and Back, 1950).

These findings seem to provide support for the proposition that direct interaction with a computer—available with a time-shared computer system—is likely to result in higher levels of accuracy and performance, in a shorter amount of time, than would a non-interactive computer system. Further, we might expect a higher level of satisfaction when the subject interacts directly with the computer.

Several studies comparing the use of interactive computers with the more traditional method of teaching seem to provide support for these conclusions. Bilzer and Easley (1962) compared the results of using a computer to give students regular classroom instruction. They found the time spent on the lesson material was significantly less for the students using the computer. However, there appeared to be no measurable difference in final performance for the two groups of students. In a similar experiment, Porter (1959) found that students taught spelling via teaching machines performed significantly better than students exposed to regular classroom instruction.

There are several studies which indicate that students react more favorably to machine teaching than to standard classroom instructional methods. In one, Holland (1960) studied students after completion of a one-semester course in psychology. The students were overwhelmingly in favor of the teaching machines and stated that: 1) they would have have gotten less from the course if the machine had not been used; 2) they learned more on the machine than they would have had they only studied the text, given equal amounts of time and effort; and 3) they would prefer to use the machine for another similar course.

A word of caution is in order on the apparent bandwagon effect for machine teaching. Unlike the computer sciences, the educational field has had a long tradition in experimental testing of human performance. With the advent of computer-assisted instruction (CAI), many traditional educational problems were transferred to the computerized setting, such as: forced pacing vs. self-pacing; comparisons of CAI, lecture methods and noncomputerized programmed instruction; massed vs. spaced learning; multiple-choice vs. constructed response modes; comparisons between different programmed instruction procedures for step size, sequencing, and branching; comparisons between various reinforcement schedules and prompting techniques; graphic versus symbolic displays, and comparisons among various types of audiovisual presentations. The list of experimental problems can be extended almost indefinitely. There is a vast experimental literature on educational performance and much of it overlaps and interpenetrates the mounting literature on computer-aided performance as automation grows and proliferates in the educational setting.

Although many experiments show a superiority of some form of CAI over a presumably comparable traditional educational technique, the cost of developing, installing and maintaining CAI software may be prohibitive, it is frequently not mentioned, it is often deliberately withheld as proprietary information, or it may be misleadingly reported at an excessively low figure if a commercial interest is at stake. Although effectiveness data may be accurately presented, cost data are often unreliable, and objective cost-effectiveness comparisons cannot be made.

A related factor is that the lion's share of the experimenter's time and attention is devoted to the innovative computerized method, whereas the traditional method gets perfunctory treatment—often resulting in a Hawthorne effect (Roethlisberger and Dickson, 1939), for the computerized version, and a negative bias for the conventional method. Objective experimental comparisons of user performance in computer-based educational methods require *cost*-effective experimental designs. Standardized software accounting procedures, such as those proposed by Weinwurm (1965), should be adapted to educational use to facilitate more meaningful comparison between different forms of computerized educational services.

Turning to community considerations, some evidence for the long-range social effects of a close-knit community of computer users has been described by Fano and Corbató (1966). Their observations stemmed from Project MAC experience at Massachusetts Institute of Technology. They chose to compare this system to a growing organism—as opposed to a chance collection of changing, independent users—primarily because of the increasing tendency for users to employ one another's files, programs, and techniques. The users have "taken over" in the sense that they create and produce their own programs. Most programs have been written by users rather than by professional programmers responsible for designing, implementing, and maintaining the central system. The users have organized their own "editorial board" to decide upon new commands to be incorporated into the system and they serve as referees for information to be stored in public files.

Real-time, joint problem-solving was starting to take place between users at different stations working with the same programs and data base, as with students and teachers, and with members of a research team. Fano and Corbató predicted that communities of organizational users in time-shared systems may evolve into closely knit real-time systems. This observation suggests a possible major evolutionary pattern for time-shared systems—a trend moving from individual, online problem-solving, to real-time, cooperative control.

The historical context, as developed in this initial chapter, reveals a general picture painted in bleak overtones from the user's point of view: computers were originally designed for highly specialized users employing esoteric and difficult languages for man-computer communication; narrow technical considerations and immediate cost constraints dominated computer technology, in large part at the expense of human ease, convenience, and social effectiveness; computer system professionals were not equipped or trained to measure and test human performance in computer-aided systems, and an endemic experimental lag has grown between computer applications and verified knowledge of user performance; the time-sharing systems which appeared in the 1960's have inherited and compounded user problems during this decade; and, with the prospect of public information utilities developing in the 1970's, the user is the forgotten man, and the general public stands to suffer in the long run from the pervasive experimental and humanistic lag in information services.

2

PORTRAIT OF THE COMPUTER USER

THE remaining chapters in Part I are concerned with initial, exploratory studies of online/offline man-computer effectiveness. These studies may be subdivided into those dealing with all types of users (the user community) and those primarily concerned with programmers. Accordingly, the general user is the subject of this chapter and programmer studies are covered in the next chapter.

In this chapter we encounter some hard empirical data bearing on system and user performance. All of the cited studies were performed on pioneering, first-generation time-sharing systems. In breaking new ground, these forerunners of computing utilities had to develop empirical statistics for user traffic, central system accounting, and for the development of more efficient scheduling procedures. This effort led to simulation and recording techniques to time and measure various characteristics of users and the central system. The main findings of studies on user statistics are reviewed. Early studies on individual and organizational user attitudes are also reviewed to round out this preliminary portrait of the computer user.

2.1 USER STATISTICS IN TIME-SHARING

The leading studies from which these data were gathered include Scherr (1967) and Raynaud (1967) at Massachusetts Institute of Technology using the Compatible Time-Sharing System (CTSS); Totschek (1965) and McIsaac (1966) using the System Development Corporation (SDC) Time-Sharing System (TSS); and Shaw (1965) and Bryan (1967) at RAND with the Johnniac Open-Shop System (JOSS). To keep the review within manageable bounds, none of these systems are described in any detail here. The reader is referred to the numerous publications in the literature (including the articles cited). Parkhill's book on the computer utility (1966) is a useful single source containing comparative descriptions of these and early commercial time-sharing systems.

The data on JOSS is reproduced in Table 2.1 from Shaw (1965). The JOSS data refer to a 40-hour sample, from 10 AM to 6 PM over one week. Table 2.1 is a simple, descriptive introduction to user activity in time-sharing. Some basic user characteristics in time-sharing may be readily observed.

Table 2.1. EARLY USER STATISTICS ON JOSS (from Shaw, 1965)

- JOSS worked for 77 different users in one week.
- On the average day, 31 users conducted 49 sessions.
- The sessions averaged 58 minutes, with 50% less than 35 minutes.
- The system was saturated with 8 users 18% of the time, and 4% of the time someone was waiting in the queue.
- There were 5.7 simultaneous users, on the average.
- The input rate was 1.9 lines per minute per user. The output rate was 3.9 lines per minute per user. That is, a line of input or output every 10 seconds for every user.

The median time spent by a user at a console at one sitting is roughly half an hour, and most users interacted with JOSS for only one console session during the day. The frequency distribution is positively skewed since the mean user session is almost one hour. For RAND users (primarily in scientific and technical areas), the total input/output (I/O) conversational rate averages out to one line every 10 seconds, and the mean computer output is twice as large as the input. The other figures are more or less unique to the JOSS facility and its working capacity.

In a more recent study on JOSS, Bryan (1967) confirmed most of the above statistics and provided some further useful information. For example, mean user program size was 650 words with the median at 200 words. Of particular interest is the "typical" profile for a complete user cycle from one message to the next. "Typical" is interpreted as median rather than as mean values because of the large positive skew created by the small proportion of very long user cycles. The typical JOSS user (for the PDP-6 computer version in operation in 1966) inserts new commands at a median rate of once every 11 seconds. After he completes his message and strikes the carriage return key at his terminal, it takes about 2 seconds for the computer to respond and complete the typed output. Control of the keyboard is then returned to the user who then spends some 9 seconds "thinking" about his next command and typing it out. The new cycle starts at the end of his message when he strikes the carriage return. In contrast, the *average* user cycle is 34 seconds, broken down into approximately 10 seconds for computer response and completed output, and 24 seconds for user thinking and typing.

Before considering the next study, it is of interest to note an important difference in the work pattern between human operators in dedicated real-time systems as contrasted with users of time-shared systems. In real-time command and control systems such as SAGE, the military operator usully works full-time at his console, monitoring and responding to the changing air defense situation. In online reservation systems such as American Airlines SABRE and in outline banking systems, the agent or teller continually interacts with the central computer throughout his working day. In contrast to such full-time interaction in real-time systems, the time-sharing user is not permanently stationed at a console, and he uses the facility only when he has a need for such use. Programmers, who are probably the most frequent and intensive users of time-shared facilities, spend most of their working time away from the interactive terminal, except for relatively short periods requiring man-computer interaction. This difference in user patterns between dedicated real-time systems and more general-purpose time-shared systems should be appreciated at the outset: the total time-and-motion, problem-solving behavior of the time-sharing user is characterized by "manual" activities most of the time and by interactive communication with the computer for only a comparatively small proportion of total working time.

Scherr (1967) has provided extensive data on Project MAC at MIT for some 300 users with 112 hours of system operation for approximately 80,000 user commands over a three-month period. About 10% of the usage was attributed to staff programmers with the remainder utilized by research-oriented personnel on a variety of projects involving the many disciplines serviced by Project MAC in the university setting. His study was written primarily from the central system rather than the user's point of view.

Table 2.2 lists key empirical finding in Scherr's study. "N" represents sample size, and "SD" is the standard deviation. Each of the variables in this table requires some explanation, since time-sharing terminology varies between facilities and among authors. A user cycle is described as: thinking time, typing input, and waiting for the completed computer system response. See Figure 2.1, taken from Scherr, for the elements comprising a typical man-computer message cycle. "Thinking" time as used in Table 2.2 is essentially the interval between program output and the next user input, shown as "input wait" time in Figure 2.1. Processor Time per Interaction refers to central computing time required for a completed response to an input command; it is the sum of the computer time slices for servicing the user's request. Interactions per Command refers to the number of times the user's program is serviced, that is, the number of round robins through all active users that are necessary to produce the completed output for each input command. Program Size refers to the length of the user's program in machine words.

Although Scherr did not provide statistics for a complete user cycle at any one point, he did provide pieces in separate con-

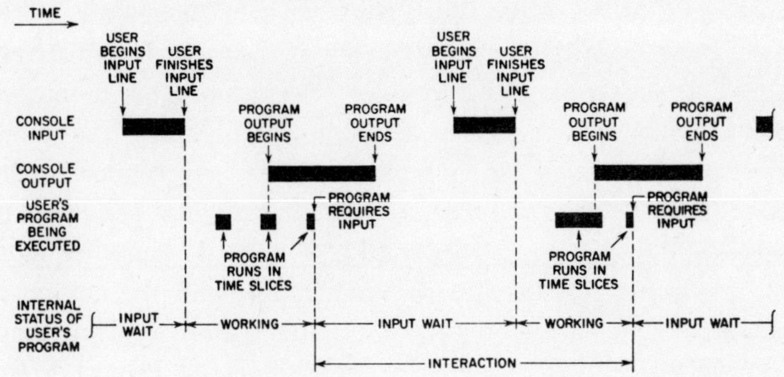

Figure 2.1. MAN-COMPUTER INTERACTION IN THE MAC TIME-SHARING SYSTEM (FROM SCHERR, 1967)

texts that presumably add up to the complete cycle. These "pieces" are apparently as follows. It took the user an average of some 35 seconds (Table 2.2) to "think" or decide what he wants to tell the computer. He then typed his input command. Next, he waited an average of about 7 seconds for the system response (estimated for 25 simultaneously active users, higher for more users). During this waiting period, the central processor cycled through an average of 2.8 time slices (Table 2.2) to respond to the input command. For most users, only a small fraction of a second of computer running time was consumed to process the command and produce the typed output. Note that these figures are fairly similar to JOSS user data previously reviewed.

Table 2.2 makes it clear that user performance is characterized more by variability than by central tendency. As with RAND JOSS statistics, mean values are much larger than median values for "thinking" time and processor time, standard deviations are comparatively large, and the frequency distributions are strongly skewed. User programs are typically small—Table 2.2 shows a median value of 1,500 machine instructions—but, here too, there is considerable variation.

System saturation, a central problem in time-sharing systems, is discussed from two approaches. A simple approach, as Scherr suggests, is to calculate the quotient between average "think" time and the sum of mean processor time and mean swap time—(35.2)

Table 2.2. PROJECT MAC USER STATISTICS (from Scherr, 1967)

Variable	Mean	Median	SD	N
"Thinking" Time (sec.)	35.2	11.0	23.0	238,308
Processor Time per Interaction (sec.)	.88	>.05	.7	237,645
Interactions per Command	2.8	2.0	—	84,697
Program Size (words)	6.3K	1.5K	9.0K	37,632

/(.88+.56) for Project MAC data. This ratio results in a saturation point of 24.4 users; that is, if each user, on the average, needs about 1½ seconds of machine time for every 35 seconds of "thinking" time, then there is room for about 24 users before the system becomes "saturated." The system load imposed by additional users would stretch system response time out past the saturation point by forcing all users to wait longer, presumably without any productive thinking going on. This scheme has some merit, basing system capacity on empirical measurement of user behavior. But it begs the question of system capacity because it is exclusively concerned with the efficiency of machine system throughput, and overlooks the more fundamental question of the empirical effectiveness of user performance.

The second approach to system saturation mentioned by Scherr is user evaluation of system response time, the time between a user's input command and the completed computer response at his console. Scherr reports that the number of users was varied, and that user reaction was somehow obtained and balanced against system efficiency. The upshot of this trial-and-error technique was that the maximum acceptable number of users was 30, associated with a system response time of about 10 seconds. This approach raises the whole issue of user opinion, an issue that is consistently treated in the technical time-sharing literature as a nuisance factor to be dispensed with by subjective commentary rather than as an object of scientific study in its own right.

Scherr indicated that under the saturation condition with 30 users, CPU utilization for serving users was 61%, and that drum and disk swap time was 10% and 29%, respectively. These estimates were considered roughly comparable to the efficiency of conventional batch processing with the same computer.

Some discussion was devoted to recording and reduction techniques that were employed to obtain user data. The recording routines were located within the time-sharing scheduling algorithm which already possessed the appropriate timing characteristics to extract the required system data. In addition, the reduction of raw data into desired tabular form was accomplished online, at trivial cost in terms of central processor, or CPU, time, and with relatively low core storage requirements (2000_{10} locations). The moral of this methodology is that considerable data may be directly collected and reduced online from users, with minimal cost and disruption to the operation of the central system.

Scherr also indicated that comparatively simple simulations of user timing characteristics could be constructed from statistical characteristics of the data, providing a close fit in simulated runs against empirical user performance. He considered this finding "the most important result of the research in this report." This use of parsimonious rather than elaborate simulation, and the verification testing of models against real data reflect sensible and practical approaches that should be applied more extensively in this field.

Scherr's work is a valuable ground-breaking contribution to the study of user behavior in time-sharing systems. Although the emphasis was primarily on system scheduling and machine efficiency, rather than on user behavior, it nevertheless provided extensive empirical data on some fundamental timing relationships between users and the central system.

The remaining two studies on user statistics were conducted at SDC. The first was reported by Totschek (1965) and the second by McIsaac (1966). Both studies were primarily concerned with improving central system scheduling from empirical measurement of time-sharing utilization at TSS.

Totschek's study was essentially a statistical compilation and analysis of central system timing characteristics relative to user requests, based on 13 samples of one hour per sample, recorded early in 1965. The sampling plan took four factors into account—location of user, day of week, time of day, and security classification of system operation. Although the sampling plan could not be implemented in its entirety, the final sample represented most combinations of these variables.

The terminology is different from the MIT and RAND studies. For example, the interval between the last computer response and the insertion of the next input by the user, is referred to as "thinking time" by Scherr, and as "interarrival time" by Totschek. Similarly, the system response time to the user's request—the interval between the command input and the computer response—is described as "request elapsed time" by Totschek, and as "response time" by Scherr. Other variables are not only labeled differently, but are defined differently, which makes comparisons more difficult and ambiguous.

Unlike Scherr, the recording technique reported by Totschek consumed a substantial amount of total system time, averaging close to 10% of total computer time for the 13 samples. This inefficiency could not be avoided because of space limitations in interfacing the recording routines with the time-sharing executive system. In contrast to Scherr's online data reduction, user data was transferred to magnetic tape as it was collected and was later reduced offline.

Recording design has received little attention in the computer literature. Too often recording is grafted onto the system after all other software components have been designed and produced, as a kind of afterthought. If user performance studies are to be pursued systematically, the various tradeoffs between continuous, sampled, or mixed recording, between online vs. offline data reduction, and between minimal accounting information and detailed user performance characteristics—to mention but a few considerations—have to be weighed against the objectives of user research and expected system costs early in system design.

Totschek presented some valuable normative data on user characteristics. For example, the number of simultaneous users was normally distributed, with a mean of 11.7 and a standard deviation of 4.0. (Scherr also reported day-to-day stability in system usage.) The average time spent by a user at a console was about 25 minutes, with a standard deviation of roughly 25 minutes, indicating great variability and a positively skewed distribution in console time. However, the relatively short one-hour samples biased these results by precluding measurement of longer console sessions.

Mean job size was 25,000 instructions, with a median at 24,000, in contrast to much smaller typical jobs reported in the MIT and RAND studies. This difference in comparative job size may be related to differences in types of users in the two systems. For example, Project MAC has comparatively more student users and nonprogrammer users than TSS, and these users are more likely to employ smaller programs.

System capacity was treated by Totschek as an analytical problem in machine efficiency with respect to a generalized user. As with Scherr, no consideration was given to differential user performance effectiveness. Human behavior in time-sharing was briefly described in the summary as an unpredictable "sociological" consideration and that was the end of it. This attitude is characteristic of the user avoidance syndrome found in the literature on time-sharing system design, although, in all fairness, Totschek's study was primarily concerned with system scheduling rather than user characteristics. Totschek did mention that the frequency distributions for most measures in his study were positively skewed, suggesting that they were probably composites of different types of jobs and user requests, and that these elements should be analyzed into their key components in future work.

McIsaac's paper (1966) on TSS user statistics is the first that made some attempt to compare empirical data on users for different time-sharing systems. McIsaac described central objectives of time-sharing systems—fast system response time for the user is primary, and efficiency of machine throughput is secondary. As in the other studies, the nature and determination of optimal system response time and its relation to user performance was left in limbo, propped up by the tacit understanding that a faster system is, ipso facto, a better system.

McIsaac's user data were collected in 1966, and included a total sample of approximately 30,000 user requests. The sampling plan incorporated continuous recording over a five to seven hour period each day for several days. This procedure permitted a more complete picture of individual user characteristics than the one-hour samples used to Totschek's study. Key measures included service time, input/output times, interarrival times, request elapsed times, and some characteristics of individual jobs (see Figure 2.2 from McIsaac for a description of these measures).

The typical positively skewed frequency distributions for various system timing measures reinforced the notion that these frequencies were probably pooled composites of different classes of user events. One way to classify the activities of the user is by the type of program that he employs. McIsaac provided data on frequently used programs, as shown in Figure 2.3. The ordinate in Figure 2.3 represent relative frequency of occurrence (labeled as "probability density") and the abscissa is log scale of processor time in seconds. Figure 2.3 reflects two notable findings. The most obvious is that there are consistent and substantial differences between user programs with respect to processor time. A less obvious but related finding is that nonprogrammer users tend to use less processor time per request than programmers. This is shown by shortest processor times for TINT (a simplified version of JOVIAL adapted for nonprogrammers) and for "other programs" which consist, in large part, of small, special-purpose routines developed for nonprogrammers.

Another noteworthy feature of Figure 2.3 is the learning and adaptation that takes place with users with increasing time-sharing experience. More experienced users, programmers, and nonprogrammers, learn how to exploit the central system more effectively. Unless constrained by the system, more experienced users tend to use larger programs, more primary and secondary storage, and more central processor time. Continuing user learning and adaptation, long after the user has mastered the basic elements of a given time-sharing tool, is another unexplored area for understanding user differences; this is analogous to "overlearning" in the psychological literature. How many time-sharing systems, current and projected, have a built-in evolutionary capability to expand and adapt to more sophisticated information services with increasing user experience?

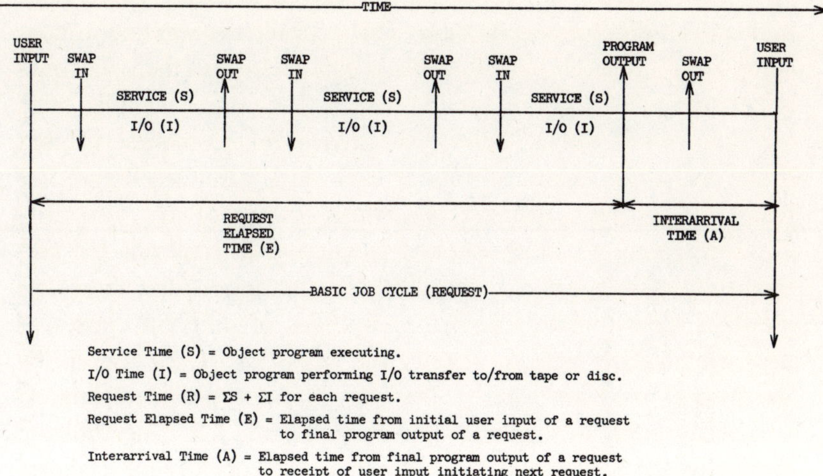

Figure 2.2. USER JOB CYCLE IN THE SDC TIME-SHARING SYSTEM (FROM McISAAC, 1966)

2.2 USER CHARACTERISTICS

The various studies cited in the previous section, and an additional study by Raynaud (1967) provide the basis for a preliminary portrait of user characteristics in time-sharing. The results of these statistical studies, involving approximately a million man-computer messages, reveal significant characteristics of users and overall man-machine effectiveness in time-sharing. A summary of these characteristics, extracted and summarized from these studies, is shown in Table 2.3.

Three key findings bearing on user effectiveness in Table 2.3 are briefly discussed—system response time, the nature of human problem-solving in man-computer communication, and the significance of individual differences. Contrary to popular folklore, users may be willing to live with relatively long delays in computer response time (satisfactory ratings were given for delays up to 10 minutes in Raynaud's study) if they know that their job requires considerable computation and if they know about how long the system will take to respond to their request. This finding underscores the vast differences between various types of prob-

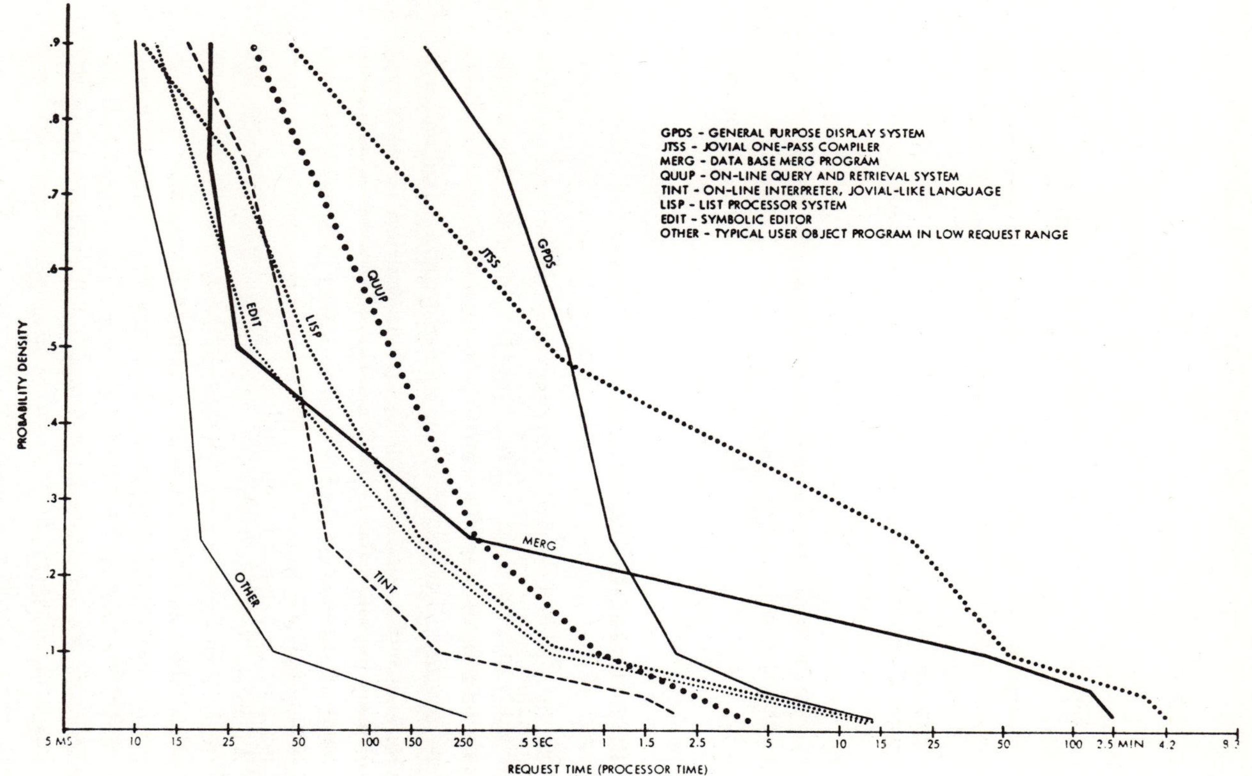

Figure 2.3. COMPARATIVE COMPUTER TIMES OF FREQUENTLY OCCURRING JOBS IN THE SDC TIME-SHARING SYSTEM (FROM McISAAC, 1966)

Table 2.3. PRELIMINARY SUMMARY OF USER CHARACTERISTICS IN TIME-SHARING

Timing and Pacing

1. More often than not, the time-sharing user will employ a terminal only once a day, and not every day; this rule is subject, however, to numerous exceptions for individual users and between different users.
2. The typical user spends between half an hour to an hour at his console at each session; this rule is also subject to great intra- and inter-subject variability.
3. Approximately 10% of the typical user's total working time is spent in man-computer communication at his console, whereas 90% of his working time is spent away from the console.
4. His median input rate is at the general order of three requests every minute, whereas his average input is roughly one per minute at the terminal.
5. Half of the time he will insert a new command some 10 seconds after he has received a complete output from the computer; only on comparatively rare occasions will he wait as long as a minute before making a new request after receiving an output.
6. The ratio of human time to central proessor time is at the general order of magnitude of 50:1; that is, approximately 50 seconds of elapsed human time is associated with one second of computer operating time on the user's program.

System Effectiveness

7. Users with tasks requiring relatively small computations become increasingly uncomfortable as computer response time to their requests extends beyond 10 seconds, and as irregularity and uncertainty of computer response time increases; users with problems requiring much computation tolerate longer intervals, up to as much as 10 minutes for the largest jobs.
8. As system load rises with increasing numbers of users, system response time increases, and, at high-load levels, both central system effectiveness and user performance tend to deteriorate.

Individual Differences

9. The computer is generally more verbose than the human; each line of human input tends to be accompanied, roughly speaking, by about two lines of computer output. New users tend to be more verbose; more terse inputs occur with increasing experience.
10. Programmers seem to use, on the average, larger object programs and more computer time than nonprogrammers.

11. As the central system matures, and as users become more experienced, there is a tendency for object programs to grow in size and complexity and for experienced users to require more computing time and a larger share of system capacity. Experienced users are more adept in exploiting central system resources.

lems, not only in computation time and data storage requirements, but also in the potential flexibility of human attitudes toward system response time, providing that the user is well informed and knows what to expect from the system.

The data on user timing and pacing raises critical questions on the nature of human problem-solving at the computer terminal. The implied hypothesis of man-computer symbiosis effectively states that man-computer interaction directly enhances human creativity, that major insights in human problem-solving are likely to occur more often at the computer terminal. The results in Table 2.3 show that most human time is spent away from the console (typically on the order of 90%). The critical question then arises of where the major insights occur—at the terminal, or at the desk, away from the computer?

The data from five independent studies, in remarkable agreement, show that user "thinking" time—the interval between the last computer output and the user's next message to the computer —is typically only 10 seconds (see Table 2.4). That is, the median value for this interval for these five studies, involving hundreds of thousands of user messages, was consistently close to 10 seconds. This agreement suggests that time-sharing users go to their terminals with well-formulated problems, and that they go through fast-moving, tactical problem-solving to see if their solutions will work. Ten seconds seems too short to achieve significant insight. Instead of man-computer symbiosis, an alternative hypothesis is suggested, namely, that problem-solving is a human-directed process first and foremost, with major insight occurring away from the computer when the individual has the time and the leisure to mull his problem over and come up with a fresh approach.

While these data are suggestive, they are by no means definitive, and the question is still an open one. For example, it may be

TABLE 2.4. COMPARATIVE INTERARRIVAL STATISTICS FROM VARIOUS TIME-SHARING SYSTEMS

Author	Totschek (1965)	McIsaac (1966)	IBM Memo (1966)	Scherr (1967)	Bryan (1967)
Time-Sharing System	SDC Q-32 System 1965 Study	SDC Q-32 System 1966 Study	IBM 7090 System	MIT Project MAC System	RAND JOSS System
Mean (sec.)	27.7	70.7 (35.3) *	20.0	35.2	24
Median	12.8	9.0	10.0	11.0	9.3

* Adjusted by removing all interarrival times greater than 30 minutes (1.55% of total).

argued that fast-moving trial and error may regularly precede major insight at the terminal. These preliminary data, however, suggest that most problem-solving occurs away from the computer whether or not the individual is working with his problem in an online or offline mode. Man-machine effectiveness may primarily be a matter of human rather than machine effectiveness. This brings us to the matter of individual differences.

If any generalization can be made on individual differences, it is that users are characterized far more by their variability than by any central tendency among them. New users are more verbose with the computer, they tend to use smaller programs and smaller amounts of computer time. With increasing experience, the size, variety, and running time of their programs tends to increase. This trend is reflected in the differences between programmers and non-programmers: programmers, as more experienced users, exploit the available computing system more fully.

There is a significant point here in comparing time-sharing vs. small computers. If it is a natural human tendency to use increasing computer power and more computer facilities with increasing experience in computer applications, then the small computer with its relatively limited resources will, sooner or later, inhibit the user in expanding the range and scope of his skills, and the kinds of problems he tackles.

2.3 COMPARISON OF COMPETITIVE COMPUTER SYSTEMS

This section is concerned with a broad, exploratory study on the comparative cost-effectiveness of four basic types of computer configurations conducted by Erikson (1967). This doctoral dissertation was based on the development of a programmed analytic model incorporating numerous parameters bearing on the cost of representative computer systems—time-sharing, batch processing, multiple-console batch processing, and small, personally operated systems. Parametric values for the model were empirically derived from a few extensively documented systems and from specially recorded data on human, machine, and software characteristics. With this data, numerous runs were conducted on the model for varying conditions, which generated a variety of tradeoff curves on the four computer configurations.

The model was limited to human and equipment costs incurred in computer facility operations. It did not include human costs away from the time-shared console, nor did it incorporate specific types of jobs, except for a distinction between interactive vs. non-interactive tasks. This investigation also encompassed experimental data on debugging performance for students. While these debugging studies clearly indicated striking performance differences under different computer configurations, the relations were too complex and the empirical data were too meager to incorporate them into the analytic cost model.

Erikson's work demonstrated the versatility of the analytic model in estimating computer system costs, for future as well as current systems. Perhaps the most valuable use of this modeling technique lies in its heuristic and educational possibilities, rather than in the specific cost figures that it produces, which are always only partial costs derived from data having a high obsolescence rate in the swiftly changing computer field. Erikson emphasized the point that no one computer configuration may be categorically considered as better than any other in any absolute sense; meaningful comparisons can only be made under highly specified conditions permitting quantitative measurement, and even these are subject to guarded qualification by factors not incorporated in the model, as well as by differential unreliability in the empirical data.

With the above qualifications in mind, Erikson's model did indicate several interesting conclusions in regard to time-sharing vs. batch systems and the small computer. As one might expect, batch systems were less costly than time-sharing for noninteractive jobs, whereas time-sharing was less expensive for interactive jobs. Less obvious was his finding that when mixed jobs were run on his model, time-sharing proved less costly for mixes ranging from 100% interactive all the way up to about 90% noninteractive and 10% interactive.

The only conditions under which Erikson found the small computer more economical than time-sharing were in relatively extreme cases in which the workload and tasks were well known and tightly scheduled in advance, when the jobs required little or no interaction, and when there was only a small number of users, so that none of the user's waiting time was lost. These conditions probably preclude most scientific and engineering tasks which are marked by unpredictable hunch and subsequent trial and error. Erikson predicted that the small computer would probably have restricted use in three limited areas in the 1975 time period: as a teaching tool, for well-defined, large workloads such as payroll computations, and as powerful (programmable) desk calculators.

Erikson came across some interesting kinds of adaptive user behaviors in compiling empirical parametric data from the literature. In one case, he found that as turnaround time increased in batch systems, the users tended to assemble larger jobs requiring longer running times. The relationship was such that total computer running time would remain approximately constant as lower job submission rates were counterbalanced by the longer running times associated with increased job size. In another case, in a large time-sharing installation, it was noted that average user program size was significantly reduced when it was announced that longer programs would receive lower-priority service.

The merit of Erikson's study was reflected in several departures from previous analytic studies in this area. One was the development of a model amenable to cross-system comparisons as opposed to the more usual case of models describing costs for only one kind of system. A second feature was the heavy and extensive use of differential empirical data from real-world computing facilities to obtain cost and effectiveness estimates, as opposed to hypothetical, armchair exercises. A third difference was the deliberate attempt, admittedly limited, to incorporate and account for significant human parameters in the analytic model, also derived from empirical data, in contrast to the studied avoidance and gross oversimplification of human factors in traditional cost models.

2.4 SURVEY OF THE BUSINESS COMMUNITY

Only one early study was found that offered any empirical data on the business user, a book by Popell, et al, (1966) which includes a questionnaire survey on attitudes and expectations of the business community toward time-sharing and competitive computer systems. This study is useful for sketching a preliminary profile of organizational attitudes toward time-sharing and for evaluating the questionnaire technique.

The questionnaire sampling scheme is shown in Table 2.5. Five types of business organizations were queried: large companies using computers regularly; smaller companies using computers only occasionally or not at all; leading computer manufacturers in the United States and in foreign countries; computer system management consultants; and manufacturers of peripheral equipment for computer systems. Table 2.5 indicates that 415 questionnaires were mailed and, of these, 164 were answered, for an overall response level of 40%. Systematic sampling differences between those answering and not answering the questionnaires were not indicated, consequently it is not possible to assess the representativeness of the available data. These sampling problems, as well as the small number of responses to most of the sampling categories, make this a tentative and exploratory study rather than a definitive assessment of attitudes toward time-sharing in the business community. Key results for each of the five classes of companies are discussed in turn.

The companies using computers included manufacturers, banks, insurance agencies, railroads, retailers, utilities, and air-

Table 2.5. QUESTIONNAIRE SAMPLE FOR TIME-SHARING SURVEY OF BUSINESS ORGANIZATIONS

Type of Organization	Questionnaires Sent Out	Questionnaires Answered	Percent Responding
Companies Using Computers	160	79	49%
Companies Not Using Computers (smaller firms)	160	48	30%
Computer Manufacturers	30	15	50%
Management Consultants	30	14	47%
Manufacturers of Peripheral Equipment	35	8	23%
Totals	415	164	40% (average)

(Adapted from Popell, 1966)

lines. Operational hardware and software costs ran approximately 50% for each. Accounting was the prime application for computers, consuming approximately 60% of computer time; all other types of activities required less than 10% of computer time. In contrast to this usage, the major expectations of these firms for time-sharing were in the areas of engineering and research, information retrieval, data communications with remote field locations, and online inventory management. The overwhelming majority of these firms (91%) preferred and expected *dedicated* time-sharing systems for their purposes, consisting of their own consoles tied to their own central computers and data banks. The dedicated system was seen as the preferred way of protecting proprietary company information from accidental or deliberate misuse.

These suggestive findings point up the need for normative statistics on types of tasks performed under time-sharing, and also at batch facilities, for different types of users and for the determination of user attitudes. According to the above data, it is apparent that accounting is the prime computer activity for these firms, and that accounting is viewed as a batch-processing task. Applications more suitable for time-sharing, in the view of these respondents, would probably play a relatively minor role in future computing activity.

Whether one agrees with these implications or not, the stereotypes nevertheless exist and represent a potent force in shaping the form and direction of time-sharing in the business community. By extension, analogous stereotypes on what information utilities can or cannot do, will, in turn, significantly mold the form and direction of social applications for other types of users. From an experimental view, the development of adequate user task statistics in conjunction with appropriate sampling of user attitudes is essential for determining what, in fact, is being done in time-sharing and in competitive computer facilities, whether users practice what they preach, and what course "user readiness" for time-sharing is taking.

The nonuser firms were primarily concerned with anticipated excessive costs of computers for their requirements. They also viewed computer applications primarily for accounting purposes and secondarily for production control, sales forecasting, and information retrieval. Providing that costs were not prohibitive, these firms were interested in eventually having a time-shared terminal at their plant. However, they would carefully investigate whether a small, free-standing computer of their own might be better suited for their purposes. They were especially concerned about the possible loss of control over company information stored at the time-sharing center. As might be expected, there was also great concern over possible government regulation of the security of user information in time-shared facilities—88% of the firms were against government supervision. A common thread running through most of these responses was the need for considerably more information in time-sharing costs and services.

The findings of these smaller firms indicate the importance of attitude surveys for potential users to assess their readiness for computer utilities. For example, special attention would have to be devoted to educational efforts to achieve greater familiarity with time-sharing for the above potential users, and special system design effort would be required to protect company information and provide adequate fallback and recovery procedures in the event of system failure. Indoctrination programs that, at a minimum, emphasize these and related points would probably be required for such users before they would commit company resources to time-sharing services. The methods and efficacy of such indoctrination programs, to achieve user competence for initial standard tasks and to develop positive attitudes toward time-sharing, are vital areas for experimental investigation.

The questionnaire responses of computer manufacturers were interesting on several counts. They also ranked engineering and scientific applications as best suited for time-sharing, with information retrieval second. However, they emphasized that time-sharing would thrive best in an environment marked by a multiplicity of user tasks rather than limited and stereotyped tasks. For these and related cost considerations, they believed that larger companies would probably be the most suitable initial targets for time-sharing services. The median cost estimate was that time-sharing systems would run about 25% higher than comparable batch-processing systems (excluding the costs of typewriter consoles). The manufacturers apparently did not share the opinion of some time-sharing enthusiasts that time-sharing equipment and operating costs were less than comparable batch-processing costs. (Since the time of this survey, however, comparative costs have grown closer and have dropped substantially.)

These firms wanted to know much more about potential users of time-sharing, such as: the kinds of tasks they would like to do on time-sharing; how fast an answer they need for their queries; the kinds of languages the user wants; and whether the console operator will be the boss, a technician, or the secretary. Concern was expressed over the protection and security of clients' information. As with other respondents, the manufacturers wanted more definitive and objective evaluative information on user performance under time-sharing.

The manufacturers' replies point to several directions for possible experimental work on user performance. They need to know what users actually do with time-sharing—another indication of the central importance of real-world statistics on user tasks. Since time-sharing is held to be more expensive than comparable conventional computer services, experimental effort should be directed toward comparative cost-effectiveness of time-sharing relative to competing computer services, rather than to comparative effectiveness without regard for costs.

Skill levels of users need to be determined and the ability of various classes of users to master time-sharing languages and tools ought to be experimentally evaluated. Designers not trained in human factors evaluation often assume, unreasonably, that users will be able to do what the designer can do with his own system. Finally, although manufacturers may know their products best of all, they are understandably uncertain as to how effective they will turn out to be for various kinds of users. They will not know this, nor will others, for that matter, until object data are collected on representative user performance in live system settings.

The responses of management consultants were in general agreement with the observations of computer manufacturers, but with a stronger orientation toward user problems as opposed to central system problems. For example, they singled out the lack of trained personnel, the lack of knowledge of time-sharing, and man-computer language difficulties as prime problems for users. They saw information management and retrieval as the most promising use of time-sharing, with engineering and scientific applications as second in importance. Their prediction that online data management may become the chief use of time-sharing in the business setting stood out against the predictions of the others who selected engineering and scientific utilization. The management consultants felt that much more information was needed from users on the nature of user populations, user tasks, expected cost levels, and cost allocation for time-sharing. Experimental implications with regard to consultant management responses are primarily in the areas of training and user statistics.

The eight questionnaire responses from peripheral equipment manufacturers comprised the smallest sample for the five types of respondents. This group expected fierce competition from batch-processing quarters, a prediction that has since materialized in the form of remote batch services with fast turnaround. They cited the relatively high costs of remote user terminals, and they underscored the greater costs and complexities of programming time-shared systems. They felt that too much attention was paid to engineering and scientific use of time-sharing with too little effort devoted to business applications.

These manufacturers would like to see a simple, rugged, "idiot-proof" typewriter console with facilities for punched card and punched tape inputs. The emphasis on "idiot proof" is an interesting example of impatient, wishful thinking; the lowest common denominator (as we have seen again and again in the mass media of communication) is not the same as the optimal denominator, and no amount of semantic legislation is going to abolish the brute fact of individual differences. The responses from this group also emphasized the need for comparative cost-effectiveness studies between time-sharing and competing systems for representative classes of user tasks. Measuring, observing and understanding the varieties and types of user behavior at all skill levels for a broad spectrum of tasks is essential for developing human-engineered consoles and associated software services.

It should be pointed out that the commentary on experimental implications of Popell's survey did not come from Popell. As a matter of fact, systematic experimentation with users is not mentioned at any point in his book on time-sharing in the business setting. This indifference to experimental testing of users, frequently encountered in the business context, is a stumbling block in the path of productive applied research on organizational effectiveness with computer utilities. The experimental recommendations have been added as interpretive commentaries to point up the value of questionnaire surveys as useful exploratory aids—aids that uncover and highlight key problem areas based on expressed attitudes and opinions of current and potential users. These anticipated problem areas help guide investigators toward experiments dealing with real rather than imagined problems of users. The combined use of exploratory questionnaires and follow-on experiments, acting as checks and balances on each other, is more powerful than either technique taken alone. Stated somewhat differently, test and measurement of user attitudes and motivations should always be part of an integrated experimental approach to user performance.

3

EXPLORATORY STUDIES WITH PROGRAMMERS

3.1 INTRODUCTION

IN the early 1960's, while the pioneering time-sharing systems were being designed and used for the first time, and while initial user statistics and user questionnaires were gathered, as indicated in the previous chapter, the anecdotal arguments between proponents for batch and time-sharing systems came to a head. The stage was set for the first exploratory experiments comparing the effectiveness of the two competing computer systems.

Between 1966 and 1969, eight experimental studies have appeared in the literature, each comparing some form of online and offline data processing with respect to man-machine measures of system performance. These pioneering studies comprise the first substantive data base for comparing and evaluating the growing and changing competition between time-sharing and batch processing (Adams and Cohen, 1969; Erikson, 1966; Gold, 1967; Grant and Sackman, 1967; Sackman, 1969; Sackman and Gold, 1968; Schatzoff, Tsao, and Wiig, 1967; and Smith, 1967). The two exploratory studies at SDC conducted on programmers, are the subject of this chapter. The Gold, and the Sackman-Gold experiments are described in detail in Part II. The large-scale study conducted by the author at the Air Force Academy comprises Part III of this book.

The two exploratory studies summarized here are found in

Grant and Sackman (1967) and in Erikson (1966). The original studies should be consulted for technical details that are beyond the scope of this chapter. They were performed by the System Development Corporation for the Advanced Research Projects Agency of the Department of Defense. The first study is concerned with online vs. offline debugging performance for a group of 12 experienced programmers (average of seven years experience). The second investigation involved 9 programmer trainees in a comparison of interactive vs. noninteractive program debugging. The highlights of each study are discussed in turn. For easier reference, the first experiment is described as the "Experienced Programmer" study, and the second as the "Programmer Trainee" study.

The two experiments were conducted using the SDC Time-Sharing System (TSS) under the normal online condition and simulated offline or noninteractive conditions. TSS is a general-purpose system (see Schwartz, Coffman, and Weissman, 1964) similar in many respects to the Project MAC system (see Scherr, 1966) at the Massachusetts Institute of Technology. Schwartz (1965) has characterized this class of time-sharing system as providing four important properties to the user: "instantaneous" response, independent operation for each user, essentially simultaneous operation for several users, and general-purpose capability.

TSS utilizes an IBM AN/FSQ-32 computer. The following is a general description of its operation. User programs are stored on magnetic tape or in disk file memory. When a user wishes to operate his program, he goes to one of several Teletype consoles; these consoles are direct input/output devices to the Q-32. He instructs the computer, through the Teletype, to load and activate his program. The system then loads the program either from the disk file or from magnetic tape into active storage (drum memory). All currently operating programs are stored on drum memory and are transferred, one at a time, in turn, into core memory for processing. Under TSS scheduling control, each program is processed for a short amount of time (usually a fraction of a second) and is then replaced in active storage to await its next turn. A program is transferred to core only if it requires processing; otherwise it is passed up for that turn. Thus, a user may spend as much time as he needs thinking about what to do next without wasting the computational time of the machine. Although a time-sharing system processes programs sequentially and discontinuously, it gives users the illusion of simultaneity and continuity because of its high speed.

3.2 EXPERIENCED PROGRAMMER STUDY

3.2.1 Experimental Design

The design used in this experiment is illustrated in Figure 3.1.

	ONLINE		OFFLINE	
GROUP I	Algebra	(6)	Maze	(6)
GROUP II	Maze	(6)	Algebra	(6)
TOTALS		(12)		(12)

Figure 3.1. EXPERIMENTAL DESIGN FOR THE EXPERIENCED PROGRAMMER STUDY

The 2 x 2 Latin-Square design with repeated measures for this experiment should be interpreted as follows. Two experimental groups were employed with six subjects in each; the two experimental treatments were online and offline program debugging; and the Algebra and Maze problems were the two types of programs that were coded and debugged. Repeated measures were employed in that each subject, serving as his own control, solved one problem task under online conditions and the other under offline conditions. Note in Figure 3.1 that each of the two program problems appears once and only once in each row and column to meet the requirements of the 2 x 2 Latin-Square. Subjects were assigned to the two groups at random, and problem order and online/offline order were counterbalanced.

The statistical treatment for this design involves an analysis of variance to test for the significance of mean differences between the online and offline conditions and between the Algebra and Maze problems. There are two analyses of variance, corresponding to the two criterion measures, one for programmer man-hours spent in debugging and the other for central processor time. A leading advantage of the Latin-Square design for this experiment is that each analysis of variance incorporates a total of 24 measurements. This configuration permits maximum pooled sample size and high statistical efficiency in the analysis of the results—especially desirable features in view of the small subject samples that were used.

3.2.2 Method

A number of problems were encountered in the design and conduct of this experiment. Many are illustrative of problems in experimenting with operational computer systems, and many stemmed from lack of experimental precedent in this area. Key problems are described below.

Online and Offline Conditions. Defining the online condition posed no problems. Programmers debugging online were simply instructed to use TSS in the normal fashion. All the standard features of the system were available to them for debugging. Defining the offline condition proved more difficult. It was desired to provide a controlled and uniform turnaround time for the offline condition. It was further desired that this turnaround time be short enough so that subjects could be released to their regular jobs and the experiment completed in a reasonable amount of time; on the other hand, the turnaround time had to be long enough to constitute a significant delay. The compromise reached was two hours—considerably shorter than most offline systems and yet long enough so that most of the programmer-subjects complained about the delay.

It was decided to simulate an offline system using TSS and the Q-32 by requiring the programmer to submit a work request to a member of the experimental staff to have his program operated. The work request contained specific instructions from the programmer on the procedures to be followed in running the program—essentially the same approach used in closed-shop computer facilities. Strictly speaking, then, this experiment was a comparison between online and *simulated* offline operations.

Each programmer was required to code his own program, using his own logic, and to rely on the specificity of the problem requirements for comparable programs. Program coding procedures were independent of debugging conditions; that is, regardless of the condition imposed for checkout—online or offline—all programmers coded offline. Programmers primarily wrote their programs in JTS (JOVIAL Time-Sharing—a procedure-oriented language for time-sharing).

Experimental Problems. Two program problem statements were designed for the experiment. One problem required the subjects to write a program to interpret Teletype-inserted algebraic equations. Each equation involved a single dependent variable. The program was required to compute the value of the dependent variable, given Teletype-inserted values for the independent variables, and to check for specific kinds of errors in Teletype input. All programmers were referred to a published source (Samuelson and Bauer, 1960) for a suggested workable logic to solve the problem. Programs written to solve this problem were referred to as Algebra programs.

The other problem called for writing a program to find the one and only path through a 20 x 20 cell maze. The programs were required to print out the designators of the cells constituting the path. Each cell was represented as an entry in a 400-item table, and each entry contained information on the directions in which movement was possible from the cell. These programs were referred to as Maze programs.

Performance Measures. Debugging time was considered to begin when the programmer had coded and compiled a program with no serious format errors detected by the compiler. Debugging was considered finished when the subject's program was able to process, without errors, a standard set of test inputs. Two basic criterion measures were collected for comparing online and offline debugging: programmer man-hours and central processor (CPU) time.

Man-hours for debugging were actual hours spent on the problem by the programmer (including turnaround time). Hours were carefully recorded by close personal observation of each programmer by the experimental staff in conjunction with a daily time log kept by the subjects. Discrepancies between observed time and reported time were resolved by tactful interviewing. TSS keeps its own accounting records on user activity; these records provided accurate measures of the central processor time used by each subject. The recorded CPU time included program-execute time, some system-overhead time, and times for dumping the contents of program or system registers.

A variety of additional measures were obtained in the course of the experiment to provide control data, and to obtain additional indices of programmer performance. Control measures included: TSS experience, general programming experience (excluding TSS experience), type of programming language used (JTS or machine language), and the number of computer runs submitted by each subject in the offline condition. Additional programmer performance measures included: man-hours spent on each program until a successful pass was made through the compiler (called coding time), program size in machine intructions, program running time for a successful pass through test data, and scores on the Basic Programming Knowledge Test (BPKT)—a paper-and-pencil test developed by Berger, et al, (1966) at the University of Southern California.

3.2.3 Results

Criterion Performance. Table 3.1 shows the experimental data base: all performance and control variables, raw scores, descriptive statistics, and mean-difference tests between time-sharing and batch groups. Table 3.2 shows the means and standard deviations for the two key criterion variables, debug man-hours and CPU time. These raw-score values show a substantial superiority for online debug man-hours, varying from 50% to 300% faster than the offline condition. CPU time shows a reverse trend: the offline condition consistently required about 30% less CPU time than the online mode. The standard deviations are comparatively large in all cases, reflecting wide-ranging individual differences. Are these results statistically significant with such small samples?

Table 3.3 shows three types of analysis of variance applied to the Latin-Square experimental design. The first is a straight-

Table 3.1. EXPERIMENTAL DATA MATRIX

	Criterion Measures for Debugging Performance				Additional Measures for Programmer Performance						Control Variables				
	Debug Hours Algebra	Debug Hours Maze	CPU Time Algebra (seconds)	CPU Time Maze (seconds)	Code Hours Algebra	Code Hours Maze	Program Size Algebra	Program Size Maze	Run Time Algebra (seconds)	Run Time Maze (seconds)	TSS Experience (months)	Gen. Prog. Experience (years)	Prog. Lang. (SCAMP=0, JTS=1)	BPKT 1 (Programming Knowledge)	BPKT 2 (Coding Skill)
Group I On/Off	On	Off	On	Off											
S 1	15	4.5	749	82	11	20	4433	1538	3.2	6.8	2	2	*J*	32	8
S 2	29	20.5	1781	240	76	23	3215	1371	2.0	3.7	0	7	*J*	51	14
S 3	6	7.0	678	57	24	4	1050	651	3.5	2.8	9	11	*J*	35	12
S 4	57	26.0	1228	273	58	6	4957	3227	3.5	.6	4	3	*J*	38	6
S 5	15	8.0	1434	401	66	5	4042	1890	7.9	3.9	6	5	*J*	45	13
S 6	85	8.0	1727	91	111	50	2460	1286	2.4	4.2	2	11	*S*	47	5
Group II On/Off	Off	On	Off	On											
S 7	170	12.5	3075	257	88	16	2140	1501	3.5	2.4	30	4	*S*	47	12
S 8	31	2.0	370	541	19	2	3550	2188	5.0	5.4	3	2	*J*	50	11
S 9	20	3.0	403	115	12	2	1186	1000	3.0	2.3	18	10	*S*	43	10
S 10	27	2.0	527	269	60	16	6137	3287	6.6	8.0	12	9	*J*	25	5
S 11	23	3.5	416	141	7	2	2286	933	2.2	2.0	10	8	*J*	46	12
S 12	30	1.0	652	50	24	10	2690	1348	1.6	1.8	32	4	*J*	32	4
Mean I	34.50	12.33	1266.16	190.66	57.66	18.00	3359.50	1660.50	3.75	3.66	3.83	6.50	0.83	40.50	9.00
SD I	30.52	8.72	473.38	136.42	36.22	17.67	1437.63	867.72	2.12	2.01	3.25	3.88	0.40	9.81	3.57
Mean II	50.16	4.00	907.16	228.83	35.00	8.00	2998.16	1709.50	3.65	3.65	17.50	6.16	0.66	41.33	9.66
SD II	58.85	4.25	1067.06	174.64	32.01	6.92	1719.26	894.19	1.85	2.51	11.51	3.25	0.51	7.44	3.82
F-test	0.33	4.42	0.56	0.17	1.31	1.66	0.15	0.00	0.00	0.00	7.82	0.02	0.38	.02	.09

Table 3.2. EXPERIENCED PROGRAMMER PERFORMANCE

Debug Man-hours

	ALGEBRA		MAZE	
	Online	Offline	Online	Offline
Mean	34.5	50.2	4.0	12.3
SD	30.5	58.9	4.3	8.7

CPU Time (sec.)

	ALGEBRA		MAZE	
	Online	Offline	Online	Offline
Mean	1266	907	229	191
SD	473	1067	175	136

forward analysis of raw scores. The second is an analysis of square-root transformed scores to obtain more normal distributions. The third is also an analysis of variance on the square-root scores, but with the covariance associated with programmer coding skill partialed out statistically; that is, individuals were effectively equated on coding skill (individual score on program coding time) so that online/offline differences could be tested more directly.

These applications resulted in six analyses of variance (three for each criterion measure) as shown in Table 3.3. The columns

Table 3.3. COMPARATIVE RESULTS OF THREE ANALYSES OF VARIANCE

	Significance Levels		
Performance Measures	Raw Scores	Square Root	Square Root with Covariance
1. Debug Man-Hours			
Online vs. Offline	None	.10	.025
Algebra vs. Maze	.025	.001	.10
2. CPU Time			
Online vs. Offline	None	None	None
Algebra vs. Maze	None	.001	.05

in Table 3.3 represent the three kinds of analysis of variance; the rows show the two criterion measures. For each analysis of variance, tests for mean differences compare online vs. offline performance, and Algebra vs. Maze differences. The entries in the cells show the level of statistical significance found for these two main effects for each analysis of variance.

The results in Table 3.3 reveal key findings for this experiment. The first row shows results for online vs. offline performance as measured by debug man-hours. The raw-score analysis of variance shows no signficant differences. The analysis on square-root transformed scores shows a 10% level of significance in favor of online performance. The last analysis of variance, with covariance, on square-root scores, shows statistically significant differences in favor of the online condition at the .025 level. This progressive trend toward more clear-cut mean differences for shorter debug man-hours with online performance reflects the increasing level of statistical control over individual differences in the three types of analyses. In contrast to debug man-hours, no significant trend is indicated for online vs. offline conditions for CPU time. If real differences do exist, along the lines indicated in Table 3.3 for more CPU time in the online mode, these differences were not strong enough to show statistical significance with these small samples and with the large individual differences between programmers, even with the square-root and covariance transformations.

The results for Algebra vs. Maze differences were not surprising. The Algebra task was obviously a longer and harder problem than the Maze task, as indicated by the performance measures (see Table 3.1). The fairly consistent significant differences between Algebra and Maze scores shown in Table 3.3 reflect the differential effects of the three tests of analysis of variance, and, in particular, point up the greater sensitivity of the square-root transformations over the original raw scores in demonstrating significant problem differences.

Individual Differences. The observed ranges of individual differences are listed in Table 3.4 for the 10 performance variables measured in this study. The ratio between highest and lowest values is also shown.

Table 3.4. RANGE OF INDIVIDUAL DIFFERENCES IN PROGRAMMING PERFORMANCE

Performance Measure	Poorest Score	Best Score	Ratio
1. Debug Hours Algebra	170	6	28:1
2. Debug Hours Maze	26	1	26:1
3. CPU Time Algebra (sec.)	3075	370	8:1
4. CPU Time Maze (sec.)	541	50	11:1
5. Code Hours Algebra	111	7	16:1
6. Code Hours Maze	50	2	25:1
7. Program Size Algebra	6137	1050	6:1
8. Program Size Maze	3287	651	5:1
9. Run Time Algebra (sec.)	7.9	1.6	5:1
10. Run Time Maze (sec.)	8.0	.6	13:1

Table 3.4 points up the very large individual differences, typically by an order of magnitude, for most performance variables for this highly experienced group of programmers. To paraphrase a nursery rhyme:

When a programmer is good,
He is very, very good,
But when he is bad,
He is horrid.

The "horrid" portion of the performance frequency distribution is the long tail at the high end, the positively skewed part in which 1 poor performer can consume as much time or cost as 5, 10, or 20 good ones. Validated techniques to detect and weed out these poor performers could result in great savings of time, effort, and cost.

To obtain further information on these striking individual differences, an exploratory factor analysis was conducted on the intercorrelations of 15 performance and control variables in the experimental data. The main results were:

- A substantial performance factor designated as "programming speed," associated with faster coding and debugging, less CPU time, and the use of a higher-order language.

- A well-defined "program economy" factor marked by shorter and faster running programs, associated to some extent with greater programming experience and with the use of machine language rather than higher-order language.

This concludes the description of the method and results of the first study. The second study on programmer trainees follows.

3.3 PROGRAMMER TRAINEE STUDY

3.3.1 Experimental Design

A 2 x 2 Latin-Square design was also used in this experiment. With this design, as shown in Figure 3.2, the Sort Routine problem was solved by Group I (consisting of four subjects) in the noninteractive mode and by Group II (consisting of the other five subjects) in the interactive mode. Similarly, the second problem, a Cube Puzzle, was worked by Group I in the interactive mode and by Group II in the noninteractive mode.

	INTERACTIVE	NONINTERACTIVE
GROUP I (4)	Cube Puzzle	Sort Routine
GROUP II (5)	Sort Routine	Cube Puzzle
TOTAL	9 Subjects	

Figure 3.2. EXPERIMENTAL DESIGN FOR THE PROGRAMMER TRAINEE STUDY

Analysis of variance was used to test the significance of the differences between the mean values of the two test conditions (Interactive and Noninteractive) and the two problems. The first (test conditions) was the central experimental inquiry, and the other was of interest from the point of view of control.

3.3.2 Method

Nine programmer trainees were randomly divided into two groups of four and five each. One group coded and debugged the first problem interactively while the other group did the same problem in a noninteractive mode. The two groups switched computer system type for the second problem. All subjects used TINT (Kennedy, 1965) for both problems. (TINT is a dialect of JOVIAL that is used interpretively with TSS.)

Interactive and Noninteractive Conditions. Interactive, for this experiment, meant the use of TSS and the TINT language with all of its associated aids. No restrictions in the use of this language were placed upon the subjects.

The noninteractive condition was the same as the interactive except that the subjects were required to quit after every attempted execution. The subjects ran their own programs under close supervision to assure that they were not inadvertently running their jobs in an interactive manner. If a member of the noninteractive group immediately saw his error and if there were no other members of the noninteractive group waiting for a Teletype, then, after he quit, he was allowed to log in again without any waiting period. Waiting time for an available console in the noninteractive mode fluctuated greatly, but it typically involved minutes rather than hours.

Experimental Problems. The two experimental tasks were relatively simple problems that were normally given to students by the training staff. The first involved writing a numerical sort routine, and the second required finding the arrangement of four specially marked cubes that met a given condition. The second problem was more difficult than the first, but neither required more than five days of elapsed time for a solution by any subject. The subjects worked at each problem until they were able to produce a correct solution with a run of their program.

Performance Measures. CPU time, automatically recorded for each trainee, and programmer man-hours spent debugging the problem, recorded by individual work logs, were the two major measures of performance. Debugging was assumed to begin when a subject logged in for the first time—that is, after he had finished coding his program at his desk and was ready for initial runs to check and test his program.

3.3.3 Results

Criterion Performance. A summary of the results of this experiment is shown in Table 3.5. Analysis of variance showed the difference between the raw-score mean values of debug hours for the interactive and the noninteractive conditions to be significant at the .13 level. The difference between the two experimental conditions for mean values of CPU seconds was significant at the .08 level. In both cases, better performance (faster solutions) was obtained under the interactive mode. In the previous experiment, the use of square-root transformed scores and the use of coding hours as a covariate allowed better statistical control over the differences between individual subjects. No such result was found in this experiment.

If each of the subjects could be directly compared to himself as he worked with each of the systems, the problems of matching subjects or subject groups and the need for extensive statistical analysis could be eliminated. Unfortunately, it is not meaningful to have the same subject code and debug the same problem twice; and it is extremely difficult to develop different problems that are at the same level of difficulty. One possible solution to this problem would be to use some measure of problem difficulty as a normalizing factor. It should be recognized that the use of any normalizing factor can introduce problems in analysis and interpretation. It was decided to use one of the more popular of such measures, namely, the number of instructions in the program. CPU time per instruction and debug man-hours per instruction were compared on the two problems for each subject for the interactive and noninteractive conditions. The results showed that the interactive subjects had significantly lower values on both compute-seconds-per-instruction (.01 level) and debug-hours-per-instruction (.06 level).

Individual Differences. One of the key findings of the previous study was that there were large individual differences between programmers. Because of differences in sampling and scale factors, coefficients of variation were computed to compare individual differences in both studies. (The coefficient of variation is expressed as a percentage; it is equal to the standard deviation

Table 3.5. PROGRAMMER TRAINEE PERFORMANCE

Debug Man-hours

	SORT ROUTINE		CUBE PUZZLE	
	Interactive	Noninteractive	Interactive	Noninteractive
Mean	0.71	4.7	9.2	13.6
SD	0.66	3.5	4.2	7.0

CPU Time (sec.)

	SORT ROUTINE		CUBE PUZZLE	
	Interactive	Noninteractive	Interactive	Noninteractive
Mean	11.1	109.1	290.2	875.3
SD	9.9	65.6	213.0	392.6

divided by the mean, multiplied by 100.) The overall results showed that coefficients of variation for debug man-hours and CPU time in this experiment were only 16% smaller than coefficients of variation in the experienced programmer study (median values of 66% and 82%, respectively). These observed differences may be attributable, in part, to the greater difficulty level of the problems in the experienced programmer study, and to the much greater range of programming experience between subjects which tended to magnify individual programmer differences.

In an attempt to determine if there are measures of skill that can be used as a preliminary screening tool to equalize groups, data were gathered on the subject's grades in the SDC programmer training class, and, as mentioned earlier, they were also given the Basic Programming Knowledge Test (BPKT). Correlations between all experimental measures, adjusted scores, grades, and the BPKT results were determined. Except for some spurious part-whole correlations, the results showed no consistent correlation between performance measures and the various grades and test scores.

The most interesting result of this exploratory analysis, however, was that class grades and BPKT scores showed substantial intercorrelations. This is especially notable when only the first of the two BPKT scores is considerd. These correlations ranged between .64 and .83 for Part I of the BPKT; two out of these four correlations are at the 5% level and one exceeds the 1% level of significance even for these very small samples. This implies that the BPKT is measuring the same kinds of skills that are measured in trainee class performance. It should also be noted that neither class grades nor BPKT scores would have provided useful predictions of trainee performance in the test situation that was used in this experiment.

This observation may be interpreted in three basic ways: first, that the BPKT and class grades are valid and that the problems do not represent general programming tasks; second, that the problems are valid, but that the BPKT and class grades are not indicative of working programmer performance; or third, that interrelations between the BPKT and class grades do in fact exist with respect to programming performance, but that the intercorrelations are only low to moderate, which cannot be detected by the very small samples used in these experiments. The results of these studies are ambiguous with respect to these three hypotheses; further investigation is required to determine whether one or any combination of them will hold.

The interpretation of the results of these two experiments is considered in conjunction with the remaining two exploratory studies in the next chapter. The combined results of the four exploratory investigations sets the stage for the comprehensive experiments described in Parts II and III.

4

ANALYSIS OF THE EXPLORATORY ONLINE/OFFLINE STUDIES

THIS chapter completes the review of the exploratory online/offline studies and analyzes the combined results of all six experiments. Leading issues and key hypotheses in man-computer problem-solving arise from these findings, which, in turn, provide the critical scientific mass necessary for follow-on experimentation. With these initial experiments, there is the emergence of a preliminary conceptual framework for extended research, a framework arrived at inductively from experimental experience, rather than deductively from abstract considerations.

4.1 EXPLORATORY STUDIES WITH STUDENTS

The four exploratory studies on college and graduate students are summarized from Adams and Cohen (1969), an unpublished Air Force Academy study, Sackman (1969), Smith (1967), and Schatzoff, Tsao, and Wiig (1967). Tables 4.1, 4.2, 4.3, and 4.4 are summary profiles of these two experiments. These tables are self-explanatory and should be carefully examined to understand the scope, strengths, and limitations of each study. These tables cover subjects, problems, online/offline facilities, experimental procedure, performance measures, and key results.

Table 4.1. PROFILE OF THE SMITH STUDY

METHOD	
Subjects	
Sample Size	127
Type of Subjects	Undergraduate and graduate students in an introductory programming course
Experience Level	Most subjects had less than a year experience
Problems	
Number and Type	Two easy "warmup" problems and four experimental problems; cosine infinite series, matrix sorting, language translation, heuristic program
Difficulty Level	Moderately difficult for beginners
Average Completion Time	Approximately 60 hours to complete all problems
Online/Offline Facilities	
Online Facility	Burroughs B5500 batch system at Stanford with "instant" turnaround
Batch Facility	Same facility, with normal turnaround
Language Used	Burroughs extended ALGOL
Batch Turnaround Time	Variable, usually hours
Experimental Procedure	
Experimental Design	Match groups of subjects, each subject taking two problems on "batch" and two on "instant"
Statistical Tests	Descriptive statistical comparisons; no tests of statistical significance
Experimental Controls	Counterbalanced order of "batch" and "instant" modes
Motivational Controls	Class grades
Recording Procedures	Computer recording, student logs and questionnaire

RESULTS

Performance Measure	"Instant" * Mode	Batch * Mode
Initial Program Preparation (min.)	440	405
Time to Keypunch Original Program (min.)	109	108
Time to Prepare New Run	311	293
Number of Runs per Student	7.1	6.6
Computer Runs per Trip	2.5	1.9
Elapsed Time (days)	3.0	3.7
Computer Time (average min. per run)	.277	.186
Student Preference	70%	24%

* No tests of statistical significance were reported.

BOX SCORE

1. Instant turnaround results in less elapsed time than conventional batch to prepare, code and debug programs for a relatively large sample of student users.
2. Instant turnaround results in heavier computer time expenditure than conventional batch processing.
3. Instant turnaround is preferred by substantially more students than conventional batch processing.
4. Instant turnaround is associated with changes in programming working patterns that are characterized by shorter intervals between successive job runs and earlier completion of the experimental task.
5. The above conclusions are contingent upon the variability of the data and derived tests of statistical significance which were not reported in the published study.

Table 4.2. PROFILE OF THE SCHATZOFF, TSAO, AND WIIG STUDY

METHOD	
Subjects	
Sample Size	4
Type of Subjects	Undergraduate students with high programming aptitude
Experience Level	"Some" programming experience
Problems	
Number and Type	Four problems: Monte Carlo integration, algebraic sorting, Pig Latin translator, text format conversion
Difficulty Level	Moderately difficult for skilled student subjects
Average Completion Time	Approximately 40 hours to complete all problems
Online/Offline Facilities	
Online Facility	MIT Time-Sharing, IBM 7094
Batch Facility	IBM 7094 scientific batch facility
Language Used	Not mentioned
Batch Turnaround Time	Not mentioned
Experimental Procedure	
Experimental Design	Graeco-Latin Square: 4 problems, 4 subjects, vs. on/off comparison
Statistical Tests	Analysis of variance, correlational analysis
Experimental Controls	Counterbalanced order of experimental design
Motivational Controls	Not mentioned
Recording Procedures	Computer recording, work logs, paper and pencil test

RESULTS

Performance Measure	Time-Shared Mode	Batch Mode	Statistical Significance
Elapsed Time (days)	29.5	46	.08
Analysis Time (min.)	3059	2295	—
Programmer Time (min.)	5672	2737	.02
Computer Time (min.)	92	101	—
Total Cost (dollars)	1579	1075	.08
Range of Individual Differences for above variables			3:1 to 4:1

BOX SCORE

1. Students experienced in batch techniques and who are inexperienced in time-sharing techniques, and who essentially use batch procedures under both modes, use less of their own time and incur lower man-machine costs to prepare, code, and debug programs under the batch mode than in time-sharing.
2. Time-sharing, even with subjects unfamiliar with its use, requires less total elapsed time than batch processing to prepare, code, and debug programs.
3. In a select group of students, individual differences in performance are larger than system differences between time-sharing and batch processing.
4. The above conclusions are contingent upon the type of programming languages used in both modes and the extent and variability of batch turnaround times—neither of which were reported in the original article.

Table 4.3. PROFILE OF THE AIR FORCE ACADEMY STUDY

METHOD	
Subjects	
Sample Size	53 (33TS, 20B)
Type of subjects	Undergraduates
Experience Level	Beginners
Problems	
Number and Type	Introductory
Difficulty Level	Moderate
Average Completion Time	9 hours
Online/Offline Facilities	
Online Facility	GE 635
Offline Facility	B 5500
Language Used	BASIC (TS) ALGOL (B)
Batch Turnaround Time	Two hours
Experimental Procedure	
Experimental Design	Matched groups
Statistical Tests	Mean difference tests
Experimental Controls	Class indoctrination
Motivational Controls	Grade
Recording Procedures	Student logs, computer printouts
Key Performance	Man-hours
Measures	Program runs, instructor rating, objective exam

RESULTS

Performance Measure	Time-Sharing Group	Batch Group	Statistical Significance
Sample Size	33	20	—
Man-Hours	7.9	9.4	—
Computer Runs	21	12	.01
Problem Grade	85.5	79.8	—
Range of Individual Differences (Man-hours)	2.6 to 27.2 man-hours (10:1)		
Range of Individual Differences (Program Runs)	3 to 79 (26:1)		

BOX SCORE

1. Time-sharing tends toward fewer man-hours to complete a standard problem and toward a higher-quality end product. However, neither of these tendencies was statistically significant.
2. Batch required fewer computer runs and required less computer time to solve the standard problem.
3. Individual differences in man-hours and in computer time are much larger than computer system differences.

Table 4.4. PROFILE OF THE ADAMS, COHEN STUDY

METHOD

Subjects

Sample Size	8
Type of Subjects	Students
Experience Level	Broad range

Problems

Number and Type	2 math problems
Difficulty Level	Easy to moderate
Average Completion Time	5 hours

Online/Offline Facilities

Online Facility	GE 265
Offline Facility	Control Data 6600
Language Used	FORTRAN
Batch Turnaround	Immediate (mins.)

Experimental Procedure

Experimental Design	Matched groups
Statistical Tests	Mean difference tests
Experimental Controls	One-week warmup
Motivational Controls	Volunteers
Recording Procedures	Student logs, questionnaires, automatic recording
Key Performance	Man-hours
Measures	Questionnaire, computer time

RESULTS

Performance Measure	Time-Sharing	Instant Batch
Man-Hours (both problems combined)	11.0	10.2

Problem Grade	5.5 correct solutions,	5 correct solutions
Student Preference	Rapid batch preferred, 7 to 1	
Individual Differences	Ranges from 3:1 to 37.5:1 for five measures of student time	
Computer Costs	$1000	$150

BOX SCORE

1. Time-sharing and instant batch were equally effective in regard to man-hours and quality of problem solutions.
2. Instant batch computer costs were much cheaper than time-sharing costs to solve the two test problems.
3. Individual differences overshadowed computer system differences.
4. The students overwhelmingly preferred instant batch over time-sharing; however, previous experience in both modes was not reported; student preference could have been associated with greater familiarity with batch.

4.2 METHODOLOGICAL PROBLEMS

The aim of this section is to review comparative methodology for the six exploratory studies to help determine technical scope and limitations. Subjects, problems, computer system facilities, experimental procedure, and performance measures are each discussed in turn.

There are a total of 213 subjects in all six studies. Students and trainees form the bulk of this population, with only one sample showing a highly experienced group of programmers (Grant and Sackman, 1967). The studies with small samples were organized around relatively efficient experimental designs to optimize the information yield from the results.

A critical experimental control factor, not previously discussed, enters into the selection of subjects. This factor is the nature of the computer-related experience of the subjects and their bias, as a result of their experience, toward time-shared or batch systems. For example, Erikson's (1966) subjects were trained primarily in online programming, whereas Schatzoff, Tsao, and Wiig indicated that their subjects had most of their previous experience in batch systems and used batch-oriented procedures in the experimental time-sharing mode. The other studies had subjects with various degrees of mixed online and offline experience. Obtaining equal familiarity and equal skill in online and offline activities is a difficult kind of experimental control. An antidote to the problem, only partially encountered in these studies, is to select subjects deliberately on the basis of equal experience and to offer them extensive and equal practice sessions in both modes up to some standard level of proficiency.

The problems cover a fairly wide area of programming and problem solving. They include mathematical problems, various puzzles, sorting procedures, and translation tasks. While many of these are typical of program tasks, they can hardly be put forth as representative. For example, there are no large data-base or statistical analysis problems—the kinds requiring large data storage and much computation, which tend to lend themselves more efficiently to batch processing. On the other hand, neither were there any particularly long, involved programs, such as those encountered in graphic and display-centered systems, that lend themselves more efficiently to time-sharing. All problems were individual rather than team-oriented tasks. Perhaps most basic of all, there are no empirical norms available to determine the representativeness of the various data-processing tasks.

The difficulty level of most studies varies from conceptually simple to moderately difficult. The time for subjects to complete experimental tasks varied from a few hours to 60 hours. The longer problems give some idea of the considerable manpower costs in conducting this kind of research and underscore the general tendency to use students or trainees.

The online/offline facilities reveal key dilemmas faced by the experimenters in attempting to construct unbiased and equal conditions for an objective comparison between time-sharing and batch processing. In the two SDC studies described in the previous chapter, time-sharing was real and batch processing had to be simulated on the Q-32 Time-Sharing System. In Smith's study, the basic system of batch and time-sharing was effectively simulated by providing "instant" turnaround time (several minutes); there were no conversational or interactive features in this simulated online condition. While Smith's study is primarily a comparison between conventional batch and fast-turnaround batch, it is included because of the useful information it contributes to timing and feedback aspects of the time-sharing/batch controversy. The Adams-Cohen study and the Schatzaff, Tsao, and Wiig study were the only ones offering ostensibly comparable online and offline modes without resorting to some form of simulation.

The computer language employed is another difficult control variable. In three studies, subjects used the same language, equally applicable and useful for both modes. Erikson used TINT, an interactive language, for the nointeractive mode. In the Grant-Sackman (1967) study, most subjects used JTS, originally a batch-processing language, later adapted to time-sharing. Schatzoff, Tsao, and Wiig do not mention any languages at all. Since they indicate that their subjects used batch procedures in the time-sharing mode, and that their subjects only had a brief indoctrination in time-sharing, one cannot help but wonder whether their comparison provided reasonably comparable starting conditions under both experimental modes. This same criticism applies, at least in part, to the other studies.

Experimental control problems are compounded further with respect to turnaround time under the batch mode. These turnaround times vary from minutes to hours to next-day turnaround. Grant and Sackman controlled this variable at a constant value of two hours; Adams and Cohen provided "instant" turnaround. While this procedure provided rigorous experimental control over turnaround time, it was obviously unrealistic in not providing variability in turnaround service. The other investigators apparently left their subjects to the vagaries of their particular operational batch system without obtaining exact measures of turnaround time for each run.

In addition, for all studies, it is not clear whether subject waiting time during batch turnaround was spent working on the problem, or not working on the problem. For some studies, it was not clear whether turnaround time was included or excluded in subject logs of man-hours spent on the experimental task. Future studies should incorporate systematic variation and control of machine turnaround time, and careful recording of what the subject does during this time. Lack of experimental controls in this area unquestionably increases error variance in performance measurement and decreases the reliability of the final results.

The next category, experimental procedure, reveals a remarkable spectrum of experimental designs. The Graeco-Latin Square configuration of the Schatzoff, Tsao, and Wiig study is the most sophisticated design, whereas the Smith study and the Adams-Cohen study merely compared mean scores of matched groups without any reported measures of dispersion or any tests of statistical significance. With a sample of four subjects, the Schatzoff, Tsao, and Wigg study had to have optimal statistical efficiency to demonstrate reliable results, whereas with Smith's sample of 127 subjects, observed mean differences are correspondingly more reliable. Nevertheless, the absence of statistical tests, as well as the neglect in reporting measures of dispersion in the data from which statistical tests may be constructed, are to be deplored, since these practices reduce the cost-effective yield of an experiment, leave quantitative results ambiguous, and deprive the larger community of useful information on individual differences.

The three experiments using Latin-Square designs employed analysis of variance and correlational techniques to the findings, which not only provided statistical tests for online/offline comparisons, but also yielded valuable information on problem and individual performance differences. The Grant-Sackman study was the only one which included an exploratory factor analysis of subject performance.

The experimental controls included matching of groups primarily on the basis of questionnaire items. The three studies using Latin-Square designs, involved stratified samples of subjects (e g, experienced programmers, high-performance students, trainees) with random assignments of subjects to the various test conditions in accordance with the experimental design. Motivational controls essentially consisted of class grades for students and fulfillment of job assignments for experienced programmers. Individual competition probably spurred most subjects to work hard at their assigned tasks and to keep most of their problem strategy and tactics to themselves, at least in the small sample experiments.

These motivational constraints were probably less effective in Smith's large sample.

The recording procedures characteristically included computer recording for machine usage, subject logs for man-hours spent on experimental tasks, questionnaires for selecting and matching subjects and for collecting observations and ratings on computer system preference and self-performance. Paper and pencil tests of programmer ability were used in three studies. Schatzoff, Tsao, and Wiig selected students who received a grade of A on the IBM Data Processing Aptitude Test; and in the two SDC studies, the Basic Programming Knowledge Test (BPKT) was administered to the subjects. Of the various recording procedures, the computer records were probably the most objective, whereas subject logs were open to intentional and unintentional errors. In the four studies with small samples, it was easier to keep the subjects under surveillance, to monitor their manual reporting procedures, and to resolve discrepancies tactfully as they arose. In the larger sample studies, experimenter monitoring of individuals had to be more indirect. Possible errors or bias in subject reporting procedures are typically not discussed in any detail.

The last category covers the experimental payoff. The two key performance measures running through all studies are man-hours and computer time required to complete experimental tasks. The computer time measure is the most straightforward. Man-hour measures appear in various forms and are partitioned in different ways. For example, the two SDC studies and the Adams-Cohen study distinguish coding time from debugging time; the other studies incorporate an overall measure of elapsed time with different ways of slicing man hours spent on experimental tasks. Cross-comparisons are somewhat difficult because measures are defined differently for different contexts.

The three studies utilizing Latin-Square designs devote some attention to the analysis of individual performance differences. Although individual differences were not originally a key objective of these studies, there was serendipitous fallout of human differences from the analysis of variance in each investigation.

The SDC studies used final program size and running time as measures of performance. It is surprising that these objective, easily obtainable, and obvious measures of programming efficiency were not reported in the other two studies. It would be of value to test whether programs are written more efficiently, as measured by these two indexes, in the online or the offline mode.

The performance measures in the Schatzoff, Tsao, and Wiig study include estimates comparing online/offline costs which incorporate man and machine factors. These costs were derived from experimental measures of human and machine time which were used as empirical parameters in simple cost models.

In an attempt to explore the relation between paper and pencil tests and performance on experimental tasks, the two SDC studies incorporated scores on the BPKT in their analyses of individual differences. Since sample sizes were small, and since validity correlations of successful paper-and-pencil tests of job performance are traditionally moderate to low, these tests, at best, were highly tentative probes.

Summing up, what are the chief methodological characteristics, strengths, and weaknesses of these six exploratory studies in regard to subjects, problems, computer facilities, experimental procedure, and performance measures? The subjects were primarily students or trainees; experienced data-processing personnel were used in only one study. While the experimental problems ranged over a broad area, involving many types of data-processing tasks and procedures and requiring many hours for successful solutions, certain types of tasks prominently occurring in batch processing and in time-sharing were not encountered in such studies, and it is difficult to assess how representative these problems are for data processing in general, and how well they are balanced for an objective online/offline comparison. Some of the toughest problems arose in providing comparable time-sharing/batch facilities; matched computer and equivalent languages posed many problems; and the crucial variable of batch turnaround time was generally not systematically controlled.

The experimental procedures showed diverse levels of experimental sophistication, with the most critical problems occurring in the observation and measurement of human performance. Even at this early stage, the range of performance measures is impressive, covering a variety of man-machine indexes; on the other hand, the paucity of automatically collected measures of human and program performance, particularly in the online setting, is somewhat disappointing. More powerful online techniques, such as regenerative recording of user performance—a technique for capturing the complete real-time interaction between the user and the computer so that it can be played back in its entirety for later analysis (Sackman, 1967)—should be developed and applied to the experimental investigation of a broad spectrum of user tasks.

4.3 INTERPRETIVE PROBLEMS

What are the consistent patterns, the ambiguities, and the gaps in the findings of the four exploratory studies? Six types of performance measures in the data are reviewed: subject time, computer time, system costs, user preference, individual differences and special measures.

Four out of six studies show time-sharing (or its simulated equivalent) to result in less human time in producing programs or solving problems than batch processing (or its simulated equivalent). The Schatzoff, Tsao, and Wiig study and the Adams and Cohen study show a reverse trend. The former study shows less elapsed time for completion of experimental tasks under time-sharing. On the other hand, the Erikson study, which shows the greatest relative performance advantage for time-sharing (almost 2:1 in trainee man-hours), was based on the use of an interactive interpretive language in both modes, which created a favorable bias for time-sharing. With these qualifiers at both extremes in mind, it appears that time-sharing does tend to require less elapsed time and fewer man-hours to produce programs and solve problems. The magnitude of this performance advantage is moderate—the median improvement for all six studies is 20% less human time under time-sharing than in batch processing. No claims are made for the meaning or the stability of this or the other medians, but they do give a crude rule of thumb for the pooled results of these six studies.

The comparative results on computer time show a reverse

trend. The median ratio is 1.5:1 in favor of batch for computer time. That is, time-sharing requires some 50% extra computer time to perform standard tasks for these six studies.

The combined results for human time and computer time, assuming that the reported trends are reliable, reinforce the hypothesis that in time-sharing the user trades off computer time for his own time. To state the extreme case, the time-sharing user is less likely to check out his program as thoroughly as he can at his desk, and is more likely to take a rough version or only a partially checked program to the computer for a trial run than his batch counterpart. Time-sharing critics assail this practice by claiming that the user develops careless and lazy work habits through excessive reliance on extra computer runs; time-sharing advocates assert that such behavior allows more intelligent exploration and testing of alternative solutions at a natural pace for the user when and as problems arise. While there is probably some truth to both positions (which are not mutually exclusive), we should look to further experimental analyses of problem-solving stages in both modes that lead to improved hypotheses in the dynamics of man-computer communication—improved hypotheses to supersede these rather crude stereotypes of user behavior under time-sharing and batch processing.

The data on system costs shows a standoff. These estimates are based on immediate man-hour and computer time costs only. While only two studies reported cost estimates, the overall results indicate that one study shows definitely less expense for time-sharing (less computer time and fewer man-hours), three studies show roughly equal costs for both modes (computer time and man-hour results in opposite cost directions), and the remaining two show a cost advantage for batch processing. In essence, the time-sharing advantage in man-hours is neutralized by the batch advantage in computer time. Here again the results are contingent upon unique experimental conditions.

The comparative results on user attitudes show a trend for time-sharing over batch. As batch evolves toward shorter turnaround times, the competition is narrowing down to time-sharing vs. fast batch. The available experimental data result in a draw between these two competitors. The Erikson study shows an advantage for time-sharing over simulated fast batch. The Adams-Cohen study shows essentially equivalent performance for time-sharing and fast batch, but with strong user preference for batch. User preference and demonstrated superior performance for the interactive conversational features of time-sharing over fast batch is still a moot point.

Individual differences were systematically investigated in those three studies using analysis of variance techniques. In each case, performance differences between subjects were dominant and overshadowed system differences between time-sharing and batch processing. The observed ranges were sometimes at an order of magnitude between best and poorest performers—even with relatively stratified subject samples.

Except for the Grant-Sackman exploratory factor analysis of individual performance differences, no systematic analysis of human problem-solving differences was attempted. This factor analysis resulted in two well-defined and essentially independent factors —one concerned with programming speed (low coding and debugging time, and low computer time) and the other with program economy (smaller and faster-running programs). While the entire area of individual differences in man-computer communication, from economic, system-performance, and humanistic points of view, is probably more important than operating system differences; nevertheless, little has been done and virtually nothing is known about such individual differences.

The distribution of successive computer runs in Smith's study reveals interesting differences between the instant and the conventional batch modes. Median turnaround time for subjects to prepare their next run is only about half as long in the instant mode as in conventional batch. Problem-solving speed is apparently slower under conventional batch. As time-sharing adherents have often pointed out, ready accessibility of computer services lends itself to natural pacing in problem-solving tasks, whereas the forced delays inherent in conventional batch turnaround time tend to disrupt normal problem-solving patterns and inhibit spontaneous closure. Unfortunately, the intervals between successive computer runs under batch, and between successive console sessions under time-sharing were not reported in the other studies; thus, the above hypothesis is still conjectural. Nor does this hypothesis bear upon the differences between instant batch versus interactive time-sharing.

The two SDC studies, at least as far as program size and running time are concerned, are neutral with respect to program differences between time-sharing and simulated batch modes. It would be of interest if online/offline experiments were conducted in which subjects were instructed to write short and fast-running programs in addition to solving the experimental tasks. Without such instructions subjects are likely to concentrate primarily on working solutions rather than on operating costs of the finished product. Program size and running time can be used to measure comparative "quality" of final programs—a useful measure in real-time computer systems, for example, where space and running time are often at a premium.

What is the composite picture of experimental comparisons of time-sharing and batch systems, at least as depicted by the available studies, and what are the main gaps in this portrait? The preliminary portrait that emerges seems to show that time-sharing is more likely to get the job done faster, at a working pace preferred by users. Batch requires less computer time and consequently less cost than time-sharing. The balance could easily be shifted if there is prior familiarity with batch or time-sharing and built-in individual or institutional bias toward one or the other. Especially if this familiarity or bias is coupled to computer system tools or languages built for one mode rather than the other, the balance could be tipped in the familiar direction. Overshadowing these relatively small system differences are wide-ranging individual differences which account for most of the observed variance in performance.

Virtually nothing was done on human creativity in the online/offline setting in these exploratory studies. No studies were performed on the distinctive characteristics of conversational interaction in time-sharing and the extent to which these characteristics offer any advantage over fast batch systems. No work has been done on a comparative error analysis of user performance between time-sharing and batch processing except for some preliminary tabulations listed by Smith (1967). There are no detailed case histories on the real-time pattern of problem-solving that occurs under online and offline conditions, away from the computer as well as at the computer—a kind of time-and-motion study of human decision making. Until we understand the behavioral dynamics of man-computer communication, we can hardly expect to understand the relative tradeoff between alternative modes of data processing.

4.4 SUMMARY AND CONCLUSIONS

The contributions of the six exploratory studies are summarized below to set the stage for the more comprehensive studies which follow. This capsule review is treated under two main heads: methodology and findings.

4.4.1 Methodology

Initial Studies. Six initial experimental studies were reviewed that compared some form of time-sharing with a contrasting version of batch processing taking into consideration standard tasks and various measures of user and system performance.

Subjects. The subjects in these studies were primarily college students or trainees; experienced data-processing personnel were employed in only one study. Four studies had 12 subjects or less, and were highly exploratory, while the other studies had samples of 127 and 53 students.

Problems. The experimental tasks varied over a broad range of problems, often requiring days or even weeks for successful solutions. While the variety and difficulty levels of the experimental problems were impressive, some types of tasks prominently encountered in both modes were not employed. It was not possible to assess how representative the experimental problems were with respect to data-processing in general, or, more particularly, with respect to an objective comparison between online and offline operations.

Method. Difficult methodological problems arose in arranging comparable time-sharing and batch facilities; equivalent computers, languages, and facilities often had to be simulated; turnaround time in the batch mode was generally uncontrolled.

Experimental Design. Experimental procedures showed diverse levels of sophistication, ranging from a Graeco-Latin Square design to descriptive statistics without tests of significance. The most critical problems arose in the observation and measurement of human performance.

Performance Measures. The performance measures included human time, machine time, comparative costs, user preference, program efficiency and a variety of special measures. There was a paucity of online and automatically collected measures of human and program performance, and, except for one preliminary study, no reported analyses of man-computer errors.

Cost Effectiveness. The above combination of methodological problems and pitfalls led to large variations in reported comparative cost effectiveness of time-sharing vs. batch processing—variations that were very sensitive to the precise man-machine conditions and constraints under which the experimental comparisons were made.

4.4.2 Results

Man-Hours. Time-sharing required fewer man-hours than batch processing for completion of experimental tasks. The median value for the pooled results of all six studies showed a 20% advantage for time-sharing.

Machine-Time. The results on computer time showed more machine time under time-sharing than under batch processing for the pooled set of experimental tasks, with 50% extra machine time as the median value for time-sharing.

Use of Resources. The tendency toward fewer man-hours and more computer time under time-sharing suggests the hypothesis that time-sharing users tend to trade off computer time for human time—more exploratory computer runs with less polished programs—which may be positively interpreted as more intelligent exploration of a wider variety of problem alternatives, or negatively as careless use of computer resources, or both.

Costs. Comparison of man-machine system costs on available data seemed to show no definite advantage under either mode, except, as indicated above, for a tendency toward reduced manpower costs under time-sharing, and lower computer facility costs for the batch mode.

User Preference. When ratings were formally collected, a decided user preference was demonstrated for time-sharing over conventional batch. Attitudinal data comparing fast or "instant" batch against time-sharing showed a standoff between these two modes.

Individual Differences. Whenever data were available on individual differences in subject performance, such individual differences generally overshadowed time-sharing/batch system differences. Only initial, exploratory probes were conducted to determine the nature and basis of the large variations observed in individual man-machine effectiveness.

Program Size and Time Differences. Available data indicated no significant differences in final program size or running time when produced under time-sharing and batch conditions.

Other Features. While tentative evidence was gathered indicating shorter intervals between successive computer runs for fast batch as compared to conventional batch, no definitive evidence was available on systematic variations of turnaround time nor on the interactive features of time-sharing.

Experimental investigation of man-computer problem solving is seen to have been virtually nonexistent in the formative years of computing, from World War II until the early 1960's. This was the predisciplinary era in which the humanistic lag and the associated experimental lag in man-computer communication took hold and became firmly entrenched in the first generation of computer professionals for a variety of technical, economic, and social reasons. The advent and rapid development of time-sharing in the 1960's and the glittering prospects of public computer utilities broke the quarantine on scientific study of the human use of computers. User statistics appeared from pioneering time-sharing systems. A portrait of user features in man-computer communication began to emerge. The first experimental studies of users with standard problems under controlled online and offline conditions made their appearance. With these studies the transition was made from predisciplinary to early experimental investigation of man-computer problem solving. Key experimental parameters emerged and the richness and diversity of human behavior in computerized environments became apparent. Finally, the stage was set for studies focusing more on human problem-solving and less on technical computer system differences; it was also time for a cross-fertilization of the method and findings of man-computer studies with the behavioral and social sciences.

PART II

AN EXPERIMENTAL INQUIRY INTO HUMAN PROBLEM-SOLVING

5

EXPERIMENTAL METHOD AND COMPUTER SYSTEM RESULTS

THE comprehensive study which is the major concern of Part II is an extension of the original experimental comparison of time-sharing and batch processing conducted at MIT by Gold (1967). In this extension (a collaborative effort by the author and Gold, 1968) the experimental data were analyzed with primary emphasis on human problem-solving and individual differences. The experimental design involved two matched groups of students, 33 working under time-sharing and 33 in the batch mode. The students' task was an open-end, computerized simulation of the construction industry in which each student, as an independent builder, tried to maximize his profit score by improving his decision rules and optimizing available parameters. In this extension of the original study, a total of 53 measures were statistically analyzed, including automatically recorded variables on man-machine performance, a great variety of questionnaire data, and class grades. As the next three chapters will show, the results yielded a considerable amount of new information on time-sharing and batch differences in man-computer communication; on the factor-analytic structure of individual differences in man-computer performance; on systematic changes in user attitudes and motivation; on the variability and extent of human error; and on the behavioral dynamics of problem-solving in an open-end task. The findings generally confirm expectations from earlier exploratory studies—batch is more efficient for economical machine operations, whereas time-sharing is more effective throughout virtually all stages of human problem-solving for the experimental task.

5.1 THE EXPERIMENTAL PROBLEM

The exploratory literature on time-sharing vs. batch has consistently pointed up the overwhelming importance of individual differences and has offered some hints on the underpinnings of such differences in problem-solving and human creativity. We have seen that human performance differences overshadow computer system differences, typically by an order of magnitude.

The pervasive presence of large individual differences has profound implications for the future development and growth of man-computer communications. From an economic viewpoint, managers of computer centers can realize greater cost savings through improved techniques for testing, selecting, training, and motivating programmers and other computer personnel. Technically, faster and better solutions to data-processing problems are determined primarily by the effectiveness of individuals and secondarily by the particular computer system, languages, or facilities that are used. Educationally, allowance should be made for wide-ranging individual differences by designing and constructing software at graded difficulty levels commensurate with the full spectrum of user proficiency. Psychologically, we need to explore individual user style and pacing to tailor information services to fit the large variations in human problem-solving. Socially, we are only beginning to recognize the great diversity of human skills and needs for information services, all of which require the computer utility to be responsive to individuals rather than to the mass or the crowd.

Only the surface has been scratched in experimental attempts to understand problem-solving behavior in man-computer communication. The available results from the six exploratory online/offline experiments offer little data on recognizable stages in problem-solving (such as preparation, incubation, illumination, and verification). Very little is known on the correlates and extent of human error in man-computer communication, nor on the existence of error-prone individuals. This is an ironic commentary on the data-processing field in view of the central economic importance of program debugging.

The impact of man-computer communication on human creativity has not been experimentally measured even though it is the subject of endless speculation with professionals and laymen. The literature is almost devoid of case histories of individual problem-solving in a man-computer setting. How can we expect to extend mass information services to the public when we are still in the dark on the fundamental elements of human behavior in man-computer dialogue?

The purpose of this study was to extend experimental method and findings more deeply into the area of human problem-solving in computerized settings. In the original experiment, considerable data on human problem-solving was collected but was not analyzed, since the main effort was directed toward development and verification of a methodology for evaluating time-sharing usage. Costs, usage, and performance difference between time-sharing and batch systems were key considerations. In contrast, this study was primarily concerned with human behavior and individual differences in problem-solving under online and offline conditions. Accordingly, the present inquiry contains much new data and new analyses at a level of detail and comprehensiveness that, to our knowledge, was not present in previous work in this area.

5.2 EXPERIMENTAL PROCEDURE

Table 5.1 summarizes the experimental design and procedure followed in the original study. The original dissertation (Gold, 1967) should be consulted for full details, complete listings of data forms, and individual scores. Each of the listed items in Table 5.1 is briefly discussed to point out special features and limitations.

Table 5.1. SUMMARY OF EXPERIMENTAL PROCEDURE

Subjects	
Sample Size	66
Type of Subjects	Undergraduate and graduate students
Experience Level	78% of subjects had taken at least one programming course
Problems	
Number and Type	One problem, simulation model of construction industry
Difficulty Level	Moderately difficult, open-ended problem
Average Completion Time	15 to 20 man-hours
Online/Offline Facilities	
Online Facility	MIT Time-Sharing, IBM 7094
Batch Facility	MIT Batch Facility, IBM 7094
Language Used	Dynamo—simulation language used in time-sharing and batch
Batch Turnaround Time	6 hours (daytime), 10 hours (overnight), variable
Time-Sharing Availability	Maximum of one hour per console session per day for each student
Experimental Procedure	
Experimental Design	Two matched groups of subjects
Statistical Tests	A variety of nonparametric statistics comparing the two groups
Experimental Controls	Questionnaire items, deadline for completed problem
Motivational Controls	Class grades
Recording Procedures	Computer records, student logs and questionnaires

The original sample included 33 individuals in the batch group and 33 in the time-sharing group. Some students did not complete their experimental assignment and others turned in incomplete data. The listed sample size of 66 is thus a maximum figure which varies with particular measures. In relation to the other online/offline studies, the student sample should be viewed essentially as a group of trainees, since most had less than one year's experience in computer programming courses.

The problem was a computerized simulation model of the construction industry and its market. The student's task was to learn how to operate and work with the model, its parameters, and constraints, in accordance with a set of written rules and instructions. When the subject could produce an error-free run with the model, his initial profit score was $1000, which was equivalent to the decision rule followed by the industry as a whole, the initial baseline. His task was to devise improved decision rules over and above the industrial baseline, in order to maximize his profit as an independent, small-scale builder in this simulated, cyclical market. When he worked out and plugged in a new decision rule and adjusted available parameters, he would run his revised model. The simulation pass would either output an error statement, if some mistake were made in format or syntax, or it would run to completion, indicating a new profit score.

The task was open-ended in the sense that a revised decision rule or a more optimally adjusted parameter could lead to a higher profit score. The student continued working at the problem until he felt he had reached a satisfactory profit level or until the elapsed time for the assignment ran out. This task had the methodological advantage of measuring how well the student did throughout the entire course of the experiment; this was the only study to date with this useful feature.

The problem is described as "moderately difficult" in Table 5.1 on several counts. First, the students had to master the mechanics of the Dynamo simulation language and the Industrial Dynamics model to reach the level where they could execute an error-free run to obtain a score of $1000 (equivalent to the industrial norm). If they could not do this, they received no profit score; 21 subjects in the total initial sample of 66 were unable to reach this point. Next, the students had to learn how to manipulate and change the decision rule and associated parameters to increase their profit beyond the average for the industry. There were 3 students who never got beyond the $1000 baseline. The remaining 42 students were able to augment their profits, but even these scores were strung out in a positively skewed distribution (most scores tending to pile up near the low end). These general results indicate that the model was very difficult for some, moderately difficult for most, and easy for only a small proportion of the total sample.

The online/offline modes, as shown in Table 5.1, involved the same computer and the same simulation language and model. With an average six-hour turnaround in the batch mode, the student could submit two batch runs per day if he turned in the first job early in the morning and the second by late evening. If he wished, he could submit several runs at a time to try out more than one alterative.

Students were matched on experience, background, and attitudes, as derived from questionnaire responses, and then they were randomly assigned to each of the two experimental groups. The basic experimental design in the original study was a straightforward comparison of nonparametric distributions for various measures of performance between the batch and time-sharing groups.

The students were notified that their grades would be determined by their highest profit score in the simulation model, and by a written report on the assigned problem that they were required to turn in, with equal weight for each requirement. Their basic motivation was the class grade. The written instructions were explicit on the point that they would not be graded on their questionnaire responses nor on the time that it took them to complete the problem. The students were constrained, however, in terms of lapsed time to turn in their work—the end of the 10-day assignment was their deadline. While the maximum profit score was open-ended, maximum elapsed time was not, and in this sense, the experimental problem was not a true "power" test, nor a completely open-ended problem.

5.3 DATA ANALYSIS IN THIS INQUIRY

The primary aim of the current study was to assemble the unanalyzed questionnaire and performance data of the original study and subject these data to exploratory, multivariate analyses with respect to behavioral attributes under online and offline conditions. The plan of the analysis was fivefold:

- Obtain descriptive statistics such as frequency distributions, means, standard deviations, and bivariate correlations for each of the experimental groups and the combined sample. This initial pass would decribe the extent of individual differences and set the stage for follow-on analyses of such differences.
- Analyze the mean differences and variance differences between the online and offline groups, distinguish group differences from individual differences, and establish an initial behavioral profile contrasting problem-solving patterns in the two groups
- Analyze bivariate correlations among the various performance measures in the total sample to explore empirical relationships, test for similarities in problem-solving behavior cutting across both groups, and lay the groundwork for subsequent factor analyses.
- Conduct exploratory factor analyses of the available data base, for each group separately and for the combined group; test for the presence or absence of a general factor in problem-solving; test for group factors under both modes.
- Conduct special multivariate tests on particular subsets of the total data base as suggested by leads drawn from the previous steps.

The five-step plan places strong emphasis on exploratory techniques. The orientation of the analysis was to conduct an eclectic and iterative test and evaluation of hypotheses derived from initial hypotheses, as well as new ones suggested to us by the data in the course of the analysis. Such an omnibus approach in test and evaluation seemed appropriate for this new field in man-computer problem-solving, in which so little is known.

The possibility of online statistical analysis of the data was considered and dropped in favor of offline analysis. Available online statistical services were adequate for data inspection, descriptive statistics, and various types of bivariate analyses but they could not handle more complex techniques such as analysis of variance, factor analysis, and regression analysis. Rather than set up the overhead twice for two separate data bases, one for offline and another for online analysis, we selected the offline option at the System Development Corporation which included all the statistical procedures we expected to use (see McCornack,* 1968, for a description of SDC statistical services).

5.4 PERFORMANCE MEASURES

The data base of this study essentially consisted of a matrix of 53 measures related to performance for the 66 subjects in the original sample. The 53 variables listed in Table 5.2 show the various types of measures employed in this study. Four groups are indicated in this table: pretest questionnaire, posttest questionnaires, study grades on the experimental task, and various man-machine measures of performance.

The pretest questionnaire (items 1 to 6 in Table 5.2) includes control variables such as experience items and attitudes toward time-sharing and batch processing at the beginning of the experiment. The posttest questionnaires include a second administration of the pretest questionnaire (items 13 to 18) to test for attitudinal and control variable changes, and a great variety of other measures concerned with problem-solving behavior with special emphasis on the allocation of the students' time and effort. These measures (7 to 35) range from yes/no answers, to

* We are indebted to R. McCornack for statistical consultation and services throughout this study.

Table 5.2 EXPERIMENTAL VARIABLES

A. PRETEST QUESTIONNAIRE

No.	Name	Description	Type of Measure
1	*Dynamo Experience	How much experience have you had writing Dynamo programs?	Rating Scale, 1-9
2	Industrial Dynamics Experience	How much experience have you had analyzing Industrial Dynamics problems?	"
3	Batch Dynamo Experience	How much experience have you had using Dynamo on the batch-processing computer system?	"
4	Batch Evaluation	What is the value of the batch-processing system in helping you analyze Industrial Dynamics problems?	"
5	Dynamo Time-Sharing Experience	How much experience have you had using Dynamo on the time-sharing computer system?	"
6	Time-Sharing Evaluation	What is the value of the time-sharing system in helping you analyze Industrial Dynamics problems?	"

B. POSTTEST QUESTIONNAIRES

No.	Name	Description	Type of Measure
7	Sufficient Time	Have you had sufficient time to complete your analysis of the Construction Industry case?	Yes, 1; No, 0
8	Completion Date	If your answer to question 1 is yes, when did you complete your analysis?	Day of Month
9	Time Needed	If your answer to question 1 is no, how much more time	Hours

Table 5.2 EXPERIMENTAL VARIABLES (Cont'd)

No.	Name	Description	Type of Measure
		would you have needed to complete your analysis?	
10	Computer System Usefulness	How useful was the computer system you used (batch processing or time-sharing) in helping you solve the Construction Industry case?	Rating Scale, 1-9
11	Satisfaction with Results	How satisfied are you with your final results?	"
12	Usefulness of Other System	How useful would the other computer system have been in helping you solve the Construction Industry case?	"
13	*Dynamo Experience	How much experience have you had writing Dynamo programs?	"
14	Industrial Dynamics Experience	How much experience have you had analyzing Industrial Dynamics problems?	Rating Scale, 1-9
15	Batch Dynamo Experience	How much experience have you had using Dynamo on the batch-processing computer system?	"
16	Batch Evaluation	What is the value of the batch-processing system in helping you analyze Industrial Dynamics problems?	
17	Dynamo Time-Sharing Experience	How much experience have you had using Dynamo on the time-sharing computer system?	"
18	Time-Sharing Evaluation	What is the value of the time-sharing system in helping you analyze Industrial Dynamics problems?	"

* These and the five successive variables are pretest and posttest administrations of the same questionnaire.

19	First Decision Rule Hours	When did you develop the general concept that resulted in your first decision rule for Mr. Z? After .... hours of work on the project?	Hours
20	First Decision Rule Date	On March ....?	Day of Month
21	Alternate Decision Rules	How many different general concepts (leading to decision rules) did you devise for possible use by Mr. Z?	Integer
22	Last Decision Rule Hours	If you devised more than one general concept, when did you devise the last concept you used? After .... hours of work on the project?	Hours
23	Last Decision Rule Date	On March ....?	Day of Month
24	Successful Decision Rule	If you devised more than one general concept, which one did you find most successful? (First, second, etc.)?	Integer
25	Successful Decision Rule Hours	When did you devise your most successful concept? After .... hours of work on the project?	Hours
26	Successful Decision Rule Date	On March ....?	Day of Month
27	Total Problem Time	How much total time did you expend on this problem?	Hours
28	Reacquaintance Time	Approximately what percentage of your time was spent on the following: Reacquaintance time?	Percent
29	General Concept Time	General Concept Time?	"
30	Parameter Time	Parameter Time?	"

Table 5.2 EXPERIMENTAL VARIABLES (Cont'd)

No.	Name	Description	Type of Measure
31	Editing Time	Editing Time?	Percent
32	Time on Results	Time on Results?	"
33	Waiting for Results	Waiting for Results?	"
34	Diversion of Attention	How much attention did you divert from your other courses because of this project?	Rating Scale, 1-9
35	Time from Courses	How much time did this assignment take from your other courses? .... hours?	Hours
	C. CLASS GRADES ON EXPERIMENTAL TASK		
36	Grade A: Understanding Model Dynamics	Teacher evaluation of student's written reports.	Teacher Rating 1-15
37	Grade B: Strategy with Model	"	"
38	Grade C: Flexibility of Model	"	Teacher Rating 1-10
39	Grade D: Perceptiveness and Understanding	"	"
40	Sum of Grades	"	Sum of Four Grades
	D. MAN-MACHINE MEASURES OF PERFORMANCE		
41	Maximum Performance (Both Groups)	Maximum profit score on Dynamo simulation model	Profit in Dollars

42	CPU Time (Both Groups)	Computer time, excluding overhead	Seconds
43	Elapsed Time (Both Groups)	Elapsed days on problem	Days
44	Total Interactions (TS Only)	Total online user inputs	Integer
45	CPU + Input/Output (TS Only)	Computer time, including overhead	Seconds
46	Percent Individual Throughput (TS Only)	CPU/(CPU + I/O)	Percent
47	Percent Edit (TS Only)	Edit time/total computer time	"
48	Percent Print (TS Only)	Print time/total computer time	"
49	Percent Compile and Run (TS Only)	Compile time/total computer time	"
50	Percent Successful Interactions (TS Only)	Successful/total interactions	"
51	Total Runs (Batch Only)	Total batch runs	Integer
52	Percent Successful Runs (Batch Only)	Successful/total runs	Percent
53	Batch vs. Time-Sharing	Experimental groups	Batch, 1; Time-Sharing, 0

a standard nine-point rating scale for attitude scores, to percentage scores for functional allocation of problem-solving time, to estimates of man-hours and the reporting of exact dates for computing sub-tasks. These various items were designed to provide some insight into describing attitudes toward competitive computer systems, problem-solving style, and in testing for differences between online and offline behavior.

The third group of variables listed in Table 5.2 (36-40) refers to teacher grades of written student reports on the experimental task. Four grades on various aspects of the students' written performance are indicated, including a fifth measure which is the arithmetic sum of the separate grades. The fourth and last group of variables covers various objective measures of performance that were automatically recorded. These include the highest profit score on the business simulation model, machine time, elapsed time spent on problems, error scores and a percentage breakdown of task activities under the time-sharing mode. Throughout the rest of Part II, variable names are usually accompanied by their numbers, as listed in Table 5.2, for more convenient reference.

5.5 DIFFERENCES BETWEEN TIME-SHARING AND BATCH PROCESSING

The initial results cover computer system differences. Statistical tests are described, observed findings are tabulated, and preliminary interpretations are given.

Mean difference comparisons between the time-sharing and batch groups are shown in Table 5.3. This table is read as follows. The first six columns to the right of the stub refer to the sample size and observed mean and standard deviation for each listed variable for the two experimental groups. The Probability of Mean Difference column refers to the level of significance obtained for the calculated t-value (or F-test) for the observed mean difference. The probabilities are reported to three significant figures; only values significant at the 5% level are listed and probabilities of .001 or less are reported as .001. Only nonredundant variables that apply equally to both groups were included in Table 5.3 for a total of 43 measures.

The next column, Probability of Standard Deviation Difference, refers to the observed significance of the difference between variance of the two groups, as determined by the Bartlett test for homogeneity of variance which is produced by the statistical routine employed. In the event that unequal variances were found, the results of Welch's test for mean differences are reported under the Mean Difference column (the Welch test, also produced by our statistical routine, does not require equal variances for testing mean differences). The last column, Correlation Ratio, lists the obtained correlation between the online/offline groups for the given variable. For correlations between the dichotomized experimental groups against continuous, normally distributed variables, the correlation is equivalent to a point-biserial coefficient. The correlation ratio measures the strength of the observed relationship; the square of this coefficient is equal to that proportion of total variance associated with group differences. As in the other statistical results, only those coefficients significant at the 5% level are listed (the significance level of the correlation ratio is the same as that shown for the mean difference).

Notable findings are briefly discussed in their listed order in Table 5.3. Variable 6, Time-Sharing Evaluation, shows that the time-sharing group had a higher pretest evaluation of time-sharing than the batch group; this finding, while significant, is simply a chance fluctuation of the random assignment of students to experimental groups.

Variable 10, Computer System Usefulness, shows a decided posttest preference for the online mode. This finding is borne out in very similar findings for the next two variables (11 and 12), Satisfaction with Results and Usefulness of Other System. The time-sharing group was more satisfied with its final product than the batch group; the online group was also more consistent in its ratings than the offline group, as shown by a significantly smaller standard deviation. The ratings on the Usefulness of the Other System are among the most striking results of this study. The batch group showed an average rating of eight for time-sharing on a scale that runs from one to nine, whereas the time-sharing group rated batch at three—there was almost no overlap between the two groups, as indicated by the very high correlation ratio of .86. Further, while the online subjects showed a standard deviation of some two points on this scale, the offline subjects

Table 5.3. TIME-SHARING AND BATCH GROUP DIFFERENCES

Variable		Time-Sharing Group			Batch-Processing Group			Prob. Mean Diff.	Prob. SD Diff.	Correlation Ratio
No.	Name	N	Mean	SD	N	Mean	SD			
1	Dynamo Experience	29	2.103	.9763	29	1.965	1.267	—	—	—
2	Industrial Dynamics Experience	30	2.233	1.135	29	2.137	1.355	—	—	—
3	Batch Dynamo Experience	30	1.366	1.098	29	1.206	.6198	—	.003	—
4	Batch Evaluation	30	1.766	1.430	29	1.827	1.559	—	—	—
5	Dynamo Time-Sharing Experience	30	2.733	1.257	29	2.586	1.323	—	—	—
6	Time-Sharing Evaluation	28	6.928	1.844	28	5.321	2.373	.006	—	.36
7	Sufficient Time	25	.6400	.4899	20	.4000	.5026	—	—	—
8	Completion Date	16	17.43	1.459	8	16.87	2.642	—	—	—
9	Time Needed	9	9.222	10.76	11	9.818	6.289	—	—	—
10	Computer System Usefulness	25	7.800	1.825	22	4.181	2.174	.001	—	.68
11	Satisfaction with Results	25	6.760	1.362	22	4.363	2.786	.009	.001	.49
12	Usefulness of Other System	24	3.125	1.848	22	8.090	.9211	.001	.002	.86
13	Dynamo Experience	25	4.760	1.451	22	3.863	1.457	.040	—	.30
14	Industrial Dynamics Experience	25	4.600	1.290	22	4.000	1.380	—	—	—
15	Batch Dynamo Experience	25	1.320	1.144	22	3.136	1.909	.001	.017	.51
16	Batch Evaluation	16	2.187	1.276	22	3.227	1.950	—	—	—
17	Dynamo Time-Sharing Experience	25	5.480	1.782	22	3.500	1.263	.001	—	.54
18	Time-Sharing Evaluation	25	8.000	1.040	22	7.545	1.010	—	—	—
19	First Decision Rule Hours	26	4.269	2.201	25	5.600	4.272	—	.001	—
20	First Decision Rule Date	26	13.96	2.125	20	13.55	2.327	—	—	—

21	Alternate Decision Rules	26	2.461	.9478	25	2.680	2.135	—	.001	—
22	Last Decision Rule Hours	26	7.461	3.972	25	12.08	7.604	.010	.001	.36
23	Last Decision Rule Date	26	15.42	1.792	21	16.61	2.355	—	—	—
24	Successful Decision Rule	26	2.192	1.059	25	2.320	1.676	—	.026	—
25	Successful Decision Rule Hours	26	6.538	3.227	25	12.08	6.744	.001	.001	.47
26	Successful Decision Rule Date	26	15.19	1.789	21	16.09	1.578	—	—	—
27	Total Problem Time	26	16.03	7.022	25	19.00	8.098	—	—	—
28	Reacquaintance Time	26	10.57	9.625	21	18.42	14.77	.043	.045	.31
29	General Concept Time	26	30.96	16.18	24	24.58	15.08	—	—	—
30	Parameter Time	26	13.30	11.46	20	11.75	6.495	—	.012	—
31	Editing Time	26	15.07	9.736	25	15.24	10.49	—	—	—
32	Time on Results	26	17.46	8.645	21	24.66	18.07	—	.001	—
33	Waiting for Results	26	5.692	10.74	15	18.93	21.11	.035	.003	.39
34	Diversion of Attention	26	6.461	2.063	25	6.280	2.264	—	—	—
35	Time from Courses	26	6.384	4.418	24	9.041	7.497	—	.011	—
36	Grade A: Understanding Model Dynamics	26	9.500	3.313	24	9.958	3.168	—	—	—
37	Grade B: Strategy wtih Model	26	8.653	3.643	24	8.375	3.785	—	—	—
38	Grade C: Flexibility	26	3.038	3.515	24	2.583	3.282	—	—	—
39	Grade D: Perceptiveness and Understanding	26	5.346	2.189	24	3.916	1.954	.019	—	.33
40	Sum of Grades	26	26.53	10.15	24	24.83	9.765	—	—	—
41	Maximum Performance	25	1444.	203.2	20	1244.	226.7	.003	—	.43
42	CPU Time	27	343.9	157.6	28	71.78	59.63	.001	.001	.76
43	Elapsed Time	27	4.296	1.996	28	4.071	1.998	—	—	—

showed a significantly smaller standard deviation of only one, indicating the strength of their positive stereotype on time-sharing.

The significant mean difference for variable 13 (Dynamo Experience) indicates that the online experience was interpreted as more effective than the offline experience in increasing the user's skill in the Dynamo simulation language. This result suggests the hypothesis that the immediate knowledge of results characteristic of online experience leads to bettter mastery of user languages than the delayed reinforcement occurring in offline experience.

The significant mean differences for variables 15 and 17 represent trivial results. In effect, they show that the online group gained more online experience, and that the offline group gained more offline experience as a result of the experiment.

Variable 19, which is the number of hours that the student spent in arriving at his first decision rule for making more profit, shows a substantial, but not a significant advantage for time-sharing. The 24% time advantage is statistically wiped out by the relatively large variance shown for the batch group. Whereas all online subjects got their first useful decision rule after 9 hours of work, four students in the batch group required 10 to 20 hours to arrive at their first decision rule. Taken together, the mean and variance differences suggest the hypothesis that time-sharing facilitates quicker initial progress in problem-solving and tends to reduce large individual differences in getting underway, particularly among poorest performers.

Variable 22, Last Decision Rule Hours, and variable 25, Successful Decision Rule Hours (highly correlated and similar measures), show results consistent with the trends mentioned above for First Decision Rule Hours; that is, successful and final decision rules were reached earlier under time-sharing and there was significantly less variation among online subjects in reaching these points. Mean times and standard deviations are smaller for online subjects than for offline subjects, which reinforces the hypothesis that time-sharing not only makes for earlier and faster solutions, but for reduced individual differences in the time required to arrive at solutions, especially for poorest performers. For example, only two time-sharing subjects required more than 15 man-hours to arrive at their final decision rule as compared to nine subjects in the batch group.

Variable 27, Total Problem Time, shows a fairly substantial three man-hour advantage in favor of the time-sharing group, but is not statistically significant. This result is probably due to a combination of two factors—the open-ended nature of the simulation problem, which allowed students to keep increasing their profit score, coupled with the deadline for turning in their solution. If they were told to stop after reaching a specified level of proficiency, the man-hour difference probably would have been more pronounced as indicated by the significant group differences described previously for decision rule man-hours throughout the course of the problem.

Variable 28 shows significant results for Reacquaintance Time, which is the student's estimate of the proportion of time spent in warming up and refamiliarizing himself with the experimental problem. The offline group spent almost twice as much of its time warming up and showed a standard deviation 50% larger than the online group. These findings support the hypothesis that the virtual elimination of machine turnaround time and the interactive features of time-sharing make for more continuous application and more natural individual closure on the overall man-computer task and on component subtasks.

The similar findings for variable 33, Waiting for Results, reinforces the above hypothesis. The online subjects estimated that only 6% of their total time was spent waiting for results, as compared to offline subjects who averaged 19%. The standard deviation is twice as great for offline subjects, indicating greater uncertainty as to when they would get their results. A disruptive effect of this uncertainty in offline waiting time is reflected in the results for variable 35, Time from Courses. The significantly larger variation in the offline group suggests that the length and uncertainty of batch turnaround disrupted student schedules and required more time to be taken from other courses.

Of the four grades given to students by the teacher from written student reports on the experimental task, only one successfully differentiated the two groups. This is Perceptiveness and Understanding (variable 39), which showed a significantly higher grade for the time-sharing group. Even in this case, the correlation ratio is only .33, indicating that teacher ratings, at least in this case, show only moderate to low correlation with online/offline group membership.

The results for variable 47, Maximum Performance, are of central significance for this study. The score represents the maximum profit obtained by students with the best decision rule that they were able to devise for the simulation construction industry. Since $1000 represents the baseline at the beginning of the task, the mean score of $1444 for online subjects is almost twice as good as the average $1244 score for the offline group, and the difference is statistically significant. The true difference is even larger when one takes into account the higher dropout rate under batch.

The results for CPU time (variable 48) show a very large advantage for the batch group, which used only about one-fifth of the machine time that was required by the time-sharing group. Part of this difference is attributable to additional computer time spent on editing in time-sharing, an editing load that is not present in batch for this particular problem. The high correlation ratio of .76 shows that most of the variance in reported CPU time is attributable to computer system differences rather than individual differences.

6

PROBLEM-SOLVING BEHAVIOR

THIS chapter is primarily focused on multivariate problem-solving relationships in the data. These relationships are derived from correlational analyses, factor analyses, and special pretest/posttest comparisons. These various procedures cover the remaining results for this experiment. Although some initial interpretations are offered as each of the findings are described, the burden of extended interpretation is carried in the next chapter.

6.1 CORRELATION ANALYSIS

The intercorrelation matrix for all variables used in this study constitutes the data base for comparative factor analyses of time-sharing and batch-processing groups and is of interest in its own right. Rather than present the complete correlation tables for the two separate groups and the combined group, each of which includes some 1400 coefficients, most of them insignificant, Table 6.1 lists only those correlations of .50 or higher for the total sample, including thumbnail interpretations of individual results. Separate correlations for the two experimental groups are not listed because of smaller sample size and large error variance in obtained coefficients. The correlations are shown in rank order of absolute value. Omitted from this listing are: spurious part-whole correlations, such as CPU time vs. CPU + I/O time; obvious artifacts of the experimental situation (e g, positive correlations between course experience and simulation language ex-

Table 6.1. HIGHEST OBSERVED CORRELATIONS

Rank Order	Correlation Coefficient	N	Variable Numbers	Name of Variables	Comments
1	.86	46	12 53	Usefulness of Other System Batch vs. Time-Sharing	Both experimental groups decisively considered time-sharing to be more useful than batch-processing.
2	—.76	55	42 53	CPU Time Batch vs. Time-Sharing	Much more CPU time was consumed under time-sharing than in batch operations.
3	.76	50	27 35	Total Problem Time Time from Courses	More time on the experimental problem was associated with more time taken from other courses.
4	.74	50	37 38	Gr. B: Strategy with Model Gr. C: Flexibility	Separate grades on the written report were highly intercorrelated.
5	.74	44	10 42	Computer System Usefulness CPU Time	The more the student used the computer system for a given task, the more useful he believed the computer system to be.
6	.70	47	10 11	Computer System Usefulness Satisfaction with Results	Computer system usefulness was largely a projection of personal satisfaction with results.
7	.69	50	37 39	Gr. B: Strategy with Model Gr. D: Perceptiveness and Understanding	Grades on separate aspects of student's written report were highly intercorrelated.

8	—.68	47	10 53	Computer System Usefulness Batch vs. Time-Sharing	Experimental experience accentuated student preference for time-sharing over batch processing.
9	.67	39	10 41	Computer System Usefulness Maximum Performance	Better performers rated their computer system higher; poorer performers rated their system lower.
10	.66	50	38 39	Gr. C: Flexibility Gr. D: Perceptiveness and Understanding	Separate grades on same report were substantially intercorrelated.
11	.66	50	25 35	Successful Decision Rule Hours Time from Courses	Those who took a longer time to arrive at successful decision rules tended to take more time away from other courses.
12	—.65	23	23 50	Last Decision Rule Date Percent Successful Interactions	In the time-sharing group, slower performers tended to have higher man-computer error rates.
13	.63	16	9 22	Time Needed Last Decision Rule Hours	Slower performers believed they would have done better with more time on the experimental task.
14	.61	22	11 52	Satisfaction with Results Percent Successful Runs	In the batch group, error-prone individuals were less satisfied with their results.
15	—.61	44	12 42	Usefulness of Other System CPU Time	The more computer time a subject uses, the less useful he rated the competing computing system.
16	.60	15	9 29	Time Needed General Concept Time	Slower performers required more time to develop effective general concepts.
17	—.60	46	10 12	Computer System Usefulness Usefulness of Other System	Those who found their computer system more useful tended to evaluate the other computer system as less useful.

Table 6.1. HIGHEST OBSERVED CORRELATIONS (Cont'd)

Rank Order	Correlation Coefficient	N	Variable Numbers	Name of Variables	Comments
18	—.59	27	43 47	Elapsed Time Percent Edit	In the time-sharing group, faster performers spent more of their time editing results.
19	.59	39	11 41	Satisfaction with Results Maximum Performance	Winners were more satisfied with their results than losers.
20	.58	9	9 49	Time Needed Percent Compile and Run	In time-sharing, slower performers spent more time recompiling and rerunning their programs.
21	—.58	43	20 43	First Decision Rule Date Elapsed Time	Those who started later had less elapsed time to get their work done.
22	.57	28	43 51	Elapsed Time Total Runs	In the batch group, more computer runs resulted in longer elapsed time to complete the assignment.
23	—.57	24	8 11	Completion Date Satisfaction with Results	Those turning in their work earlier tended to be more satisfied with their results.
24	.56	45	7 11	Sufficient Time Satisfaction with Results	Those who were more satisfied with their results felt they had sufficient time.
25	.55	22	10 52	Computer System Usefulness Percent Successful Runs	In the batch condition, those who had more successful runs found the batch mode to be more useful.

26	.55	44	17	Dynamo Time-Sharing Experience	The more experienced students interacted more frequently with the time-sharing system.
			42	CPU Time	
27	.55	44	11	Satisfaction with Results	Those who tended to use the computer more extensively were more satisfied with their work.
			42	CPU Time	
28	.54	23	24	Successful Decision Rule	In the time-sharing group, slower performers spent a greater proportion of their time on nonproductive printouts.
			48	Percent Print	
29	—.54	25	19	First Decision Rule Hours	In the batch group, fewer errors led to faster initial problem-solving.
			52	Percent Successful Runs	
30	.53	27	43	Elapsed Time	In time-sharing, longer elapsed time was associated with more computer time.
			45	CPU + *I/O*	
31	—.53	23	20	First Decision Rule Date	Under time-sharing, a lower man-computer error rate was accompanied by faster problem-solving.
			50	Percent Successful Interactions	
32	—.53	23	20	First Decision Rule Date	In time-sharing, those who got off to an earlier start tended to use more computer time.
			45	CPU + *I/O*	
33	.53	22	10	Computer System Usefulness	In time-sharing, those who used more computer time tended to rate their system as more useful.
			45	CPU + *I/O*	
34	.53	46	20	First Decision Rule Date	Those who performed faster at the beginning of the task tend to arrive at their successful decision rule earlier.
			26	Successful Decision Rule Date	

Table 6.1. HIGHEST OBSERVED CORRELATIONS (Cont'd)

Rank Order	Correlation Coefficient	N	Variable Numbers	Name of Variables	Comments
35	.52	46	20 23	First Decision Rule Date Last Decision Rule Date	Those who started and made progress earlier tended to stay ahead and finish earlier.
36	—.52	42	11 19	Satisfaction with Results First Decision Rule Hours	Those who got off to a fast start tended to be more satisfied with their final results.
37	.51	43	41 42	Maximum Performance CPU Time	Those who performed more effectively tended to use more computer time.
38	.51	39	18 41	Time-Sharing Evaluation Maximum Performance	Those who performed more effectively tended to rate time-sharing more favorably.
39	.50	24	36 52	Gr. A: Understanding Model Dynamics Percent Successful Runs	A higher grade on the written report was associated with fewer errors under the batch mode.
40	.50	27	43 44	Elapsed Time Total Interactions	Under time-sharing, longer elapsed problem time was associated with increased use of the computer.
41	.50	47	10 17	Computer System Usefulness Dynamo Time-Sharing Experience	Those who had more time-sharing experience with the Dynamo language tended to rate their computer system as more useful.

perience); and intercorrelations with most data missing. All of the reported coefficients are product-moment correlations. Some are point-biserial correlations where one of the variates is continuous and the other dichotomous (e g, time-sharing vs. batch processing). The listed coefficient of .50 or higher is significantly different from a zero correlation at the .002 level for the median sample size of 42 in Table 6.1; the .50 figure was selected as a convenient cutoff point for significant and "substantial" correlations.

Table 6.1 is read as follows for the first entry. The correlation between variables 12 and 53, Usefulness of Other System and Batch vs. Time-Sharing, is .86, based on a sample of 46 subjects; the strong positive correlation shows that after the experiment was over, batch subjects rated time-sharing very highly, whereas the time-sharing group gave low ratings to the batch method. In the event that some entries in Table 6.1 may be ambiguous, the list of experimental variables in Table 5.2 should be consulted for the definition of each variable and the nature of the metric that was used. For example, in the above case, Batch is scored one and Time-Sharing zero, accounting for the observed direction of correlation. It is hoped that the thumbnail interpretations of observed individual correlations are self-explanatory. Correlational trends for groups of variables are treated in the factor analysis results which follow.

6.2 FACTOR ANALYSIS RESULTS

In this exploratory setting, with a large number of diverse variables relating to time-sharing and batch performance, a technique such as factor analysis is especially useful in simplifying the empirical data base by testing for behaviorally meaningful groups of intercorrelated variables that "cluster" together. Such clusters are mathematically constructed through successive factor extractions of the empirical correlation matrix (see Harman, 1967), and each cluster is interpreted in terms of those variables showing highest loadings or correlations for each factor. In this experiment, we are especially interested in three types of analyses.

First, are there consistent differences between factors found in the batch and time-sharing groups? Second, is there a substantive general factor that runs through the various man-machine, problem-solving, and attitudinal measures? Third, what are the various group factors (as opposed to a single general factor) that account most meaningfully for observed performance? To answer these questions, the factor analysis results are presented in two parts—general factor analyses and group factor analyses.

For those not versed in factor analysis, some notion of the intent of these hypotheses may be gained by an analogy to intelligence testing. The general factor approach may be used to test for a unitary trait of general intelligence. The group factor approach, on the other hand, tests for relatively independent traits such as verbal, arithmetical, and spatial skills. In this setting, we are interested in testing for a general problem-solving skill for the experimental task as opposed to specialized and independent traits, perhaps for traits corresponding to speed, accuracy, and motivation. Both approaches have led to useful findings and theories in the psychological test literature, and we might expect the possibility of similar advantages in this experiment or at least test for them.

6.2.1 Tests for a General Problem-Solving Factor

General factor analysis (or G-factor analysis) may be obtained as a by-product of group factor analysis by examining the first (and largest) of the unrotated factors. This factor is obtained by the first principal axis of the empirical correlation matrix. In preparing the correlation matrix for separate batch, time-sharing, and total group factor analyses, it was necessary to specify appropriate variables to be included in each of these three sets.

Repeated variables, such as the identical pretest and posttest questionnaire, were deleted; only the posttest questionnaire results were included. (Pretest/posttest comparisons are analyzed in a subsequent section.) Spurious part-whole variables were pruned out (e g, CPU time was retained but CPU=plus-input/output time was omitted; the four separate grades were included but the sum of these grades was excluded). Some variables were unique to each experimental group, for example, Percentage of Successful Batch Runs and Percentage of Successful Interactions. None of these and other "unique" variables could be included in the total sample factor analyses based on measures common to both groups. On the other hand, only the total sample factor analysis incorporated the critical time-sharing vs. batch variable. Accordingly, the batch and time-sharing factor analyses included 36 variables, and the total sample factor analysis included 35 measures, with most variables common to all three analyses. Specifically, all three factor analyses included variables 7, 10 to 39, and 41 to 43; with 44 and 50 for time-sharing only, 51 and 52 for batch only, and 53 for the total sample only (see Table 6.2).

Comparative G-factor results are shown in Table 6.2 for the two experimental groups. The first entry is read as follows. Variable 20, First Decision Rule Date, had the highest factor loading of —.82 in the first factor extracted before rotation for the time-sharing group. Note that factor loadings are ranked in order of absolute magnitude and that only the highest loadings are shown, those that contribute most to the description of the extracted factor.

The findings in Table 6.2 demonstrate a rational and well-defined general problem-solving factor for both groups; that is, the kinds of variables that one would expect to be associated with a general problem-solving factor are, by and large, well represented in these results. For example, included in this factor, and common to both groups, are variables relating to earlier and faster problem-solving, maximum (profit) performance in the experimental task, accuracy in man-computer communication (percentage of successful batch runs and successful time-shared interactions), positive attitudes toward the object systems (evaluation items), relevant experience with the simulation language and the computer system, and the rather interesting finding that the more successful individuals used more CPU time in both modes. For this open-ended experimental task, it appears that the more successful students were able to exploit the computer system by using more computer time to achieve higher profit.

The main differences between experimental groups are in grades for class reports which appear only in the batch group, and

Table 6.2. GENERAL FACTOR LOADINGS FOR TIME-SHARING AND BATCH GROUPS

	Time-Sharing Group			Batch-Processing Group		
Rank Order	Variable Number	Variable Name	Factor Loading	Variable Number	Variable Name	Factor Loading
1	20	First Decision Rule Date	—.82	11	Satisfaction with Results	.87
2	18	Time-Sharing Evaluation	.75	16	Batch Evaluation	.83
3	26	Successful Decision Rule Date	—.70	10	Computer System Usefulness	.81
4	42	CPU Time	.69	19	First Decision Rule Hours	—.76
5	10	Computer System Usefulness	.67	20	First Decision Rule Date	—.64
6	44	Total Interactions	.63	52	Percent Successful Runs	.61
7	23	Last Decision Rule Date	—.62	28	Reacquaintance Time	—.58
8	30	Parameter Time	.62	41	Maximum Performance	.56
9	50	Percent Successful Interactions	.59	7	Sufficient Time	.55
10	11	Satisfaction with Results	.57	26	Successful Decision Rule Date	—.54
11	27	Total Problem Time	.55	33	Waiting for Results	—.51
12	16	Batch Evaluation	—.51	38	Grade C: Flexibility	.50

13	43	Elapsed Time	.51	23	Last Decision Rule Date	—.50
14	15	Batch Dynamo Experience	—.49	36	Grade A: Understanding Model Dynamics	.46
15	34	Diversion of Attention	.46	39	Grade D: Perceptiveness and Understanding	.45
16	41	Maximum Performance	.43	15	Batch Dynamo Experience	.40
17	17	Dynamo Time-Sharing Experience	.38	35	Time from Courses	—.40
18	13	Dynamo Experience	.38	42	CPU Time	.40
19				37	Grade B: Strategy with Model	.39
20				43	Elapsed Time	.38

in reacquaintance and waiting times which also appear only in the batch group. The negative loadings (or negative problem-solving) for the two temporal measures indicate that poorer performance is associated with the longer delays and interruptions stemming from batch turnaround. This finding suggests that interrupted problem-solving results in degraded man-computer performance, and the longer the interruption, the worse the performance.

The G-factor for the batch group pulled out 21% of the total variance of the matrix, with a figure of 19% for time-sharing. On the whole, these results show a fairly substantial and meaningful general problem-solving factor which is rather similar for both groups. The main differences in the general factor patterns are clear-cut negative loadings in the batch group that are related to turnaround delays and interrupted problem-solving.

Table 6.3 shows G-factor results for the total sample, including, in this pass, the time-sharing vs. batch variable. These results confirm the general factor shown previously in the separate experimental groups, with some notable changes. By way of confirmation, note the strong showing of positive attitudes, earlier and faster problem-solving, more CPU time, and higher maximum performance, which, incidentally, shows up stronger in the combined sample than in the separate groups. Perhaps the most striking finding is that computer system differences show up very strongly (near the top) with a loading of —.73 for time-sharing vs. batch. For the given experimental conditions, not only did time-sharing lead to better performance, but the various skills and traits associated with more effective problem-solving are apparently enhanced under the online mode, as reflected in the total sample G-factor. This factor accounted for 21% of the total variance for the complete sample, in line with similar values for the separate groups.

6.2.2 Tests for Group Factors in Problem-Solving Skills

While general factor analysis is concerned with the extraction of maximal variance around a single G-factor, group factor analysis is oriented toward the extraction of a small number of

Table 6.3. GENERAL FACTOR LOADINGS FOR THE COMPLETE EXPERIMENTAL SAMPLE

Total Group

Rank Order	Variable Number	Variable Name	Factor Loading
1	10	Computer System Usefulness	.87
2	11	Satisfaction with Results	.81
3	53	Batch vs. Time-Sharing	—.73
4	42	CPU Time	.73
5	41	Maximum Performance	.65
6	26	Successful Decision Rule Date	—.63
7	12	Usefulness of Other System	—.61
8	25	Successful Decision Rule Hours	—.59
9	23	Last Decision Rule Date	—.59
10	19	First Decision Rule Hours	—.54
11	7	Sufficient Time	.51
12	22	Last Decision Rule Hours	—.50
13	18	Time-Sharing Evaluation	.48
14	17	Dynamo Time-Sharing Experience	.48
15	28	Reacquaintance Time	—.45
16	33	Waiting for Results	—.45
17	39	Grade D: Perceptiveness and Understanding	.44
18	13	Dynamo Experience	.43
19	35	Time from Courses	—.41

separate, independent factors that account for most of the correlated variance in the empirical matrix. Both techniques reflect different ways of partitioning observed variance into simpler elements, and both are explored for whatever light they may shed on the experimental results. Once again, separate factor analyses were conducted for each of the experimental groups and for the combined group with the same set of variables as used in the G-factor analysis.

A maximum of 12 factors was obtained in each pass with eigenvalues greater than one. These factors were rotated in groups of the first 4, 6, 8, 10, and 12 factors in accordance with the varimax criterion, and the results were examined for meaningful constellations of variables. We finally decided upon the 8-factor results in each of the three cases for the following reasons: smaller numbers of factors left out important results; larger numbers included trivial and unreliable findings; essentially all factors in the 8-factor pass were behaviorally meaningful; no singleton (single variable factors) occurred in the 8-factor pass; no spurious communalities over 1.00 occurred, and all factors contributed variances equal to or greater than 2%.

The comparative summarized results of these three factor analyses are shown in Table 6.4. Although separate presentation of complete factor loadings for all variables for all factors for all three sample groupings would be preferable, space constraints preclude such exhaustive presentation. Instead, we discuss the heaviest loadings and the key behavioral considerations that led to the names for each factor as listed in Table 6.4.

Note, in Table 6.4, that the eight factors for each of the three subject groupings are listed under Very Similar Factors and Related Factors. Identical factor names are shown for five factors in each of the three groupings under Very Similar Factors; these factors are not strictly identical, even though they are given the same name, because of an unknown mix of genuine differences and random jitter in factor loadings among the three groupings. The Related Factor listings include overlapping and relatively similar factors that were found in two of the three groupings.

Each of the factors is briefly discussed in turn, going down Table 6.4. Highest factor loadings for the Problem-Solving Speed occurred in measures related to problem closure and final completion of the problem—Total Problem Time (27), Last Decision Rule Hours (22), Successful Decision Rule Hours (25), and Time from Courses (35). This factor is a composite of man-hour measures not only for the experimental task but also in competition with other work. This competitive feature suggests that

Table 6.4. GROUP FACTOR ANALYSIS FOR BATCH, TIME-SHARING, AND THE TOTAL SAMPLE

Very Similar Factors

Batch	*Time-Sharing*	*Total Sample*
Problem-Solving Speed	Problem-Solving Speed	Problem-Solving Speed
Exploitation of Computer System	Exploitation of Computer System	Exploitation of Computer System
Hustler	Hustler	Hustler
Relevant Experience	Relevant Experience	Relevant Experience
Exploration of Alternatives	Exploration of Alternatives	Exploration of Alternatives

Related Factors

Batch	*Time-Sharing*	*Total Sample*
Conceptual and Applied Performance	Conceptualization of Problem	Conceptualization of Problem
———	Problem Strategy	Problem Strategy
Batch Attitude	Batch Attitude	———
Nit-Picker	———	Nit-Picker

faster problem-solvers (online and offline) concentrate on the task at hand and deliberately minimize distracting interruptions from other work.

Exploitation of Computer System is marked by a strong factor loading in CPU Time (43) for all three groupings, by a high loading with Batch vs. Time-Sharing (53) in the total sample, by Total Runs (51) under batch, and by Total Interactions (44) and Maximum Performance (41) under time-sharing. This factor is probably closest to the General Problem-Solving Factor previously discussed. First, it is the group factor which shows highest loadings for Maximum Performance. Second, as in the G-factor, it is distinctively characterized by very high loadings in CPU time, with loadings in the correct direction for Time-Sharing vs. Batch (positive association with the online condition). Third, the heavy loading for CPU Time is clearly associated in this group factor with more runs under batch and more interactions under time-sharing. This factor, related to general problem-solving skill, reveals extended exploitation of the computer system which leads to higher profit in the open-ended experiment task.

The Hustler factor stemmed from variables that suggested a personality syndrome. This factor is marked by individuals who start early (First Decision Rule Date, 20), finish early (Last Decision Rule Date, 23), take less time to arrive at their solution (Successful Decision Rule Hours, 25), make fewer errors (Percent Successful Interactions, 50), and perform well (Maximum Performance 41). The early start and early finish, coupled with superior performance, fits into the picture of a fast-moving, motivated, productive student—a portrait of an energetic "hustler," in the positive sense of the term.

The Relevant Experience factor is an obvious clustering of experience variables—Dynamo Experience (13) and Industrial Dynamics Experience (14) for all three groupings, Dynamo Time-Sharing Experience (17) in the time-sharing group, Dynamo Batch Experience (15) in the batch group, and both of these last two experience variables in the combined group. Although experience variables are intercorrelated with one another, this group factor shows that they are not strongly associated with measures of performance. Only in the general factor analysis did they make a moderate showing with performance variables.

The Exploration of Alternatives factor is simply a uniformly strong showing of Alternate Decision Rules (21) and Successful Decision Rule (24) for all three groupings. This finding may represent a spurious factor in that both variables reflect much the same measure in a part-whole relationship; most students considered their last decision rule as their most successful decision rule.

The sixth factor as listed as Conceptualization of Problem for the time-sharing and total sample groupings, and as Conceptual and Applied Performance under batch. All three groupings show high factor loadings on the four class grades; only batch has a high to moderate factor loading in Maximum Performance (41). Why Maximum Performance should only show up in batch and not under time-sharing is difficult to explain. Perhaps these results represent random variation around a moderate relationship between problem performance and class grades in these comparative analyses. This interpretation is suggested by the moderate association between problem performance and class grades that was demonstrated in the G-factor results.

The Problem Strategy factor showed up only in the time-sharing and total sample groupings. Its main distinction is a higher proportion of General Concept Time (29) with lower percentages on the other functional temporal categories; it seems to tap preparatory stages in grasping the problem as a whole before the individual can make effective headway. It is not clear why this factor should not also appear in the batch group—except, perhaps, that it is a relatively marginal factor with a small proportion of contributed variance (only about 2%, in contrast to the other group factors, which usually contributed 3% to 5%).

The next factor is concerned with attitudes toward batch processing appearing in the separate groups but not in the total sample. The Batch Attitude in the batch group was revealed by a very high loading in Waiting for Results (33) and opposite moderate loadings in Usefulness of Other System (12) and Time-Sharing Evaluation (18); that is, batch students who took a longer time waiting for computer outputs were the ones who tended to take a more favorable view toward time-sharing—the longer you have to wait for service, the greener the grass on the other side of the fence. The Batch Attitude factor for the time-sharing group is a composite of a relatively favorable attitude toward batch—high loadings on Usefulness of Other System (12) and Batch Evaluation (16)—associated with an opposite loading on Waiting for Results (33). Faster time-sharing service induced a more favorable attitude toward batch. This attitudinal factor, if valid, reveals the vagaries of psychological projection—negative waiting experience under batch made time-sharing more attractive, but positive waiting experience under time-sharing made batch more attractive.

The last factor in Table 6.4 is Nit-Picker, found only in the batch and total sample groupings. This is a marginal factor, just barely making 2% contributed variance. It is marked by large and opposite loadings in Editing Time (31) and Time on Results

(32) in both groups. The total sample loadings show the clearest profile—the profile of the individual who spends more Time on Results (32), more time on Parameter Checking (30) and less Editing Time (31), who uses more Elapsed Time (43) than others, and after all is said and done, ends up with lower Maximum Performance (41). This is the portrait of the Nit-Picker who agonizes over petty aspects of his work, sticks closely to familiar techniques and solution, and who is probably fearful of major new alternatives. This syndrome is probably accentuated under batch because the offline subjects had to protect themselves against inadvertent errors that could lead to the loss of a full day from a nonproductive computer run.

Taken together, the group factor analyses show a rather similar factor pattern for all three groupings, at least for most factors. The differences that do appear between the two groups are largely attributable to the batch turnaround delay, chance fluctuations, slightly different variable sets, and the more marginal factors. In view of the largely similar factor findings for both general and group factor analyses, the factorial results indicate common attitudinal and problem-solving processes operating in both experimental groups. Consequently, the findings for the combined sample should be taken as the most reliable indication of the factors that contribute to observed problem-solving behavior.

6.3 SPECIAL ANALYSES: PRETEST/POSTTEST QUESTIONNAIRE RESULTS

Table 6.5 summarizes analysis of variance results for the six items of the questionnaire administered to both groups before and after the experiment. The analysis of variance in each case was a 2 x 2 design—two groups (time-sharing and batch) and two conditions (pretest and posttest) for each of the six items. The results of this analysis include two main effects (time-sharing vs. batch differences, and pretest/posttest differences), and one interaction effect. Table 6.5 shows the significance of the obtained findings at the 1% and 5% levels for each of these three effects

Table 6.5. SUMMARY OF ANALYSIS OF VARIANCE RESULTS FOR THE PRETEST/POSTTEST QUESTIONNAIRE

Questionnaire Item	Time-Sharing vs. Batch Differences	Pretest vs. Posttest Differences	Interaction Effects	Comments
Dynamo Experience	—	.01	—	Both groups showed expected significant increases in Dynamo experience as a result of the experiment.
Industrial Dynamics Experience	—	.01	—	Both groups showed expected significant increases in Industrial Dynamics experience as a result of the experiment.
Batch Dynamo Experience	.01	.01	.01	The batch group showed an expected significant increase in batch Dynamo experience.
Dynamo Time-Sharing Experience	.01	.01	.01	The time-sharing group showed an expected significant increase in Dynamo time-sharing experience.
Time-Sharing Evaluation	.01	.01	.05	Both groups showed a significantly higher evaluation of time-sharing after the experiment.
Batch Evaluation	—	.01	.01	The batch group rated batch significantly higher after the experiment.

for the six questionnaire items, and it includes brief commentary on the listed results. Table 6.1 should be consulted for the cell means for batch and time-sharing groups for pretest and posttest for more detailed examination of these findings.

The first row in Table 6.5 is read as follows: The Dynamo Experience item did not show any significant group differences, but it did show an expected and significant increase in rated experience between the beginning and the end of the experiment. No significant interaction effect was found.

The four experience variables in Table 6.5 show results in the expected direction; that is, both groups showed significant increases in experience as a result of the experiment. The two computer system evaluation items show a somewhat different pattern. Both items show significant increases in the evaluation of batch and time-sharing as a result of the experiment. The pattern of these increases is quite different on two counts. First, in time-sharing the final evaluation is near the high end of the scale (total sample mean of 7.79 on a 9-point scale) whereas batch is near the low end (total sample mean of 2.79). Second, while both groups rated time-sharing higher as a result of their experience, only the batch group rated batch notably higher as a result of its experience (from a mean of 1.82 to 3.22). These evaluative results show two key trends: 1) a more tolerant attitude toward batch as a result of firsthand experience, and 2) a marked time-sharing bandwagon effect intensified by the experimental experience. These findings, based on anlysis of variance, are generally consistent with similar findings obtained in the original study through the use of nonparametric analyses of pretest/posttest change scores.

7

INTERPRETATION

7.1 LIMITATIONS OF THE METHOD

BEFORE interpreting the results, the methodological limitations and constraints of this study should be clearly understood. These fall under three main headings—the experimental task, the experimental procedures, and the performance measures.

The experimental task has many useful attributes. It is a meaningful business problem; it has clearcut feedback for the subject in unambiguous dollars and cents; the problem is not trivial, it requires sustained effort over many hours; the problem incorporates a great variety of skills including man-computer communication abilities, mastery of the Dynamo simulation language, arithmetic and logical skills, ability to construct and manipulate abstract models, and knowledge of business transactions; it is equally applicable to online and offline problem solution. Among the other tasks found in the experimental literature, this is the only open-ended task that reflects improved performance scores for better solutions.

The principal limitation is that only one problem was used and we do not know how representative or unique this problem is for data processing or man-computer communication when they are generally considered. The findings would have been more generalizable if more than one problem had been used. The validity of these results for man-computer problem-solving is admittedly contingent upon the problematic representativeness of the experimental task.

The experimental procedure involved a number of limitations, many of them unavoidable. For example, the inital sample size of 66 students was too large to permit close surveillance of the subjects, in order to make sure that the experimental ground rules and instructions were properly followed in all cases. As a result, there was uneven reporting of data, particularly for questionnaire items, and some variables had considerable missing data, among other examples.

Another case in point is experimental control over subject access to the online and offline facilities. In the batch mode, the students were subjected to the ordinary vagaries of batch service —unpredictable queues, peak periods, system delays, and unknown variability in turnaround time. In a sense, these liabilities are also experimental assets, in that they represent conditions typical of "normal" batch service.

The online mode involved four dedicated user consoles with a maximum one-hour time period per session, unless there was no other demand. This allotment worked well at the beginning of the experiment but was less effective toward the end, when student demand exceeded available terminals. This condition may also be claimed to be more representative of real-world conditions than guaranteed access at all times.

There were numerous problems with the performance measures. CPU time under both modes is not strictly comparable, because editing and compilations for this particular language and simulation model are handled less efficiently under time-sharing and therefore consume more computer time than the same kinds of program runs under batch. The questionnaire items probably involved semantic problems and differences in subjective anchoring points. For example, a uniform nine-point rating scale was used for many items, ranging from Very Little to A Great Deal. It might be argued that separate qualitative descriptors for each step in the scale for each item might have made the steps more concrete and less ambiguous. Or, perhaps, fewer steps might have served as well. As it turned out, the full range of the nine-point scale was used by the subjects, and the statistical results were usually meaningful. Nevertheless, considerable work needs to be done on standardized, comparable user ratings in man-computer communication.

Another case in point is the design of exhaustive and mutually exclusive descriptors of the user's activity. The sixfold classification used in this study was: Reacquaintance Time, General Concept Time, Parameter Time, Editing Time, Time on Results and Waiting for Results. Although it cannot be claimed that these categories are mutually exclusive, exhaustive, or unambiguous, we believe they were reasonably well understood by the subjects and that the results with these measures made sense and were useful, at least for the exploratory purposes of an initial study. Here again, further improvements need to be made with empirical categories derived from and tested on representative users working with representative tasks.

Another measurement problem stemmed from the use of teacher grades on student reports. It probably surprised no one that teacher ratings on model dynamics, strategy, flexibility, and perceptiveness were highly intercorrelated and reflected an unavoidable halo effect from the overall favorable or unfavorable impression that each report made on the teacher. Even with these limitations, these grades, arrived at independently from problem performance, were most useful in exploring and testing relationships between conceptual and other problem-solving skills. Future work might involve improvements such as multiple expert ratings and empirically derived scales.

7.2 DIFFERENCES BETWEEN ONLINE AND OFFLINE PROBLEM-SOLVING

The basic differences between online and offline problem-solving in this experiment may be summed up by saying that the batch mode favors more economical machine performance, whereas time-sharing favors more effective and more satisfactory human performance with a higher-quality end product. The bases for this capsule description are: the definite advantage of reduced machine-time costs under batch (even when liberal allowances are made for excess editing and compilation loads under time-sharing); the reduced human time and effort in time-sharing (almost all along the way); the overwhelming preference of the entire sample for the online mode; and the unequivocal superiority of the profit score for the time-sharing subjects.

7.2.1 Machine Time

What do the group differences look like from a behavioral, or problem-solving point of view? The machine-time differences should not be charged off to an economic advantage for batch and then forgotten. The matter goes deeper. Behaviorally, the online mode gives the user immediate feedback, immediate knowledge of results; the offline mode provides delayed feedback, in this case many hours later and well after immediate memory for the task has subsided. The immediate knowledge of results clearly favors the online user by providing a more effective internal reinforcement schedule. With immediate reinforcement and with the computer there, ready to be used again, the subject is tempted to try other options until he has exhausted his immediate repertoire of alternatives. This leads to greater exploitation of the computer system, and, in the pursuit of excellence, to more, rather than less, computer time. On the other hand, this temptation to extend the console session can backfire and result in nonproductive interactions in the online mode if new leads are carelessly formulated, or if the user tires from a long console session or falls into a mental rut. The key point is that computer time must be looked at from the human as well as the machine point of view, and that extra machine time may be a necessary condition not only for improved human performance but also for improved overall cost effectiveness. As computer costs go down and as human costs rise in the computer industry, the cost-effectiveness equation is rapidly becoming a human equation.

7.2.2 Transfer of Training

Other behavioral differences between the two modes are noteworthy. For example, the time-sharing group learned more about the Dynamo language from its experience than the batch group, at least as far as comparative ratings are concerned. If online problem-solving is a more effective self-educational experience, as indicated by this finding, then (all other things being equal), online users are better prepared to tackle new problems which involve the same or related skills and information tools.

7.2.3 Dropouts and Marginal Performers

A related behavioral finding, potentially of great social significance, concerns the results on how fast the subjects were able to get started on the problem and how many of them dropped out because they made no headway. Table 5.3 shows that both groups started at about the same date (variable 20), with the online group reaching their first decision rule in less time and with much less variability (variable 19). Examination of the frequency distribution for final profit scores shows 8 dropouts (no score, inability to get the model to cycle for the $1000 baseline profit) for time-sharing against 13 dropouts for batch. (This difference is suggestive, but not statistically significant.) This data indicates that it was harder for poor performers to get started under batch, and that more of them were completely discouraged from trying further. Subsequent batch scores showed that many could not pull themselves out of the low end of the performance scale.

Why? Part of the answer seems to lie in two related factors—delayed feedback and the psychology of failure. As mentioned earlier, delayed feedback results in less effective learning with less effective insight into potential problem solutions. In regard to failure, the online mode permits another and another immediate try and is essentially permissive against repeated failure; the offline mode is a one-shot affair that forces the user to wait another turnaround cycle before he can get further feedback. The hesitant, uncertain, marginal performer needs extra tries, continual support, and ample allowance for a large number of initial errors if he is ever to get going. We all learn from our mistakes, and some have to make more mistakes than others. The offline mode compels the potential dropout to stew in his own ineffectiveness and nurse his wounded pride for a period of many hours before he gets another crack at the machine (with a moderately high probability of failing again), all of which only encourages the temptation to tune out, turn off, and drop out.

It is well established in experiments on part-vs.-whole learning that less experienced and less skilled subjects tend to break down memorization problems and puzzles into small pieces that can be easily mastered and that can yield successful initial results quickly. Time-sharing permits early success in small, preparatory steps for the poor performer. In batch, however, the computer run tends more toward a win-all or lose-all type of result, a black or white outcome that excludes shades of gray. For the marginal performer, the immediate reinforcement, the permissive gradualism, and the opportunity to take successive passes at the machine make the online mode the method of choice.

7.2.4 Human Error

The error results provide further insight into the nature and extent of individual differences in online/offline problem-solving. Unfortunately, relatively little is known about errors in man-computer communication. The basic error results for this study are shown in Table 7.1. Since time-sharing and batch errors are not directly comparable because the interaction unit is different from the batch run, the table is labeled as "analogous" error rates rather than "comparative" error rates, and should be interpreted accordingly. The first two variables show mean scores and measures of dispersion for the number of man-computer interactions in the online mode and the number of computer runs in the offline mode. The last two variables are means and dispersions for percentage of online and offline man-computer errors.

Table 7.1 contains several noteworthy findings. First, note that the number of time-sharing interactions is approximately ten times the number of batch runs. Apparently, time-sharing allows the user to break down the same problem effectively into many more man-computer steps than batch. The range of individual differences in both modes is very large, as might be expected for an open-ended task.

The reported error levels confirm the computer system designer's worst suspicions about the unpredictability of the user. Error scores are quite high and they range over virtually the entire spectrum, from none to 100%. Rather than throw our hands up in despair and bypass the problem (as so many have done), let us take a closer look at these results. Time-sharing users show a statistically higher level of errors than batch users (mean differ-

Table 7.1. ANALOGOUS MAN-COMPUTER ERROR RATES IN BATCH AND TIME-SHARING

Variable	Mean	SD	Lowest Score	Highest Score
Number of Time-Sharing Interactions	51.5	22.3	19	104
Number of Batch Runs	5.8	3.5	1	15
Percent Interaction Errors	53.9%	19.4%	16%	90%
Percent Batch Errors	34.5%	29.3%	0%	100%

Mean time-sharing interaction error rate is significantly higher than the mean batch error rate.

The variability of batch errors is significantly higher than the variability of interaction errors.

ences significantly different at the 5% level for a test assuming heterogeneous variances). Time-sharing users make more errors both proportionately and absolutely in man-computer interaction than batch users. Since there is no turnaround penalty, online problem-solving permits a higher man-computer error level to be tolerated than offline problem-solving. By the same token, the online mode offers a greater opportunity to learn immediately, and faces the user with more varied and more extensive mistakes.

The variability of errors under both modes is interesting in its own right. Although batch users have a lower error rate than time-sharing users, the variability of errors in batch runs is approximately 50% greater than in time-sharing interactions. (F-ratio of the two variances is significant at the 5% level.) This result is not too difficult to interpret. If he wanted to, the batch user could opt to make small, piecemeal changes for each run; but then he would have to pay the price of more computer runs and a substantial stretch-out of elapsed time to solve his problem. To get the job done within a "reasonable" time period, the batch user is forced into packing more changes into each run. The batch user thus has a lot more riding on each computer run and has to prepare his work much more carefully to avoid a time-consuming dry run (fewer errors). In addition, the comparatively larger number of changes provides more opportunity for making an error (greater variability of errors).

Another factor that increases individual differences in error levels is the difficulty level of the experimental task. Some students were hopelessly mired and never got beyond the baseline; they simply quit after making several false starts, yielding 100% or very high error scores. At the other end of the continuum, high performers consistently turned in error-free runs. As a matter of fact, the frequency distribution for batch error levels is a J-curve, with six subjects showing all error-free runs, tapering down to two subjects who never had a single successful run. These results suggest that batch tends to magnify individual differences in man-computer errors compared to time-sharing. The spread and variation of man-computer errors is so large in both modes that we may reasonably hypothesize that "error-prone" individuals exist. By extension, we may hypothesize that error-prone individuals may constitute a large segment of user populations, and that they will require special study if information services are to be made available to the general public.

7.2.5 Problem-Solving Speed

The temporal pattern of problem-solving shows the online group getting ahead to an earlier start (first decision rule), using more computer time as they go, arriving earlier at their successful decision rule, finishing the problem in less time, and generally showing less variability and smaller individual differences than the offline group all along the way. The pattern is one of faster, more intensive, and more massed problem-solving in the online mode.

7.2.6 The Time-Sharing Bandwagon

The attitudinal differences expressed by the entire sample between the two modes of problem-solving are etched in sharp relief—they amount to nothing less than a massive bandwagon effect for time-sharing. In this context, "massive," which may seem too strong a term to use, means that not even a single responding subject rated batch-processing as better than time-sharing. One subject rated the two computer systems the same in the pretest questionnaire, and another rated them equal in the posttest questionnaire, and all others gave higher ratings to time-sharing in both questionnaire administrations. The striking differences between the ratings for the two computer systems in the posttest questionnaire are shown in the contrasting frequency distributions in Figure 7.1. This plot shows total sample ratings for each computer system; each subject rated each mode once. Recall that the highest batch ratings occurred in the posttest questionnaire. On a nine-point scale, batch tends to be bunched up at the low end, with time-sharing crowded at the high end—the overlap between the two groups in the center is for different individuals, except for the single tie score mentioned earlier.

The behavioral interpretation of the attitudinal findings involves two key considerations—comparative performance effectiveness under both modes, and the computer milieu at MIT. The correlational results make it clear that high performance breeds satisfaction with the object system, self-satisfaction with the task, and feelings of adequacy concerning the timing and techniques

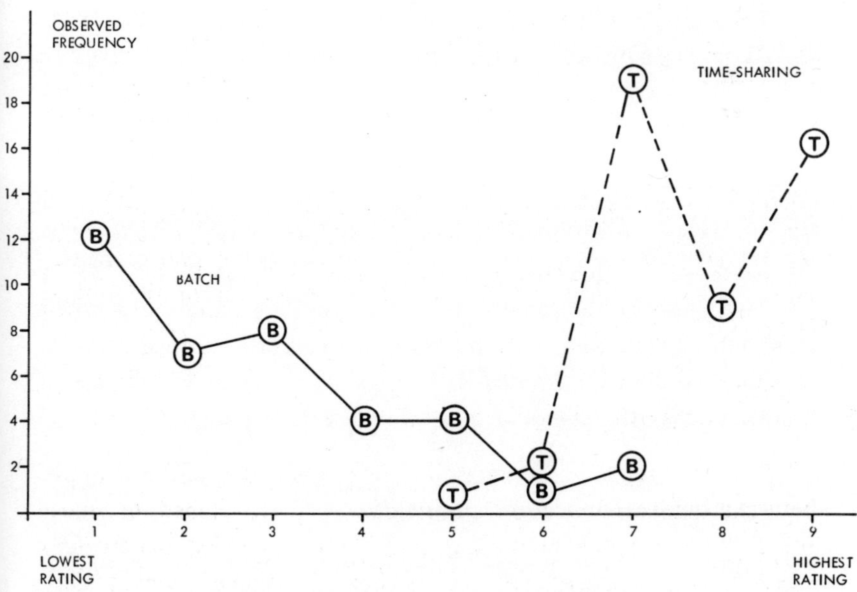

Figure 7.1 STUDENT RATINGS: TIME-SHARING VS. BATCH

used. Since the time-sharing group did almost twice as well as the batch group in the final profit score (more than twice as well if dropouts are included), their positive attitude toward time-sharing was correspondingly reinforced as a result of the experiment. Except for the highest performers, students in the batch group probably knew that the time-sharing subjects were doing better, and, in contrast to their relative failure and the unpleasant prospect of a lower grade for such performance, the grass looked especially greener on the other side of the fence—hence a bandwagon effect for time-sharing in both experimental groups.

Coupled to performance factors, and working in the same direction, was the students' bias in favor of time-sharing at the start of the experiment. MIT has been a leading pioneer in time-sharing, and it has successfully integrated the time-sharing concept into the academic community. Batch has played the role of the "heavy" and has had an uphill battle from the start. Moreover, the student sample has had more time-sharing than batch experience (see Table 6.1, variables 3 and 5). These considerations should be borne in mind in qualifying the generality of the time-sharing bandwagon effect. The attitudinal and perhaps the performance results could have been different if the computer milieu had been batch-oriented. The results obtained by Schatzoff, Tsao, and Wiig (1967), and by Adams and Cohen (1969) in exploratory online/offline comparisons with batch-trained samples, tend to support this observation. Batch is the evolutionary predecessor of time-sharing and has dominated the computer scene since computers became available in large numbers (roughly over the last 15 years). It has the force of familiarity working for it, and the dead weight that tradition can entail working against it. In the last analysis the proof is in the pudding, and only when systematic, continuing polls are taken for carefully defined samples in representative data-processing tasks will we know whether a bandwagon exists, where it is, and where it is going.

7.2.7 Conceptual and Verbal Skills

Turning to class grades on the written reports describing the experimental problem, we are faced with a dilemma. Three of the four grades showed no significant statistical difference between the two groups, with one, Perceptiveness and Understanding, showing a significant mean difference in favor of time-sharing at the .02 level. Of the other three grades, two means favored time-sharing and one mean favored batch. All four grades showed moderate to high intercorrelations. The problem: is the observed statistically significant result a substantive and meaningful indication of better conceptual insight under time-sharing, or is it merely chance fluctuation? In the context of the four grades alone, the alternatives are problematic. In the broader context of all experimental findings, the evidence is in favor of better conceptual insight under time-sharing.

The reasons are not hard to find. Time-sharing resulted in better performance and more positive attitudes, both of which may be reasonably expected to lead to more effective insight and a better conceptual grasp of the problem. Perhaps the most striking finding supporting this hypothesis is in the G-factor results for the total sample—Perceptiveness and Understanding had a moderate factor loading in the same direction as time-sharing in Batch vs. Time-Sharing, and in the same direction as higher performance, positive attitudes, and faster problem-solving. Taken together, the results support the compromise hypothesis that time-sharing leads to better conceptual insight as reflected in teacher ratings of written reports, but with the qualification that the strength of this relationship is probably low to moderate.

7.2.8 G-Factor Results

The most incisive single finding that distinguishes online from offline problem-solving lies in the general factor analysis for the complete sample. Recall that a well-defined general problem-solving factor was obtained and that the third highest factor loading (—.78) was in the Batch vs. Time-Sharing variable. As mentioned previously, time-sharing was positively associated with higher performance, faster problem-solving, more favorable motivation and attitudes, and more effective conceptualization of the problem.

A useful clue to the fundamental behavioral differences between the two modes is provided by those variables that showed general factor loadings in the same direction as batch—Reacquaintance Time (28), Waiting for Results (33), and Time from

Courses (35). The interpretation of this pattern is straightforward: batch turnaround eats up more human time and more "psychic" effort because of the forgetting that occurs with the loss of immediate memory; forgetting is accelerated by the interference effects of intervening events between job submission and completed runs; the user needs more warm-up time and more effort to plunge back into the problem again; and this extra time and effort exerts increasing pressure on competing tasks and responsibilities. These factors and others mentioned earlier are an indictment of turnaround interruptions in batch problem-solving. These factors do not cast light on the reinforcement differences between fast or "instant" batch as opposed to the relatively interactive, conversational features of time-sharing. Since this experiment only dealt with conventional batch, the effects of turnaround delay and interactive features are confounded. This interpretive problem is discussed more fully at a later point.

7.3 SIMILARITIES BETWEEN ONLINE AND OFFLINE PROBLEM-SOLVING

Although basic differences exist between online and offline problem-solving, as indicated above, the similarities are nevertheless very extensive. The most striking affirmation of the similarities is found in the factor-analysis results. Of the eight factors extracted from both groups, six were virtually identical. The comparative results for the two groups were so similar that it was recommended that the group factors for the total sample be taken as the most reliable factor results. Essentially the same conclusions were drawn for the general factor analyses—the G-factor results for time-sharing and batch were so similar that the total sample results were put forth as the most reliable indication of the general problem-solving factor for this experiment.

How can we reconcile the similarity of the factor analyses patterns in both groups with the striking performance differences between the two groups as described in the previous section? A tentative answer is that the general process of problem-solving, which is essentially a human process, is fundamentally the same in both modes when the subject is by himself, away from the computer, but that the timing, testing, and reinforcement pattern during the period of active man-computer communication is quite different. This statement may seem like a paradox, but consider the fact that even with the time-sharing group, approximately 80% to 90% of the user's time is spent away from the terminal. In the batch group, time at the computer is less, mostly to deliver job requests and pick up completed runs. Considering only the time spent on problem-solving, we find that the individual spends the far greater part of it alone, at his desk. The basic processes of problem familiarization, hypothesis formulation, and computer test preparation are much the same under both modes.

The key differences are at the man-computer interface. The batch user has minimal interaction; he merely turns in his job and receives machine output at a later time. The time-sharing user interacts directly with the computer, gets immediate knowledge of results and continues to implement and test various alternatives until he has run out of steam or out of available time. But this critical 10% to 20% of his total time serves as focal feedback for problem-solving; it tells him whether he is succeeding or failing and gives him an opportunity to try out, on the spot, options he has thought through previously or that occur to him at the moment. The batch user goes through essentially the same trial-and-error problem-solving procedure, except that he is compelled to wait for an uncertain period of time after each job submission. The online user enjoys continuous problem-solving; the offline user must submit to interrupted problem-solving. It is this difference in man-computer feedback that makes a sustained difference in performance, attitude, and understanding throughout the total problem-solving process.

The similarities in other respects are compelling. In both modes, better performers use more computer time (for the open-ended task), they make fewer machine-recorded errors, they tend to get off to an early start and stay ahead, they tend to conceptualize the problem more effectively, their attitudes are more positive toward their computer system, they tend to have more relevant experience, and they are more likely to mass their problem-solving time and work with minimal interruptions, rather than to intersperse their time with other, unrelated activities. Each group has its hustlers and slow pokes, its risk-takers and nit-pickers. General concept time, parameter time, editing time, and time on results are distributed in much the same proportions in both groups. They differ primarily in the longer reacquaintance time and time waiting for results in the batch mode.

A somewhat surprising similarity is that there was no significant difference in the number of alternate decision rules (variable 21) between the two groups—one would probably expect more alternatives under time-sharing. Our interpretation is that the formulation of a new and worthwhile decision rule (one that is worth the time and effort to try out on the computer) is an extended creative process that is best accomplished when the individual is alone and has the freedom and leisure to think things through. The evidence seems to support the hypothesis that the deepest creativity occurs when the subject is working on the problem alone, at his leisure, rather than at the time when he is interacting with the computer. A corollary to this hypothesis is that the period of man-computer communication is largely test and verification of preconceived and derivative hypotheses, as distinguished from formulation of relatively new and different hypotheses. It is not denied that time-sharing provides better reinforcement that leads to better decision rules; this is an incontrovertible fact in this experiment. But it is asserted that creative insight probably occurs as a result of sustained intellectual effort away from (rather than at) the computer terminal.

Another interesting similarity is that increased experience contributes to a more favorable attitude, regardless of the type of computer system used. This finding was reflected in moderate advances for batch and time-sharing evaluation from pretest to posttest questionnaires, an advance of approximately one point on the nine-point scale. Familiarity, at least with an inexperienced group, tends to breed respect rather than contempt.

7.4 SUMMARY AND CONCLUSIONS

This section is covered under two headings, method and findings.

7.4.1 Method

Subjects. The experiment initially included a total of 66 subjects consisting of graduate and undergraduate students, primarily in business administration. Most of the subjects (78%) had taken at least one course on computers or in programming prior to the experiment.

Problem. The experimental problem was a computerized simulation model of the construction industry in which the subject, as an independent builder, was required to maximize his profit score by developing improved decision rules with optimized parameters. This problem is the only open-ended task reported in the online/offline literature to date, a task that could be continually improved upon through more effective decision rules, and a task that had the methodological advantage of providing a continuing score on subject performance for all completed computer trials throughout the experiment. This problem was too difficult for some students, who dropped out; quite difficult for some, who got marginal profit scores; moderately difficult for most, who made significant profits, and relatively easy for several, who did very well; it typically took 15 to 20 man-hours to complete, over approximately a one-week period.

Online/Offline Facilities. The online facility was the MIT Compatible Time-Sharing System using the IBM 7094 computer; the offline mode was the MIT Batch Facility, also with the IBM 7094. The Dynamo simulation language was used under both conditions. Four typewriter consoles were dedicated for the use of the time-sharing group. The batch group typically had 6-hour turnaround for day service, and 10-hour turnaround for overnight service.

Experimental Design. The basic experimental design was two matched groups of subjects for the online and offline condition. The matching was done through biographical and experimental questionnaire items, with students in each pair randomly assigned to the two groups.

Experimental Controls. The key motivational control was the class grade for the student. Profit scores on the experimental problem and grades from a written report on the problem were weighted equally in the final grade for the course. A deadline was set for the problem; in this sense, the problem was not completely open-ended.

Performance Measures. These included computer-recorded measures, student logs and questionnaires, and teacher grades on written reports. The automatically recorded measures included such items as individual computer time, maximum profit score on the simulation model, total batch runs and number of erroneous runs, total time-sharing interactions and number of erroneous interactions, and a breakdown of online activities such as editing, printing, and compiling.

The student records included administration of identical pretest and posttest questionnaires to measure attitudinal and experience changes, and a large variety of items tracing the speed and course of problem-solving throughout the entire experiment. Difficulties with missing data were most pronounced for the questionnaire items. The instructor graded written student reports on their experimental task with respect to four categories: model dynamics, strategy with model, flexibility, and perceptiveness. A total of 53 measures were employed relating to problem-solving performance.

Statistical Design. The statistical approach featured exploratory multivariate techniques to probe into problem-solving behavior and individual differences. Descriptive statistics such as frequency distributions, means, standard deviations, and bivariate correlations were obtained to become familiar with the empirical data. Mean differences and variance differences between the two groups were then tested to develop profiles of similarities and differences in problem-solving between the two groups. This was followed by general and group factor analyses, conducted separately for each group and for the combined sample, using a data base of 35 preselected variables to test for similarities and differences in obtained factor patterns. Special analyses were conducted, as suggested by earlier leads; these included an analysis of variance of pretest/posttest changes in attitudes toward the online and offline modes, and an analysis of human error levels under both modes.

7.4.2 Results

Online/Offline Differences. Except for less computer time under batch, the tests for mean differences in performance measures showed greater effectiveness and more positive attitudes under time-sharing. There were fewer dropouts and fewer marginal performers in the online mode; subjects were able to reach their first decision rule more quickly, keep up their faster pace, arrive at their final decision rule earlier, and end up with a much higher performance score (almost twice as much profit over the baseline in time-sharing as compared to batch). The online subjects took less time to wait for results and less time to become reacquainted with their problem, and generally spent their time more efficiently and productively at their problem. Positive attitudes toward time-sharing were prominent in both groups. The time-sharing group tended to get better grades on their written reports.

General Problem-Solving Factor. A rational and consistent general factor for problem-solving appeared in each of the experimental groups and in the combined sample. This factor showed the following kinds of variables to be positively associated with better problem-solving performance: higher profit scores, the online mode (as opposed to the offline mode), more computer time (better performers exploited the computer system under both modes by using more CPU time), faster start and earlier finish, less waiting for results, less time spent on refamiliarization with the problem, more relevant experience, more positive attitudes, and higher grades on the written report.

Group Factors. Nine factors were extracted in separate group factor analyses of the two experimental groups and the total sample. Of these, five group factors appeared in all three analyses: two were closely tied to performance effectiveness, called Problem-Solving Speed and Exploitation of Computer System; a third factor described personal style and motivation, called Hustler; the fourth was concerned with Exploration of Alternatives; and the fifth referred to Relevant Experience. The four remaining factors, which were found in two out of the three groupings (batch, time-sharing, and the total sample) included Conceptualization of the Problem, Batch Attitude, Problem Strategy, and another factor on personal style called Nit-Picker. In general, the factor analyses tended to pull out characteristics that were held in common for online and offline problem-solving.

Attitudinal Differences. A decided bandwagon effect favoring time-sharing was found in both the pretest and posttest questionnaires. This finding should be qualified in light of the favorable bias toward time-sharing at MIT. At no time did any individual rate batch higher than time-sharing; there was only one tie rating in each administration of the questionnaire, and all others evaluated time-sharing as more effective. Exposure to each mode resulted in higher ratings after the experiment; familiarity with these systems led to greater appreciation of their value. But even after the experimental experience, the final ratings showed time-sharing at the high end of the rating scale with batch at the lower end of the scale. As expected, successful performance within each group was accompanied by more positive ratings.

Man-Computer Errors. Approximately one-third of all batch runs had errors, and roughly one-half of all time-sharing interactions were erroneous (computer-detected errors). The capability for immediate correction of errors under time-sharing encouraged extensive trial-and-error behavior, whereas the penalty of waiting at least half a day for batch turnaround made offline users more cautious in preparing their runs. The batch condition tended to accentuate differences in error levels among students, whereas time-sharing users had a notably smaller dispersion of error rates. Both groups showed evidence of error-prone individuals, a trait that was magnified in the batch group.

Marginal Performers. The online mode provided more favorable conditions for marginal performers, as indicated above by fewer dropouts and by reduced variation in man-computer error rates. Other factors favoring marginal performers under time-sharing include immediate knowledge of results (as opposed to forced waiting for batch turnaround) and the ability to break the problem down into manageable parts for separate interactions with the computer (as opposed to the relative all-or-none program execution under batch).

PART III

REAL-WORLD EXPERIMENTATION AT THE AIR FORCE ACADEMY

8

EXPERIMENTAL PROCEDURE

8.1 APPROACH

THE Air Force Academy and System Development Corporation have conducted a large-scale experiment at the Academy to compare time-sharing and batch processing in teaching introductory computer science to cadets. This experimental effort was motivated by two broad objectives. First, the results would contribute toward Air Force decisions on the future configuration of computer facilities and toward improved techniques of teaching computer science courses at the Academy. Second, the experiment was designed to make significant contributions to the general field of man-computer problem solving.

8.1.1 Subjects

The subjects included all cadets taking introductory computer-science courses at the Academy. It is the policy of the Academy to require every cadet to take an introductory course in computer science. The intention is to have no "computer illiterates" in the student body, a goal which is gaining increasing recognition in other leading educational centers. Three introductory courses are given, intended for students majoring in the humanities, the social sciences, and the engineering and "hard" sciences (Computer Science 230, 240, and 254 respectively). It was decided that all cadets in these three courses would participate in the experiment in order to maximize sample size (69, 179, and 167 students respectively). Thus, the experimental sample included a total of some 415 students, distributed over 29 sections taught by 9 instructors.

8.1.2 Experimental Problems

The problems assigned to the students were the same as those originally planned for the course. Each problem essentially amounts to a requirement to write a syntactically and logically correct computer program as specified on a problem sheet. The first four problems for each of the three introductory courses were used in this experiment. An example of these problems, in the form given to the cadets, is described in Section 8.2.1. Descriptor tags for the problems are listed in Table 8.1. In some cases, alternate (and essentially equivalent) forms of problems are noted as A and B variations in Table 8.1.

The problems were difficult and generally became more complex as the course progressed. While some cadets found a problem easy, most could solve it only partially or not at all. For example, a single problem characteristically took about one to two weeks of elapsed time; it required an effort on the order of 5 to 10 man-hours to reach a correct solution; and it involved roughly 10 problem runs on the computer. There were 12 experimental problems in all, 4 for each of the three introductory courses.

8.1.3 Computer Facilities

In the main experiment, all test problems were performed on a Burroughs B 5500 computer using the Burroughs Extended ALGOL programming language. The B 5500 is a medium-to-large-size computer which has been equipped at the Academy to provide essentially equivalent service under time-sharing and batch use. ALGOL (Algebraic Oriented Language) is an extensively used high-level language oriented toward mathematical and scientific applications. All students were exposed to similar introductory lessons on the computer facility and on ALGOL at the beginning

Table 8.1. EXPERIMENTAL PROBLEMS FOR THE THREE INTRODUCTORY COMPUTER SCIENCE COURSES

Computer Science 230

Problem 1	—	Flight Plan
Problem 2	—	Payroll/Timekeeping
Problem 3	—	Calendar Algorithm
Problem 4	—	Quartic Equation

Computer Science 240

Problem 1	—	Logarithmic Routine
Problem 2A	—	Newton-Raphson Algorithm
Problem 2B	—	Secant Algorithm
Problem 3A	—	Inventory Sorting
Problem 3B	—	Bid Sorting
Problem 4	—	Simplex Algorithm

Computer Science 254

Problem 1	—	Extended Euclidean Algorithm
Problem 2	—	Statistical Procedures
Problem 3	—	File Processing
Problem 4	—	Systems of Linear Equations

of the course (e g, note the Academy Computer Science texts cited in the references for this chapter).

There was a difference between batch and time-sharing that should be noted at the outset. The batch system had long been operational on the B 5500, whereas the time-sharing system was first installed immediately before the start of the experiment. Thus, there was a built-in computer-system service advantage for batch which needs to be taken into account in the interpretation of the results.

All students were required to submit their initial problem program on coding sheets that would be keypunched and run in the batch mode. In this sense, there was no procedural difference between time-sharing and batch students as far as initial coding and initial submission were concerned. Time-sharing programs were then loaded on disk, whereas batch programs were placed in the job stream.

Some time-sharing advocates might object to this early off-line procedure used in time-sharing subjects, on the ground that the potential advantages of initial online coding were not exploited. Although there may be some validity to this criticism, the above procedure was followed for two basic reasons: (1) to reduce the obviously heavy demand on time-sharing terminals, and (2) to exercise the useful experimental control of having all students in both modes initiate their computer runs from a well-defined starting point.

In the batch mode, the students typically received same-day or next-day service, depending upon whether their jobs were submitted earlier or later in the day. Batch turnaround was typically on the order of several hours.

Online terminal time was carefully regulated to assure equal opportunity for computer access for all students. Seventeen Model 33 Teletype consoles were available on a scheduled basis. Cadets had to sign up for console time in advance. They were permitted a maximum of three sessions per day, 15 minutes per session, and they were held accountable for unused sessions. Longer console sessions would have been desirable to exploit the interactive advantages of time-sharing, but the cadet load was too heavy for the available terminal capacity. In the event any consoles were free and were not scheduled, the cadets could use them on a first-come, first-served basis.

8.1.4 Experimental Procedure

The basic philosophy of the experimental procedure is the use of real-world experimentation and self-experimentation. The "real-world" approach is highlighted by the use of actual problems solved by students in each course in the normal setting and manner. The "self-experimentation" feature follows from the self-administration of tests and procedures by instructors and students in generating and collecting data, and from their systematic contribution to the analysis and evaluation of the results in each class. Each participant thus served as both subject and experimenter.

This philosophical approach was intended to enhance the real-world credibility of the overall experiment, and was expected to add to the useful output of the experiment in a manner that could not be accomplished by an individual experimenter or even by an experimental team. The cost of such experimentation is also much lower than approaches using traditional techniques of tight laboratory control and minimal subject involvement in design and analysis. Although this brief discussion is hardly a comprehensive analysis of such a complex and controversial area, it was believed that the cost-effectiveness of the final experimental yield would be greatly augmented by the proposed approach.

The experimental design was based on the individual class, or section, for better experimental control and more convenient administration. The key idea was to divide each participating section into two matched subgroups, and then assign each subgroup to time-sharing and batch in a counterbalanced order in accordance with the experimental design.

The basis for selecting matched groups was the student's overall Academy grade average. Odd ranked in subgroup 1 and even ranked in subgroup 2. Compared to random assignments to the two subgroups, this procedure had the advantages of greater control over individual differences, more homogeneous variance between groups, and reduced fluctuations from normal distributions between groups. These are useful features for more rigorous applications of analysis of variance to the results.

The two subgroups for each class, as defined above, went through the problem sequence shown in Figure 8.1 for the standardized class problem.

	Problem 1	Problem 2	Problem 2	Problem 4
Group 1	Time-Sharing	Batch	Batch	Time-Sharing
Group 2	Batch	Time-Sharing	Time-Sharing	Batch

Figure 8.1. COUNTERBALANCED EXPERIMENTAL DESIGN

The above order required that each of the two groups remain intact throughout the semester and solve each problem under the designated mode. Paired sequences were counterbalanced to permit certain types of statistical analyses and to control possible learning effects associated with computer mode sequence.

In order to test the cumulative effects of time-sharing vs. batch over the course of an entire semester, some sections worked exclusively on time-sharing or exclusively on batch for all experimental problems. Experimental control was exercised by matching each section in one mode against another section in the other computer mode taught by the same instructor. These sections did not follow the above counterbalanced order, since computer mode was constant. Each section worked independently of the other sections insofar as administration of problems and collection of data were concerned. In this sense, the experimental procedure was modularized at the individual section level.

For more convenient reference, the experimental design involving classes with counterbalanced subgroup assignments (as shown in Figure 8.1) are referred to as the "flip" experimental mode. The other classes working either on batch or on time-sharing for all problems are referred to as the "constant" experimental mode. The ratio of subjects assigned to flip and constant modes turned out to be 60% and 40%, respectively. This ratio was derived from a combination of experimental and administrative considerations in trying to achieve adequate sample sizes for both experimental modes.

8.1.5 Statistical Design

Comparison of Time-sharing and Batch Performance. The experimental design for time-sharing vs. batch comparisons essentially amounts to various analyses of variance to test for mean differences between the two modes for key performance variables, such as man-hours, problem grade, and computer time. The flip experimental mode lends itself to a Latin-Square design for the first two problems, and another one for the last two problems (see Figure 8.1). The design is a 2 x 2 x 2 arrangement which involves two groups, two conditions (online/offline), and two problems. The main advantage of this Latin-Square is that online/offline differences may be tested directly with each student effectively serving as his own control. The key disadvantage is that interaction effects cannot be tested for the joint effects of computer mode and problem differences.

Multivariate testing can be accomplished by analysis of variance, regression analysis, and factor analysis for the combined sample or major subsamples, as appropriate for selected variables. Pretest and posttest opinion ratings of the students for the two systems serve as useful controls for measuring attitude changes and motivational factors. The modular experimental design, modularized by individual class and problem, provides emergency fallback for missing data, erroneous data, incorrect sequencing of the experimental design, or other misinterpretations of experimental directions by instructors or students.

These techniques are indicative of some of the statistical procedures that can be used. The initial exploratory tests are followed by additional analyses contingent upon the initial results, the available data, constraints of the study, and new hypotheses.

8.1.6 Data Forms and Performance Measures

Consult the Appendix for cadet questionnaires and data forms. Briefly, the experimental data forms include the following:

STUDENT DATA FORMS

- *Pretest/Posttest Questionnaire.* Contains control data and attitudinal measures of the students on time-sharing vs. batch; administered before and after the experimental problems to test attitude changes; objective question forms.
- *Problem Work Log.* Contains basic performance measures on the students, the computer system, and their interaction; filled in by the student during every work session on his problem.
- *Problem Questionnaire.* Includes a variety of problem-specific questions, with objective and open-end items; the

objective items are aimed at attitudinal and timing characteristics; the open-end items are exploratory and are oriented toward qualitative aspects of individual problem-solving; filled out after the problem has been turned in.

INSTRUCTOR DATA FORM

- *Section Summary.* Individual student scores on grades and other key performance measures for the two subgroups on each problem; measures derived from student output listings; experimental control data.

The performance measures include man-hours, elapsed time, student grades on problem performance, days late in handing in assignments, and computer runs required to solve problems. Control variables include overall grade average, computer-related experience, pretest and posttest attitudes toward time-sharing and batch, evaluation of system service, and timing characteristics of sequential steps in working toward the problem solution. Open-end verbal responses are also included to discover new leads and to get a picture of the student's interpretation of his own problem-solving efforts in his own words.

8.2 THE PILOT STUDY

An integral part of the experimental plan was to design and conduct a pilot study on a relatively small, manageable sample to meet several objectives. The first was to improve the quality of the experiment by providing a small-scale rehearsal of the basic experimental cycle in connection with a single test problem. The second objective was to shake down experimental procedures and analyze the experimental data to reduce ambiguities, errors, and inconsistencies in instructions and data forms. Third, the plan aimed to assess man and machine costs to ensure that student and instructor support did not involve undue hardship or conflicts with personal schedules or Academy requirements. Fourth, the pilot experience was to allow us to develop early empirical estimates on general student performance. (It should be emphasized, however, that the pilot study was not designed to provide definitive estimates of comparative performance under time-sharing and batch, since computers, languages, and cadet experience were not comparable under both modes.) Finally, we were interested in obtaining instructor and student response to the experimental procedure to assess their motivation and involvement, and to gain a working knowledge of the adequacy of the experimental controls.

8.2.1 Method

The pilot study was run on four sections in the introductory computer science course for social science majors, 60 cadets in all. Two instructors each taught two of these sections. The flip experimental mode was used, subdividing each section into matched time-sharing and batch subgroups. This scheme allowed testing for instructor and section differences as well as time-sharing and batch differences.

The pilot problem involved simulation of a barber shop queue under specified conditions. The students were required to write a program that would simulate this waiting line for a run of up to 30,000 minutes. Table 8.2 is the pilot problem sheet handed to

Table 8.2. INSTRUCTIONS FOR THE PILOT PROBLEM

A. PURPOSES OF THE EXERCISE:

1. To simulate a queueing problem on the computer.
2. To show the use of random numbers in a simulation.
3. To show how a time span of years in real life can be simulated on the computer in terms of seconds.

B. STATEMENT OF THE PROBLEM:

Customers are arriving randomly at a barber shop at an average rate of 15 per hour. Service time per customer is 3 minutes. Find the probability distribution of waiting times (ie, how many customers had to wait zero minutes, one minute, two minutes, etc.).

Write a complete program to simulate this process for 10,000 minutes and then 30,000 minutes. Assume there is a single barber chair and queue.

C. SPECIFIC INSTRUCTIONS:

In paragraph D you will find a *partially completed* flow chart for this problem. With the aid of this flow chart write a complete program to solve this problem. Notice that we have not flow-charted an arrival. Your instructor will explain the *partially completed* flow chart.

Note: Understanding of the flow chart may be aided by the following comments,

1) Initialization of the library program RANDOM is achieved by having an eleven digit odd integer as the third parameter.

2) We can run this simulation for various lengths of time (in minutes) by reading in a new value for MINS.

3) The length of queue, service time remaining for customer in barber chair, and maximum number of minutes that any customer had to wait must be initialized to zero.

4) The LW array must be initialized to zero since we will accumulate a count of the customers that had to wait zero, one, two, etc., minutes.

5) The iteration on minutes covers one minute of time on each pass through the iteration. We have an arrival if a random number between zero and one has been generated.

6) You must supply the logic for an arrival.

the cadets. Figure 8.2 shows the flow diagram given to the students as an initial formulation and partial solution of their problem. Table 8.2 and Figure 8.2 are indicative of the format and level of detail presented to the students for the problems used in the main experiment.

The time-sharing and batch subjects worked on the different computers and different languages then in use for these two modes at the Academy. The batch mode involved the Burroughs B 5500 and ALGOL (as in the main experiment). The time-sharing mode was handled with the GE 635 computer located

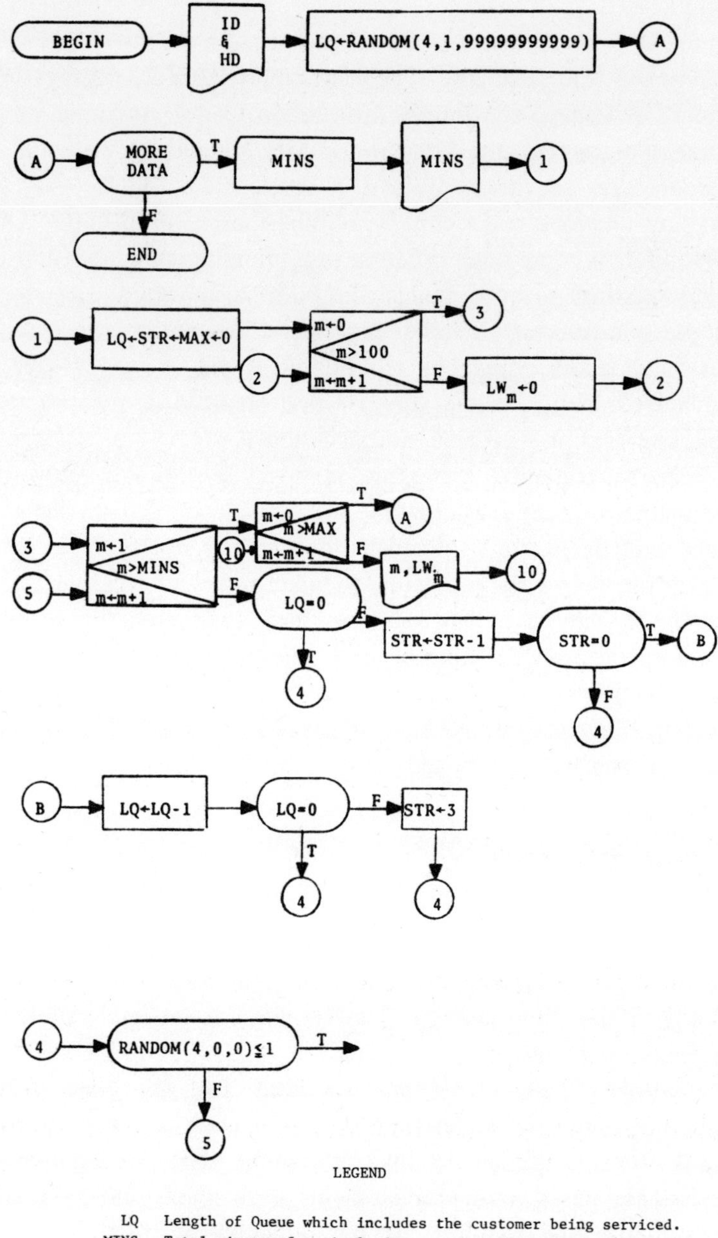

LEGEND

LQ	Length of Queue which includes the customer being serviced.
MINS	Total minutes for simulation.
STR	Service time remaining for customer in the barber chair.
MAX	The maximum number of minutes that any customer had to wait.
LW	A one-dimensional array where LW_0 contains number of customers that had to wait 0 mins., LW_1 contains number of customers that had to wait 1 minute, etc.
RANDOM (4,0,0)	Generates uniformly distributed random numbers between 1 and 4.

Figure 8.2. FLOW DIAGRAM FOR PILOT PROBLEM

at the Rome Aerospace Development Center with typewriter terminals at the Academy. The Dartmouth BASIC language (Beginner's All-purpose Symbolic Instruction Code) was used by the online subjects (see the GE 635/BASIC Manual by Walker). All students were previously trained in batch and ALGOL, very few had any previous experience with time-sharing or BASIC. Thus, with different computers, different programming languages and unequal exposure to both modes, the pilot study cannot and should not be construed as a valid experiment comparing time-sharing and batch under equivalent conditions. It did serve, however, to provide us with a useful preview and shakedown for the main experiment as it has been outlined above.

The experimental procedure involved several key steps: the instructors and the participating cadets were briefed on the pilot procedure; the students filled out their pretest questionnaire; they worked at their class problem and filled out their work log; after turning in their problem solution, they completed the problem questionnaire; finally, the posttest questionnaire was completed and turned in; data reduction and analysis followed; experimental procedures were modified and improved in joint consultation after the pilot run was completed.

8.2.2 Pilot Results

Since the pilot study was not a formal experimental test of time-sharing versus batch but primarily a rehearsal of experimental procedures, this discussion of pilot results stresses methodology rather than content. The emphasis is on implications for the main experiment.

Various changes became apparent for the data forms. Generally speaking, cadet time was at a premium, and the data forms were simplified to take minimum time for completion. Redundant items were pruned, items were made self-explanatory to minimize the requirement for rereading instructions, verbal open-end responses were made as brief as possible, and possibly ambiguous instructions were rewritten.

On the whole, the pretest, posttest, and problem questionnaires were found fast and easy to take. Relatively few changes were made in the original draft versions for the main experiment. More extensive changes were made in procedures concerning the work log. For example, it was deemed necessary to have the instructors check each student's work log after initial entries were made for the first few work sessions on the class problem. There was always the danger that the cadet would slip into the habit of filling out the work log ex post facto, imperfectly trying to remember events well after they occurred, rather than filling the log out in real time—as he worked on his problem. An instructor spot check was an effective preventive measure to minimize inaccurate or missing data.

The instructor's section summary emerged from the pilot experience. The various instructor inputs on student grades, the automatically recorded data from student problem outputs, and the overall accounting of student data forms all came from different sources and this fact led to missing and inconsistent data. Putting these instructor-related items into a Section Summary eliminated most of these problems for the main experiment.

The statistical reduction and analysis of the pilot data involved several steps: initial collating and editing of raw data, writing out the data on keypunch forms, keypunching, card-to-tape transfer, and the payoff in various statistical computer runs. Writing out the raw data by hand turned out to be a bottleneck, slowing down the entire data-reduction process. We decided to revise the data forms so that keypunching could be done directly from the raw data after relatively minor editing. Card layouts were designed and superimposed on the data forms used in the main experiment to expedite direct keypunch (see the final data forms in the Appendix).

An interesting by-product of the pilot experience was that student name turned out to be the most unambiguous and reliable way to identify each subject. The use of student codes led to numerous errors and omissions. We decided that it was easier to change student names into an appropriate statistical code for data processing, after the data were in, than to ask each cadet to use a code on his data forms. No one mixes up his own name; but it is easy to get confused over an unfamiliar and impersonal code name. However, to assuage any cadet uneasiness, each data form clearly stated that no individual names would be mentioned in the results of this experiment.

The results of the pilot study are briefly discussed under three main areas, experimental controls, man-computer performance measures, and cadet attitudes. The lack of adequate experimental control in the pilot study was mentioned earlier. Time-sharing was associated with the GE 635 computer and BASIC, whereas batch was performed on the Burroughs B 5500 with ALGOL. Thus computer mode effects were confounded with different computer and different languages. In addition, there was virtually no experience with time-sharing and BASIC as compared to a few months experience with batch and ALGOL. The time-sharing students faced the tribulations of learning a new language.

Turning to key performance results, batch students required fewer mean man-hours to complete their work on the test problem than the time-sharing group: 6.6 vs. 8.1 man-hours respectively. This mean difference was not statistically signficant ($t = 1.25$). The 23% advantage in man-hours for batch, if the trend has any meaning, could probably be attributed to the experience advantage for the batch group for computer system and computer language. This interpretation is consistent with the findings of Schatzoff, Tsao, and Wiig (1967) which demonstrated a man-hour advantage in batch for students who were more familiar with batch than time-sharing.

The spread of man-hour scores was positively skewed—most cadets put in relatively small man-hour efforts to solve the test problem with a small proportion putting in relatively long hours, up to 32 man-hours at the extreme. As in previous studies, individual differences overshadowed computer-system differences by an order of magnitude. For example, the ratio of slowest to fastest cadet performance was 32:2 man-hours, or 16:1.

The early online/offline literature shows a trend for more computer time to be consumed under time-sharing. Although cadet CPU time was not directly measured in the pilot study, the number of program executions (a correlate of CPU time) was recorded. Mean number of program executions under time-sharing was 13.2, almost twice as much as the corresponding mean of

7.5 for batch. This mean difference was statistically significant at the 5% level ($t = 2.27$). Here again, individual differences overshadowed computer system differences by an order of magnitude. The ratio between the most and least program runs for the entire sample was 59:2, almost 30:1.

The results for class grades showed almost identical mean grades for online and offline groups. Section/instructor differences, however, did turn out to be significantly different with respect to class grades. These significant differences were associated partly with instructor differences and partly with "stratified" assignment of students to sections in accordance with overall Academy grade average. Stratified assignment may occur when two or more sections of the same course are taught at the same hour. For example, if there are two sections receiving the same course at the same time, the cadets are split into equal-sized groups according to overall grade average so that there will be a more homogeneous skill level in each section to make for more effective teaching. In the pilot study, the section with the higher grade average received a substantially and significantly higher problem grade than the other section. As a result, the schedule of computer mode asignment for the main experiment was reworked to make sure that online and offline modes received equal proportions of "stratified" and unselected cadets at all skill levels. This experimental control applies only to the constant experimental mode since it refers to inter-section comparisons; the flip mode has a within-section control built into it wherein subgroups are matched on overall grade average.

The frequency distribution for problem grade essentially approximated a rectangular distribution. The maximum grade was 300 for a syntactically and logically correct solution. Approximately one-third of the sample received grades between 200 and 300, one-third between 100 and 200, and one-third between 0 and 100, corresponding to a correct or nearly correct solution, a partially correct solution, or an incorrect solution, respectively. This means that appoximately one-third of the pilot sample was unable to make any significant headway toward a correct solution. These results hold for both the regular grade received by the cadet and for a corrected grade that takes into account a penalty for late turn-in of the problem to the instructor. (Students were penalized by a 20% reduction in problem grade for each day late, with a maximum of three days late.)

The distribution of problem grades reflects an additional uncontrolled factor that enters into the interpretation of the results and the results of the main experiment concerning the nature of the experimental task. All students did not work up to the same standard of performance (a syntactically and logically correct solution); therefore, variables such as man-hours were not strictly comparable. For some students man-hours meant time until successful completion of the problem, whereas for others, they meant time until partial completion, or even for the poorest performers, no progress whatsoever. The interpretive problem lies in the tradeoff between man-hours and problem grade.

The apparent lack of control in working toward a variable standard does not mean that the experiment is invalid. What it does mean is that the task was, in part, an open-end task—at least in the sense that for most students more personal time led to a higher score or grade. On the other hand, the task was fixed or closed for cadets who arrived at a successful solution and received the maximum score. Thus, we have a difficulty continuum varying from one end where the relatively fixed problem is easily solved by most, to the other where we find a very difficult, relatively open-end problem. The pilot problem tended to fall closer to the difficult, open-end terminus of this continuum in the main experiment, the various problems will be seen to fall at different points on this continuum, depending upon their difficulty level.

The attitudinal measures in the pilot groups revealed a pattern different from that observed in the previous online/offline literature. The chief difference is that there was no time-sharing bandwagon effect. The ratings on various questions comparing time-sharing and batch generally showed middle-of-the-road ratings, with means for both modes close to the center of the scale. Mean difference changes from pretest and posttest questionnaires were generally not statistically significant. This result is an experimental bonus, in that the cadets presumably started from attitudinally neutral ground with respect to previous experience, and that they were probably more willing to judge time-sharing and batch on the basis of operational performance than if they had had a preconceived bias.

The batch mode had the advantages of familiarity and better system service working for it in the pilot run. It also had the advantage of a more powerful and a more familiar language in ALGOL. These advantages apparently neutralized the time-sharing advantages of direct access and interactive man-computer communication; the result for this sample ended up as a close draw. For example, the entire group tended to rate batch better for complex problems, individual creativity, and for more skilled users. These responses are obviously contaminated by the association of batch with ALGOL. On the other hand, the entire pilot group liked time-sharing better for beginners, self-teaching, and for debugging. These responses are equally contaminated by the association of BASIC with time-sharing. There was a notable trend for ratings to improve with experience from the pretest to the posttest period. In line with earlier findings (Sackman and Gold, 1968), increased familiarity with computer systems seems to breed respect rather than contempt. The time-sharing ratings tended to move up somewhat higher than the batch ratings in the posttest results. The design of the main experiment permitted us to determine whether these and related trends persisted over an exposure of almost a full semester to four successive problems, and to conduct a longitudinal, as opposed to a cross-sectional, test of these hypotheses.

The open-end problem questionnaire responses painted a rather consistent portrait of the test problem. The general picture was that of a tough task, marked by almost universal underestimation of the time and effort required to solve it, by numerous gripes over poor computer system service (particularly time-sharing), by great difficulties in working with the programming languages, and by a prevailing tendency for the cadets to muddle their way through to a correct solution.

Although the comments were predominantly negative, the picture was not entirely bleak. Those who solved the problem successfully were impressed with the power of the computer to compress a very large sample of simulation trials (30,000) into a short computer run; many were favorably impressed with the simplicity of BASIC and the ease of online debugging; many learned the value of careful planning and careful preparation before attempting a computer run. Numerous recommendations, ranging from broad philosophical considerations to human-engineered formats, were made for improving computer service and for making the course more useful.

Interesting observations on the nature of problem "insight," and the time and place of its occurrence were noted. For example, most "critical" insights tended to occur at private moments away from the computer rather than when working with the computer; the response of the instructor to student questions figured heavily in arriving at key insights; the type of insight listed as most important varied greatly with the skill level of the cadet—marginal students focused on overall comprehension of the problem, whereas skilled cadets focused on fine technical points in writing their programs.

Summing up, the pilot study was instrumental in meeting the basic objectives of the pilot run and in providing positive fallout as well. Experimental procedures and data forms were shaken down and made more effective. Some significant experimental control parameters were highlighted and made part of the experimental design. And preliminary pilot findings suggested some useful new hypotheses to explore in the main experiment. Although these matters have only been briefly discussed above, it cannot be too strongly emphasized how vital it is to run a precursor pilot study for the successful planning and execution of a large-scale experiment.

9

ONLINE/OFFLINE PERFORMANCE

ONLY the first phase of this study—that part concerned with time-sharing and batch performance differences—is reported in this chapter. Since the results are voluminous, only the main findings, primarily for the total sample, are listed. The presentation of the results is followed by the interpretation of online/offline findings which comprise the last part of this chapter. The next chapter is devoted to problem-solving, particularly in connection with individual differences.

9.1 ONLINE/OFFLINE RESULTS

The time-sharing/batch results are presented for the pretest and posttest questionnaire first to set the stage with respect to attitudinal and other control variables. Then the main results from the Section Summary and Work Logs are presented: the performance of the cadets on key criterion variables. Finally, the problem questionnaire findings are presented.

9.1.1 Pretest/Posttest Questionnaire

Table 9.1 shows the results for the pretest/posttest questionnaire. The first column lists the 31 questionnaire items. (The complete questionnaire with all items and scale units is found in

Table 9.1. PRETEST/POSTTEST QUESTIONNAIRE RESULTS

Variable		Pretest Results				Posttest Results				Pretest/Posttest Mean Differences	
		Humanities (230)	Social Sciences (240)	Basic Sciences (254)	Total Sample	Humanities (230)	Social Sciences (240)	Basic Sciences (254)	Total Sample	Correlation Ratio	Probability
1. Batch Experience (experience using batch processing)	M	0.29	0.21	0.77	0.45	3.08	2.85	3.20	3.03	.39	.000 *
	S	1.27	0.70	4.31	2.83	1.12	1.89	4.67	3.25		
	N	69	178	167	414	65	175	163	403		
2. Time-Sharing Experience (experience using time-sharing)	M	0.86	0.08	0.10	0.21	2.91	2.39	2.31	2.44	.46	.000 *
	S	0.39	0.38	0.56	0.54	1.20	4.08	1.86	2.97		
	N	69	178	167	414	65	173	163	401		
3. Computer Experience (experience working with computers)	M	0.99	0.30	0.80	0.61	4.40	5.01	4.82	4.83	.47	.000 *
	S	1.40	0.78	4.27	2.83	1.79	5.69	4.47	4.75		
	N	68	178	166	412	65	174	164	403		
4. Batch Value (value of batch in helping you)	M	4.39	3.74	4.29	4.08	5.74	4.93	4.49	4.88	.17	.000 *
	S	1.86	2.60	1.83	2.20	2.15	2.53	2.24	2.38		
	N	69	172	167	408	65	165	165	395		
5. Time-Sharing Value (value of the time-sharing in helping you)	M	7.23	4.34	5.72	5.39	6.03	3.78	5.34	4.78	.10	.001 *
	S	1.57	2.90	2.21	2.65	2.44	2.94	2.72	2.91		
	N	69	173	167	409	65	171	162	398		

6. Batch vs. Time-Sharing (long-term value of batch vs. time-sharing)	M	6.87	5.46	5.79	5.83	5.49	4.56	5.68	5.16	.14	.000 *
	S	1.56	2.03	1.83	1.93	2.85	2.55	2.33	2.56		
	N	69	172	166	407	65	174	165	404		
7. Coding (coding and assembling your program)	M	1.86	2.12	1.98	2.02	2.28	2.21	2.23	2.23	.11	.000 *
	S	0.90	0.82	0.89	0.86	0.90	0.87	0.90	0.89		
	N	69	179	167	415	64	175	163	402		
8. Debugging (debugging your program)	M	1.04	1.56	1.29	1.37	1.53	1.45	1.24	1.38	.00	.826
	S	0.67	0.75	0.64	0.67	0.89	0.77	0.64	0.75		
	N	69	179	167	415	64	175	164	403		
9. Computer Service (reliable and dependable service)	M	1.91	1.98	1.77	1.88	2.38	2.61	2.44	2.52	.37	.000 *
	S	0.87	0.81	0.86	0.85	0.81	0.64	0.78	0.73		
	N	69	179	167	415	65	175	164	404		
10. Faster Solution (faster solution of your problem)	M	1.03	1.47	1.23	1.30	1.60	1.70	1.29	1.52	.15	.000 *
	S	0.24	0.62	0.55	0.57	0.86	0.85	0.66	0.80		
	N	69	179	167	415	65	175	164	404		
11. Efficient Program (more efficient programs—shorter and faster-running)	M	1.25	1.53	1.51	1.47	1.78	1.79	1.71	1.76	.18	.000 *
	S	0.60	0.66	0.77	0.70	0.91	0.85	0.84	0.85		
	N	69	179	167	415	65	174	163	402		
12. Self-Organizing (easier to organize work at your own pace)	M	1.67	2.13	2.08	2.04	2.45	2.11	2.07	2.15	.06	.076
	S	0.89	0.85	0.94	0.91	0.88	0.93	0.97	0.95		
	N	69	179	167	415	65	175	164	404		

Variable		Pretest Results				Posttest Results				Pretest/Posttest Mean Differences	
		Humanities (230)	Social Sciences (240)	Basic Sciences (254)	Total Sample	Humanities (230)	Social Sciences (240)	Basic Sciences (254)	Total Sample	Correlation Ratio	Probability
13. Easy Learning (easier to learn and understand)	M	1.77	1.98	2.07	1.98	2.31	2.14	2.21	2.20	.13	.000 *
	S	0.84	0.75	0.84	0.81	0.86	0.82	0.84	0.84		
	N	69	179	167	415	65	175	164	404		
14. Greater Challenge (more challenging and interesting)	M	1.28	1.66	1.47	1.52	1.60	1.74	1.40	1.58	.03	.283
	S	0.54	0.72	0.73	0.71	0.90	0.79	0.71	0.79		
	N	69	179	167	415	65	175	164	404		
15. Analysis (easier to break problem up for stepwise solution)	M	1.86	2.07	2.05	2.03	2.09	2.06	2.10	2.08	.03	.373
	S	0.88	0.79	0.90	0.86	0.96	0.90	0.92	0.92		
	N	69	179	167	415	65	175	164	404		
16. Synthesis (see problem as a whole)	M	1.49	2.06	2.17	2.01	2.20	2.22	2.11	2.17	.09	.008 *
	S	0.78	0.80	0.89	0.87	0.92	0.85	0.93	0.90		
	N	69	179	167	415	65	175	164	404		
17. Computer Exploitation (exploit computer facilities more fully)	M	1.33	1.67	1.48	1.54	1.82	2.04	1.68	1.86	.19	.000 *
	S	0.70	0.76	0.75	0.76	0.92	0.88	0.86	0.89		
	N	69	179	167	415	65	175	164	404		
18. Insight (greater insight in problem-solving)	M	1.58	2.02	1.75	1.84	1.98	1.89	1.68	1.82	.00	.803
	S	0.79	0.75	0.83	0.81	0.93	0.80	0.83	0.84		
	N	69	179	167	415	64	175	164	403		

19. Creativity (creativity in new solutions)	M	1.59	1.80	1.74	1.74	1.55	1.75	1.57	1.65	.06	.083
	S	0.75	0.71	0.84	0.77	0.79	0.76	0.78	0.78		
	N	69	179	167	415	65	175	164	404		
20. Finding Errors (detecting and understanding errors)	M	1.14	1.72	1.58	1.57	1.80	1.79	1.71	1.76	.11	.001 *
	S	0.46	0.81	0.83	0.80	0.96	0.89	0.91	0.91		
	N	69	179	166	414	64	175	164	403		
21. Correcting Errors (helpful in correcting errors)	M	1.09	1.66	1.30	1.42	1.45	1.38	1.20	1.32	.07	.042 *
	S	0.41	0.80	0.65	0.72	0.83	0.71	0.58	0.69		
	N	69	179	166	414	64	175	164	403		
22. Self-Teaching (effective for self-teaching)	M	1.25	1.60	1.58	1.53	1.64	1.67	1.49	1.59	.03	.275
	S	0.63	0.72	0.83	0.76	0.90	0.85	0.82	0.85		
	N	69	179	166	414	64	175	164	403		
23. Exploration (explore more alternative solutions)	M	1.35	1.64	1.59	1.57	1.50	1.62	1.35	1.49	.05	.149
	S	0.70	0.72	0.84	0.77	0.82	0.81	0.72	0.79		
	N	69	179	166	414	64	175	164	403		
24. Simple Problems (effective for simple problems)	M	1.33	1.59	1.59	1.55	1.44	1.53	1.63	1.55	.00	.894
	S	0.68	0.71	0.84	0.76	0.75	0.79	0.91	0.84		
	N	69	179	166	414	64	175	164	403		
25. Complex Problems (effective for complex problems)	M	1.83	2.12	1.97	2.01	2.39	2.42	2.10	2.29	.15	.000 *
	S	0.87	0.87	0.90	0.85	0.87	0.81	0.98	0.90		
	N	69	179	166	414	64	175	164	403		

Variable		Pretest Results				Posttest Results				Pretest/Posttest Mean Differences	
		Humanities (230)	Social Sciences (240)	Basic Sciences (254)	Total Sample	Humanities (230)	Social Sciences (240)	Basic Sciences (254)	Total Sample	Correlation Ratio	Probability
26. Fixed Problems (useful for problems with fixed solutions)	M	1.80	2.13	2.08	2.06	2.09	2.21	2.05	2.13	.04	.230
	S	0.88	0.73	0.88	0.83	0.90	0.81	0.91	0.86		
	N	69	179	166	414	64	175	164	403		
27. Open-End Problems (useful for open-end problems)	M	1.59	1.84	1.76	1.77	1.81	2.02	1.78	1.89	.07	.030 *
	S	0.75	0.74	0.84	0.79	0.87	0.83	0.87	0.86		
	N	69	179	166	414	64	175	164	403		
28. Unskilled Users (effective for unskilled users)	M	1.32	1.88	2.04	1.85	2.19	2.05	2.08	2.08	.12	.000 *
	S	0.70	0.83	0.91	0.88	0.95	0.90	0.96	0.93		
	N	69	178	166	413	63	175	164	402		
29. Skilled Users (effective for skilled users)	M	1.77	1.82	1.61	1.73	1.66	1.92	1.63	1.76	.01	.611
	S	0.84	0.75	0.81	0.80	0.88	0.87	0.87	0.88		
	N	69	179	166	414	64	175	164	403		
30. Frustration Level (frustrating to work with)	M	2.36	2.24	2.46	2.35	1.59	1.63	1.90	1.73	.34	.000 *
	S	0.89	0.79	0.76	0.80	0.89	0.81	0.94	0.89		
	N	69	178	166	413	64	175	164	403		
31. Questionnaire Value (your opinion of these questionnaires)	M	1.93	1.31	1.72	1.58	1.91	1.25	1.53	1.46	.05	.095
	S	0.71	1.01	0.93	0.96	0.73	0.93	0.91	0.92		
	N	69	176	166	411	64	173	164	401		

the Appendix.) The first block of columns shows pretest results for each of the three courses and for the total sample. The mean, standard deviation, and sample size is listed for each grouping as M, S, and N, respectively. Similar information is listed in the next block of columns for the posttest results. The last block of columns in Table 9.1 shows the mean difference between the pretest and posttest administration for the complete sample. The correlation ratio column indicates the strength of the observed relationship (the square of the correlation ratio is equivalent to the proportion of total variance associated with the pretest/posttest mean difference). The last column shows the statistical significance of the observed mean difference in thousandths against the null hypotheses that the means are not different; values at or lower than the 5% level of significance are shown with an asterisk.

The correlation ratio is the generalized curvilinear coefficient of correlation. It is essentially equivalent to the square root of the ratio of correlated variance to total variance. In this context, the correlation ratio is derived directly from the t-test for mean differences; it is equal to the square root of the variance associated with the observed mean differences between the pretest and posttest scores, divided by the total variance for both tests combined.

$$\eta = \sqrt{s_m^2 / s_T^2}, \text{ where } \eta = \text{correlation ratio}$$

s = standard deviation
m = means
T = total sample

The level of statistical significance with respect to the null hypothesis (that the means are equal) is exactly the same for the correlation ratio and the associated t-test for mean differences. The advantage in reporting the correlation ratio rather than the t-value, as indicated above, is that the correlation ratio not only shows the statistical significance of the results, but also the strength of the observed relationship (see, for example, Edwards, 1949, and Ezekiel and Fox, 1959).

The units for the first six variables in Table 9.1 are self-explanatory (at least with the aid of the original questionnaire).

Items 7 through 30, however, were specially treated for ease and simplicity of presentation. The cadets were asked to respond with "T" for time-sharing, "U" for uncertain, and "B" for batch, depending upon whether they believed that one mode, or the other, or neither, was more effective for the given item (e g, debugging, as in item 9). For Table 9.1, a time-sharing (T) was scored as 1, uncertain (U) was scored as 2, and batch (B) was scored as 3. This scaling made it possible to list a single mean score and to calculate a straightforward mean difference statistic for each grouping, rather than the more cumbersome listing of raw score frequencies for T, U, and B. With this scale, means close to 1.0 indicate almost unanimous preference for time-sharing, and means close to 3.0 show almost unanimous preference for batch, whereas values close to 2.0 show an approximately even division of opinion for the given item.

Some descriptive results of the pretest/posttest findings are discussed at this point to provide a framework for control and attitudinal variables for the performance findings. The first three items in Table 9.1 are various measures of computer experience which showed expected increases as a result of the class experience itself. The only notable feature for these variables is that the cadet population started almost from scratch as far as prior computer-related experience was concerned.

Items 4 through 6 reveal a central feature of the experiment. Before the experiment, batch was rated below average, time-sharing was rated above average, and substantively higher than batch. (These scales vary from 0 to 9, with a midpoint of 4.5.) As a consequence of the experimental experience, the posttest results show a striking improvement in cadet attitudes toward batch, with overall ratings slightly above the midpoint, and the comparative rating close to but not better than time-sharing. The key question is: what happened during the experiment to invoke this shift in attitude? As we shall see, computer system service plays a pivotal role in this attitudinal shift.

The remaining items involve some interpretational complexity and are more appropriately discussed in the interpretation section. However, item 9, computer service, provides a key to the above question. Whereas the cadets were somewhat more favorably inclined toward time-sharing service at the start of the experiment (1.88 in Table 9.1), their preference shifted dramatically toward batch by the end of the experiment (2.52 mean score with a correlation ratio of .37). In a nutshell, batch service was rated as more reliable than time-sharing service by most cadets through the experiment. Note also that the "frustration level" (variable 30) shifted dramatically from expected frustration with batch at the beginning of the semester to experienced frustration directed at time-sharing at the end of the experiment.

9.1.2 Performance Measures

Table 9.2 shows basic performance results for time-sharing vs. batch for measures taken from cadet work logs and section summary forms prepared by the instructors. Only the overall results for all courses combined are listed in Table 9.2 for each of the four problems.

Table 9.2 lists six performance variables with the following scales: problem grade (percentage), days late, adjusted grade, man-hours, elapsed time (in days), and program runs. Each measure is listed with its mean, sample size, and standard deviation. As in previous results, the correlation ratio and the statistical results meeting the 5% level of significance are shown with an asterisk.

The salient characteristics of these results stand out in bold relief in Table 9.2. Most performance measures do not show reliable mean differences between time-sharing and batch. These include problem grade, days late, adjusted grade and elapsed time. The consistently significant result is with number of program runs, which is almost twice as high under time-sharing as it is with batch. The trend for more man-hours under time-sharing is consistent for all four composite problems, as far as overall means are concerned, but the difference is statistically significant in only two of the four composite problems. The pooled mean difference for the four successive problems taken as a whole is 12% more man-hours under time-sharing. There is a slight but statistically non-significant tendency for class grades to be

Table 9.2. TIME-SHARING VS. BATCH PERFORMANCE: PROBLEM 1

Variable	Time-Sharing	Batch	Correlation Ratio	Probability
• Problem Grade				
Mean	86.76	85.68	.02	.634
SD	22.81	23.04		
N	193	218		
• Days Late				
Mean	0.202	0.151	.04	.369
SD	0.642	0.499		
N	193	218		
• Adjusted Grade				
Mean	88.15	86.87	.03	.541
SD	20.84	21.49		
N	193	218		
• Man-Hours				
Mean	6.5	5.5	.12	.014 *
SD	3.9	3.7		
N	193	203		
• Elapsed Time				
Mean	11.6	10.4	.09	.072
SD	7.1	5.9		
N	191	195		
• Program Runs				
Mean	11.26	5.77	.03	.000 *
SD	8.87	2.73		
N	190	198		

Table 9.2. TIME-SHARING VS. BATCH PERFORMANCE: PROBLEM 2

Variable	Time-Sharing	Batch	Correlation Ratio	Probability
• Problem Grade				
Mean	70.08	72.19	.03	.477
SD	29.37	31.02		
N	197	220		
• Days Late				
Mean	0.289	0.291	.00	.984
SD	0.723	0.900		
N	197	220		
• Adjusted Grade				
Mean	72.77	73.94	.02	.675
SD	27.21	29.59		
N	197	220		
• Man-Hours				
Mean	7.9	7.3	.06	.206
SD	4.2	4.2		
N	181	212		
• Elapsed Time				
Mean	11.9	12.3	.04	.484
SD	4.6	5.8		
N	178	212		
• Program Runs				
Mean	12.96	8.22	.30	.000 *
SD	10.09	3.72		
N	173	210		

Table 9.2. TIME-SHARING VS. BATCH PERFORMANCE: PROBLEM 3

Variable	Time-Sharing	Batch	Correlation Ratio	Probability
• Problem Grade				
Mean	48.34	43.40	.07	.125
SD	34.11	31.11		
N	194	217		
• Days Late				
Mean	0.098	0.107	.00	.880
SD	0.600	0.549		
N	193	215		
• Adjusted Grade				
Mean	49.12	44.96	.06	.202
SD	34.31	31.24		
N	190	217		
• Man-Hours				
Mean	11.8	10.3	.07	.144
SD	5.1	4.7		
N	184	197		
• Elapsed Time				
Mean	15.9	15.6	.01	.757
SD	7.8	7.1		
N	183	197		
• Program Runs				
Mean	15.5	8.2	.29	.000 *
SD	16.5	3.8		
N	179	194		

Table 9.2. TIME-SHARING VS. BATCH PERFORMANCE: PROBLEM 4

Variable	Time-Sharing	Batch	Correlation Ratio	Probability
• Problem Grade				
Mean	48.89	45.21	.05	.279
SD	35.61	33.24		
N	183	231		
• Days Late				
Mean	0	0.049	.06	.163
SD	0	0.476		
N	183	224		
• Adjusted Grade				
Mean	48.89	45.39	.05	.301
SD	35.61	33.06		
N	183	231		
• Man-Hours				
Mean	8.3	6.9	.11	.026 *
SD	4.4	3.8		
N	169	191		
• Elapsed Time				
Mean	10.2	10.3	.00	.913
SD	5.1	4.1		
N	168	190		
• Program Runs				
Mean	14.75	6.53	.384	.000 *
SD	13.94	3.40		
N	167	187		

higher under time-sharing—the average grade for all problems combined is 4% higher for time-sharing.

9.1.3 Problem Questionnaire

Table 9.3 shows the overall results of the problem questionnaire for time-sharing and batch groupings. As in the previous tables, Table 9.3 shows online and offline means, standard deviations, sample sizes, correlation ratios, and the statistical significance of the observed mean differences. Means, standard deviations, and sample size are represented in Table 9.3 by M, S, and N, respectively. Results reaching the 5% level of significance with respect to the null hypothesis that there are no online/offline mean differences are indicated by an asterisk. Only the combined results for all courses are shown in Table 9.3.

Two items in the problem questionnaire show consistently significant mean differences for all four problem composites. These are Waiting Time and Coding/Debugging Time. As might be expected, the cadets estimated more waiting time for batch than time-sharing, about 13% more of their total time for the entire sample. Time-sharing cadets, not burdened by the forced delays of batch turnaround, were able to devote an average of 12% more of their estimated total time to coding and debugging. There was a tendency for more Time Analyzing Results in time-sharing than in batch—about 2% of total time, a result that was statistically significant for two of the four problem composites.

The other statistically significant results are scattered and sporadic. One apparently meaningful pattern does emerge, however, and it is related to a positive attitude toward time-sharing in the pretest/posttest questionnaire results. In psychological rating literature, the generalized, relatively uncritical diffusion of strong stereotypes to all or many characteristics of the object rated is often referred to as a "halo effect"; hence this name for the factor. The first three items referring to computer system ratings tend to show more positive ratings for time-sharing. For example, Table 9.3 shows statistically significant higher ratings for time-sharing for Computer System Usefulness in problem 3, and for Satisfaction with Solution in problem 3, and for Usefulness of Other System in problems 1 and 4. There were no reverse findings

Table 9.3. PROBLEM QUESTIONNAIRE RESULTS: PROBLEM 1

Variable		Time-Sharing	Batch	Correlation Ratio	Probability
1. Computer System Usefulness (rating scale, 0-9)	M	6.09	6.01	.01	.721
	S	2.23	2.11		
	N	197	208		
2. Satisfaction with Solution (rating scale, 0-9)	M	6.98	6.83	.02	.551
	S	2.50	2.68		
	N	197	207		
3. Usefulness of Other System (rating scale, 0-9)	M	4.09	5.19	.22	.000 *
	S	2.20	2.43		
	N	197	208		
4. Diversion of Effort (rating scale, 0-9)	M	6.47	6.07	.09	.062
	S	2.04	2.26		
	N	197	208		
5. Time of Insight (hours of work)	M	4.43	4.13	.02	.557
	S	4.73	5.43		
	N	188	204		
6a. General Concept Time (percent of total time)	M	20.50	22.44	.06	.211
	S	14.27	16.67		
	N	197	208		
6b. Coding/Debugging Time (percent of total time)	M	45.52	32.18	.30	.000 *
	S	21.59	19.88		
	N	197	208		
6c. Waiting Time (percent of total time)	M	15.54	26.92	.27	.000 *
	S	16.12	23.09		
	N	197	208		
6d. Time Analyzing Results (percent of total time)	M	12.87	12.32	.02	.557
	S	9.88	9.19		
	N	197	208		
6e. Reacquaintance Time (percent of total time)	M	5.56	5.69	.01	.831
	S	6.08	6.09		
	N	197	208		

Table 9.3. PROBLEM QUESTIONNAIRE RESULTS: PROBLEM 2

Variable		Time-Sharing	Batch	Correlation Ratio	Probability
1. Computer System Usefulness (rating scale, 0-9)	M	5.14	4.74	.07	.126
	S	2.64	2.76		
	N	191	246		
2. Satisfaction with Solution (rating scale, 0-9)	M	4.70	5.27	.08	.078
	S	3.34	3.22		
	N	191	212		
3. Usefulness of Other System (rating scale, 0-9)	M	4.51	4.29	.04	.403
	S	2.38	2.90		
	N	190	245		
4. Diversion of Effort (rating scale, 0-9)	M	7.40	5.96	.31	.000 *
	S	1.50	2.52		
	N	191	244		
5. Time of Insight (hours of work)	M	5.85	9.69	.18	.000 *
	S	4.62	12.50		
	N	167	224		
6a. General Concept Time (percent of total time)	M	24.33	27.06	.07	.124
	S	14.72	20.68		
	N	191	242		
6b. Coding/Debugging Time (percent of total time)	M	44.73	32.03	.28	.000 *
	S	20.60	21.13		
	N	191	242		
6c. Waiting Time (percent of total time)	M	14.37	25.32	.27	.000 *
	S	14.65	22.07		
	N	191	215		
6d. Time Analyzing Results (percent of total time)	M	11.24	10.60	.03	.467
	S	8.12	9.63		
	N	191	231		
6e. Reacquaintance Time (percent of total time)	M	5.34	9.01	.16	.000 *
	S	5.70	14.29		
	N	191	231		

Table 9.3. PROBLEM QUESTIONNAIRE RESULTS: PROBLEM 3

Variable		Time-Sharing	Batch	Correlation Ratio	Probability
1. Computer System Usefulness (rating scale, 0-9)	M	4.71	4.17	.11	.050 *
	S	2.44	2.38		
	N	135	170		
2. Satisfaction with Solution (rating scale, 0-9)	M	3.49	2.67	.12	.024 *
	S	3.28	3.02		
	N	135	171		
3. Usefulness of Other System (rating scale, 0-9)	M	3.67	4.22	.10	.061
	S	2.23	2.73		
	N	133	170		
4. Diversion of Effort (rating scale, 0-9)	M	6.95	6.72	.05	.296
	S	1.93	1.83		
	N	136	170		
5. Time of Insight (hours of work)	M	6.83	7.04	.02	.739
	S	4.63	4.99		
	N	103	118		
6a. General Concept Time (percent of total time)	M	28.89	32.66	.09	.083
	S	16.91	20.30		
	N	136	170		
6b. Coding/Debugging Time (percent of total time)	M	41.94	30.26	.29	.000 *
	S	20.07	17.86		
	N	136	170		
6c. Waiting Time (percent of total time)	M	9.62	22.08	.37	.000 *
	S	11.43	17.67		
	N	135	169		
6d. Time Analyzing Results (percent of total time)	M	13.35	10.31	.15	.007 *
	S	12.38	6.95		
	N	135	169		
6e. Reacquaintance Time (percent of total time)	M	5.65	4.85	.07	.190
	S	5.50	5.10		
	N	135	169		

Table 9.3. PROBLEM QUESTIONNAIRE RESULTS: PROBLEM 4

Variable		Time-Sharing	Batch	Correlation Ratio	Probability
1. Computer System Usefulness (rating scale, 0-9)	M	4.41	3.98	.08	.097
	S	2.76	2.35		
	N	170	216		
2. Satisfaction with Solution (rating scale, 0-9)	M	3.31	3.00	.05	.308
	S	3.07	2.87		
	N	170	216		
3. Usefulness of Other System (rating scale, 0-9)	M	3.53	4.27	.14	.005 *
	S	2.46	2.67		
	N	169	216		
4. Diversion of Effort (Rating scale, 0-9)	M	6.24	6.04	.04	.366
	S	2.21	2.09		
	N	170	216		
5. Time of Insight (hours of work)	M	6.13	5.43	.04	.435
	S	6.60	5.66		
	N	127	167		
6a. General Concept Time (percent of total time)	M	30.23	29.54	.01	.726
	S	18.47	19.49		
	N	168	215		
6b. Coding/Debugging Time (percent of total time)	M	38.99	27.71	.29	.000 *
	S	20.25	16.91		
	N	170	215		
6c. Waiting Time (percent of total time)	M	12.37	27.99	.36	.000 *
	S	15.14	23.12		
	N	170	215		
6d. Time Analyzing Results (percent of total time)	M	12.41	10.25	.10	.045 *
	S	11.97	9.10		
	N	170	215		
6e. Reacquaintance Time (percent of total time)	M	5.19	4.42	.06	.236
	S	7.49	5.14		
	N	170	215		

demonstrating higher ratings for batch that were statistically significant.

Summing up the descriptive results, we find an ambiguous portrait taking shape. The pretest/posttest questionnaire shows a moderately favorable bias toward time-sharing that was partially eroded over the course of the experiment by continuing troubles in computer system service under time-sharing. The performance measures from the instructors' summary sheet and the cadets' work logs showed about twice as many computer runs under time-sharing to solve standard problems, and practically the same performance as far as man-hours, grades, and elapsed time are concerned. The problem questionnaire results reinforce the more favorable general attitude toward time-sharing shown by the cadets throughout the course of the experiment, and they underscore the difference in more waiting time under batch. Thus, we have an initial portrait of essentially equivalent effectiveness of performance for both modes, lower computer costs for batch, with relatively more positive attitudes toward time-sharing, and all of this complicated by less reliable system service under time-sharing. This is the initial problematic framework for the interpretation of the findings which follows.

9.2 INTERPRETATION

The interpretation covers experimental controls first to set the stage for the analysis of online/offline performance and associated findings on user attitudes. The final section presents key conclusions regarding time-sharing and batch performance comparisons.

9.2.1 Experimental Controls

By and large, practically all experimental controls were carefully followed and successfully implemented, with the problematic exception of equivalent computer system service under time-sharing and batch. Instructors and students were apparently adequately briefed to follow procedures and provide experimental data, as attested by the virtually complete data in this study. Sample size and sample composition remained stable; for example, 414 students filled out pretest questionnaires, 403 filled out posttest questionnaires with the difference attributable to normal student attrition. All forms were generally properly filled out, relatively little data was lost, and instructor and student cooperation was exemplary for a study of this magnitude. The experimental design was carefully observed for flip and constant modes as well as for data recording and collection procedures. The pilot test experience proved invaluable in anticipating and ironing out procedural bugs.

The cadet sample consisted primarily of beginners in computer programming—only half a month's mean experience in computer work for the entire sample. The motivation was generally strong to achieve good grades in the highly competitive Academy context. Academy rules generally ensured that each individual worked essentially on his own with a minimum of collusion with other cadets.

The problematic experimental area that could not be rigorously controlled was equivalent computer system service. While the computer was identical under time-sharing and batch (the Burroughs B-5500), and while the same language was used in both modes (ALGOL), the fact remained that the batch mode was checked out and was relatively well established before the experiment, whereas the time-sharing configuration was new and largely untried. Computer-system procedures changed rapidly under time-sharing as new experience was gained. The time-sharing system tended to be more unreliable than batch, and, for a variety of reasons, it was easier for the cadet to lose or "clobber" his program under time-sharing.

In addition to the problem of less reliable system service, time-sharing terminals were at a premium. It was not possible for a cadet to go to the terminal whenever he wanted to, because he had to sign up in advance. And when he did get the terminal, it was for a 15-minute period, a short interval that would often be plagued by system troubles. Only during periods of reduced system demand were longer sessions at the terminals possible. All these difficulties resulted in chronic complaints over time-sharing service in cadet open-end responses.

In this context, it should also be pointed out that time-sharing adversely affected batch service. For example, when time-sharing was up from 7 to 10 PM, few if any batch jobs were processed in the background.

The comparison rating of computer service on the posttest questionnaire showed batch well ahead of time-sharing (66% of the cadets rated batch service better, 20% were uncertain, and only 14% rated time-sharing service better).

On the other hand, time-sharing received higher ratings for overall computer service for individual problems. For example, on a computer service scale running from 0 (Very Poor) to 9 (Excellent), time-sharing received an average rating of 4.04 against an average batch rating of 3.11; this was for all courses combined for problem 3; the analogous ratings for problem 4 were 4.71 for time-sharing and 3.38 for batch. (These ratings were collected only for the last two problems.) The above mean differences are statistically significant well beyond the 1% level.

Thus, we have two seemingly contradictory sets of findings on system service. On the one hand, the posttest questionnaire shows a decided preference in favor of superior batch service; on the other hand, the section work log rating scales show higher computer service ratings for time-sharing.

The wording on these scales offers a way out of this dilemma. The posttest questionnaire is specifically concerned with "reliable and dependable service," whereas the work log ratings are more broadly concerned with "class problem needs" as well as "dependable service." All factors considered, we conclude that the posttest questionnaire results are probably valid—that batch service was more reliable than time-sharing service. We also conclude, from the work log rating scales, that service in both modes was generally viewed as closer to "very poor" than to "excellent," and further, that time-sharing was more favorably viewed in helping cadets meet overall problem needs.

The upshot of these findings, from the viewpoint of experimental design, is that we were not able to achieve essentially equivalent computer service conditions under both modes. More precisely, the experimental comparison turned out to be one between relatively more reliable batch vs. somewhat less reliable time-sharing, with both systems providing marginally adequate service. All subsequent interpretation should take these factors into account.

The problem of computer service illustrates one of the pitfalls of real-world experimentation. Although we succeeded in controlling most critical variables toward an objective comparison of time-sharing and batch, and although we succeeded in designing and implementing the experiment right into the "real-world" operation of computer science courses at the Academy, the timing of the experiment was such that one of the key control variables could not be rigorously maintained. Since the study was conducted in the real-world setting, the results have a compelling credibility for the user that cannot be achieved by more highly controlled but esoteric and artificial experimentation in the laboratory. While real-world experimentation has its risks and pitfalls, it also has its rewards.

9.2.2 Time-Sharing and Batch Performance

Online/offline performance comparisons refer to the objective measures collected from the student work logs and the instructor section summary forms, as distinguished from the attitudinal data. These performance variables include problem grade, days late, adjusted grade, man-hours, elapsed time, and program runs, as shown in Table 9.2 in the previous section.

The interpretation of online/offline performance may be approached from cost-effective considerations. On the cost side, there are two key variables—computer costs and human costs in man-hours. Computer costs, at least as reflected in number of computer runs with cadet programs, consistently ran about twice as high under time-sharing as in batch—the mean ratio of time-sharing to batch runs for all courses and all problems combined is 1.92. This finding reflects the only statistically consistent result throughout Table 9.2; all other performance variables show erratic patterns of statistical significance at problem and course levels.

The results on man-hours show a fairly consistent edge for batch over time-sharing with a total composite average of 12%

more man-hours under time-sharing to solve the test problems. Although the statistical significance of man-hour mean differences is erratic, as shown in Table 9.2, the general trend is fairly clear-cut, and the 12% edge for batch man-hours may be taken as the best overall estimate derived from a composite sample of more than 1600 man-problems.

If, now, we take into account the generally less reliable machine service under time-sharing, it could be asserted that the 12% difference might disappear, or perhaps even move in the direction favorable to time-sharing. To this, the batch advocate might reply that shorter-turnaround batch, or "instant" remote batch would again tip the scales in favor of batch for man-hours. Since we have no objective way of measuring the effects of system reliability or varying turnaround time in the Academy context, these arguments must remain conjectures. Perhaps the central point is that online/offline differences lead to only relatively small differences in man-hours expended. The absence of online/offline differences for the correlated measure, elapsed time, bears this generalization out. There is no consistent pattern in favor of either mode.

The key variable for cadet effectiveness is problem grade. There is a trend, not statistically significant, for higher problem grades under time-sharing. In 9 out of 12 problems, there were higher grade averages for time-sharing subjects. The grand mean shows a 4% higher grade for time-sharing for all courses and problems combined. There is no trend for Days Late in handing in the assigned problem, nor in the Adjusted Grade which eliminates the penalty for tardiness. As in the results for man-hours, the findings for problem grades show no substantial advantage for the online or the offline mode.

Returning to the original cost-effectiveness theme, the composite objective results show one salient finding. Computer time is substantially reduced under batch to solve standard problems. While computer costs are less, objective measures of human costs and human effectiveness are virtually the same under both modes for the conditions of this experiment. But how about subjective factors that enter into the equation for human effectiveness? These are treated in the next section.

9.2.3 User Attitudes toward Time-Sharing and Batch

The data for the analysis of user attitudes are derived from the problem questionnaire and the pretest/posttest questionnaire. The problem questionnaire provides insight into problem attitudes and problem-solving style, whereas the pretest/posttest questionnaire solicits direct comparisons of perceived effectiveness between time-sharing and batch. The problem questionnaire findings are treated first, then the pretest/posttest questionnaire, followed by an integration of the attitudinal results.

A key finding pervading all questionnaire data is a small favorable bias toward time-sharing which persists as a positive halo effect for time-sharing throughout the experiment. For example, the first three rating scales of the problem questionnaire show a definite trend toward time-sharing, revealing higher ratings for System Usefulness (item 1), Satisfaction with Solution (item 2), and higher ratings for time-sharing in the Usefulness of Other System (item 3). The favorable edge is small and is often not statistically significant.

No pattern emerges for Diversion of Effort (item 4) or for Time of Insight (item 5). These measures are probably more directly related to individual differences in problem-solving skills than to online/offline effects.

The remaining five items of the problem questionnaire pertain to the estimated distribution of the cadets' time between five categories: general concept time, coding/debugging time, waiting time, time analyzing results, and reacquaintance time. The two items that revealed consistent and statistically significant results are more coding and debugging time under time-sharing, and more waiting time for batch. The interpretation of these results follows directly from the turnaround waiting time for batch, an expected result. An unexpected finding, however, is that waiting time in both modes tended to decrease substantially with increasing experience. In problem 1, waiting time was 15% for time-sharing and 26% for batch, whereas in problem 4 it was only 7% for time-sharing and 19% for batch. It seems as if the cadets became more efficient in their timing tactics for requesting computer service as they gained more experience. Other factors operated also, including increased problem difficulty level and longer man-hours per problem, which would tend to increase proportionate time for other items such as analysis time.

The pretest/posttest questionnaire results contribute toward a more balanced portrait of cadet attitudes. The findings on general attitudes toward time-sharing and batch provide an inkling of some of the dynamics at work. The value of batch went up .8 points (item 4) and the value of time-sharing went down .6 points—familiarity seemed to breed more respect for batch and more contempt for time-sharing. The previously cited results for computer-system service, with only 14% of the total sample stating that time-sharing gave better service, is the key explanation for the relative disenchantment with time-sharing over the course of the experiment. However, with item 6, in which batch is pitted directly against time-sharing, we note that time-sharing started off with a large edge over batch (5.83 as against a neutral or break-even rating of 4.50), and ended up in the posttest with a small lead, at 5.16. As with the other time-sharing and batch comparisons, with the exception of program runs, the magnitude of this observed mean difference, even though statistically significant at the 1% level, is not large.

The differential pattern of online/offline preferences seems to raise more questions than it answers. In the area of coding and debugging, the results tend to support the stereotype prevailing in much of the computer world—batch is better for coding and time-sharing is better for debugging. Although there are no direct objective measures to sustantiate these stereotypes, the supporting favorable ratings for time-sharing, in finding and correcting errors and in obtaining faster solutions and more efficient programs, indicate consistent preference for online debugging.

An interesting cluster of preferences occurred for batch in connection with ease of learning, self-organizing capabilities and the analysis and synthesis of class problems. Ease of learning seems to be a common denominator for these items. This interpretation is reinforced by the striking switch in frustration level (item 30) for batch and time-sharing over the course of the experiment. The pretest mean for the total sample is 2.35, indicating that the majority expected batch to be more frustrating to work with; this pattern was substantially and significantly reversed after the experimental experience to a value of 1.73. Two factors may have operated to create this effect. First, less reliable system service presumably raised the frustration level for time-sharing. Second, and more fundamentally, batch is probably easier to learn how to use than time-sharing in the Academy context, at least as far as initial success is concerned. The array of special calls, instructions, and online procedures, requiring direct interaction between the user and the computer, can be overwhelming for many neophytes. The time-sharing advocate might counter that ALGOL is not the optimal language for newcomers, that perhaps BASIC would have been more appropriate. On the other hand, the early inconvenience with ALGOL would later be compensated by its greater power and flexibility with growing experience.

The latter interpretation was suggested by the cadets in another cluster of questionnaire items that revealed their preference for time-sharing for more skilled users. This cluster includes: greater challenge, more insight into problems, improved exploratory capability, greater creativity, and greater amenability to open-end problems, as well as suitability for more skilled users. Apparently, the cadets regarded time-sharing as a technique more appropriate for the experienced individual who knows how to exploit the computer to solve his problem. The key contradiction to this interpretation was the preference for batch for more complex problems, and for time-sharing for simpler problems.

These gross trends and their contradictions are only suggestive. Multivariate techniques are required to take many factors into consideration at the same time. Further analysis and relation of these with the other findings is required. The key finding is that no bandwagon effects emerge from the data showing a strong, generalized preference for one computer mode over the other.

Returning to the theme of comparative cost-effectiveness of time-sharing and batch in the Academy context, we find essentially lower costs for batch and approximately equivalent effectiveness for both modes. Lower computer time requirements under batch is the principal justification for lower costs; the slight advantage in man-hours with batch contributes further to more economical operations. The tendency toward higher grades, reflecting presumably higher-quality end-products under time-sharing, together with somewhat more positive attitudes toward time-sharing, lean toward the possibility of greater effectiveness for time-sharing. The newness of the time-sharing service, its relatively lower reliability, and the stringent time constraints in its use, indicate that online cost effectiveness would probably have been better under more auspicious conditions.

9.2.4 Conclusions

Computer Costs. A consistent and statistically significant finding was that to solve the standard experimental problems almost twice as many computer runs of cadet programs were required under time-sharing than with batch. Direct computer time costs are inferred to be significantly lower under batch.

Man-Hours to Complete Problems. Time-sharing generally required 12% more man-hours for completion of test problems for the entire sample. Although this result is statistically significant for the entire sample, it was not consistently significant for individual courses and problems. No reliable mean differences between time-sharing and batch were found in the correlated measure of elapsed time to complete problems.

Problem Grades. Although there was an overall tendency toward 4% higher grades under time-sharing, this trend was not statistically significant.

User Preference. Time-sharing was consistently preferred by the cadets over batch with respect to overall ratings throughout the course of the experiment. However, the margin of preference, which was substantial at the beginning of the experiment, was significantly reduced by the end of the experiment to a relatively small edge in favor of time-sharing.

Positive Attitudes toward Batch. The batch mode was viewed as easier to learn and use, better for coding, and more conducive to individual organization of work and for problem analysis, particularly for well-defined problems.

Positive Attitudes toward Time-Sharing. The time-sharing mode was perceived as posing a greater challenge, allowing greater exploration of the problem, and as leading to a greater insight and heightened creativity, particularly for open-end problems and for more skilled users; it was the preferred mode for program debugging.

Computer System Service. The above findings are contaminated to an unknown extent by less reliable service under time-sharing (which was installed just before the start of the experiment), and by short online console sessions (15 minutes, reserved in advance) which were associated with very heavy demands for time-sharing.

Individual Differences. As in all previous online/offline experimental studies, very large individual performance differences overshadowed computer system differences, often by an order of magnitude. This central finding leads us to two chapters concerning these individual differences.

10

INDIVIDUAL DIFFERENCES: RESULTS

THIS chapter is directed toward problem-solving behaviors exhibited by the cadets, and as such, is largely concerned with the structure and dynamics of individual differences in performance. Online/offline differences are considered only to the extent that they contribute to problem-solving style.

10.1 RESULTS

Two major classes of results are presented: (1) factor analyses of cadet performance, and (2) individual verbal descriptions of problem-solving behavior. The factor analyses involve a composite of objective performance and questionnaire data gathered over this experiment, whereas the verbal descriptions are derived from the open-end responses of the Problem Questionnaire. Results are presented first, followed by interpretation in Chapter 11.

10.1.1 Factor Analyses

The primary objective of the factor analyses is to distinguish those characteristics common to problem-solving behaviors from the total set of objective measures used in this study, and to extract generalized patterns of behavior from the data. Factor analysis can provide an operational interpretation of this objective by extracting those clusters of variables that are intercorrelated among the total set subjected to analysis. A secondary objective of the factor analyses is to test for systematic differences between factor patterns for the 12 different problems. Does each problem have a relatively unique set of factors, or is the factor pattern relatively stable across most or all problems? Accordingly, one factor analysis was performed for each of the four problems in each of the three courses, 12 factor analyses in all.

A total of 49 variables were used in each factor analysis. These included all 31 pretest/posttest questionnaire items (concerned with experience and attitudes toward time-sharing and batch), performance measures (problem grades—with and without penalty for lateness, elapsed time, days late in handing in solutions, total problem runs, and man-hours), the problem-solving mode for each cadet (time-sharing or batch), the 10 problem questionnaire items (computer system ratings and estimated proportion of time spent on various aspects of problem-solving), and a score from Academy records representing overall grade point average. The appendix should be consulted for descriptions of questionnaire items and performance measures.

A problem arose with the pretest/posttest questionnaire items: which version should be used for which problems? A compromise solution was chosen. Since problems 1 and 2 were closer in time to the administration of the pretest questionnaire, the pretest responses were used for the factor analyses of the first two problems. Since problems 3 and 4 were closer in time to the posttest administration, the posttest responses were employed for factor analyses of the last two problems. Thus, among other things, the factor results are designed to test for systematic multivariate pretest/posttest questionnaire changes.

To facilitate cross-comparisons, the factor analyses were performed in the same manner for each of the 12 problems. That is, the same set of 49 variables were used; estimates of communality for each variable were based on the multiple correlation of each variable against the other variables, group factors were extracted and rotated with respect to the "varimax" criterion, and 10 factors were derived from each analysis. For a comprehensive discussion of factor analysis, consult Harman (1967); for the specific statistical routines used in this study see McCornack (1968). The 10-factor solution was arrived at by trying 5, 10, and 15 rotations and comparing the results. Five rotations yielded too few factors; 15 rotations yielded undesirable "singletons" (a factor with a heavy loading in only one variable), and too many weak or trivial factors. The 10-factor solutions provided the best overall fit for reliable, meaningful factor results.

The factor results are presented in summary form for each problem in each of the three courses in Tables 10.1, 10.2, and 10.3 for Courses 230, 240, and 254 respectively (Humanities, Social Sciences, and Basic Sciences). For the sake of brevity, and to facilitate easier cross-comparisons, only the 10 factor tags are shown for each factor analysis. Extracted factors are listed in rank order of contributed variance, as derived from the computer printout, and shown with the associated percentage of total variance in each table. The problem name accompanies the factor grouping for each problem. For example, for Course 230 with Humanities students, the first problem is concerned with flight plans.

At first glance, the factor analysis results may present a bewildering array of factors. More careful study, however, reveals some trends. For example, certain factors tend to appear consistently in most problems, such as, Overall Problem Performance, User Skill Level, and Computer Experience. Some appear consistently in the last two, but not the first two problems, such as, Batch Halo and Computer System Service. Many factors appear only once or sporadically, such as Esoteric Appeal of Time-Sharing and Questionnaire Value. Other factors fall in between these extremes. A glance at Tables 10.1, 10.2, and 10.3 indicates that while several factors tend to run consistently through each of the 12 problems, each problem seems to exhibit, at the same time, a peculiar mix of factors different from other problems. One cannot generalize at the extremes, that common factors hold across the board, nor that each problem is unique; the results are somewhere in between. These and related issues are treated in Chapter 11 which is devoted to interpretation.

Table 10.1. SUMMARY OF FACTOR ANALYSES FOR HUMANITIES STUDENTS

PROBLEM 1— FLIGHT PLAN Factor Names	Percent Contributed Variance	PROBLEM 2— PAYROLL/TIMEKEEPING Factor Names	Percent Contributed Variance
1. Overall Problem Performance	8.4	1. Overall Problem Performance	7.7
2. Complex Problem-Solving	6.4	2. Creativity	7.5
3. Debugging Skills	6.2	3. Debugging Skills	5.5
4. Speed and Ease of Time-Sharing	5.8	4. Problem-Solving Speed	5.3
5. Ease of Computer Use	5.1	5. Ease of Learning Batch	5.1
6. Batch Delays	4.8	6. Computer Experience	4.9
7. Questionnaire Value	4.8	7. Impatience with Batch Waiting Time	4.8
8. Batch Problem Planning	4.7	8. Computer Accessibility	4.5
9. Time-Sharing Experience	4.4	9. Perceived Importance of Online/ Offline Controversy	4.4
10. Computer System Exploitation	4.3	10. Efficiency of Problem-Solving	4.3

PROBLEM 3— CALENDAR ALGORITHM Factor Names		PROBLEM 4— QUARTIC EQUATION Factor Names	
1. Batch Halo (17% variance)	17.3	1. Batch Halo	16.3
2. Overall Problem Performance	6.4	2. Problem-Solving Speed	6.2
3. Computer System Service	5.5	3. Overall Problem Performance	5.8
4. Computer Experience	5.4	4. Creative Skills	5.7
5. Self-Pacing of Work	4.5	5. Time-Sharing Efficiency	5.1
6. Man-computer Effort	4.4	6. Computer Experience	4.4
7. Understanding Computer Results	4.1	7. Problem Warmup Time	3.9
8. Questionnaire Value	4.1	8. Questionnaire Value	3.9
9. User Skill	4.1	9. Esoteric Appeal of Time-Sharing	3.8
10. Diversion of Effort	4.0	10. Real Time Pressure	3.3

Table 10.2. SUMMARY OF FACTOR ANALYSES FOR SOCIAL SCIENCE STUDENTS

PROBLEM 1— LOGARITHMIC ROUTINE Factor Names	Percent Contributed Variance	PROBLEM 2— NEWTON-RAPHSON ALGORITHM Factor Names	Percent Contributed Variance
1. Ease of Batch Use	6.3	1. Overall Problem Performance	7.2
2. Overall Problem Performance	6.3	2. Ease of Computer System Use	6.4
3. Computer System Usefulness	6.2	3. Debugging Skills	5.7
4. Debugging Skills	5.9	4. Creative Skills	4.7
5. Computer Experience	4.6	5. Computer Experience	4.6
6. User Skills	4.6	6. Frustration with Computer Service	4.2
7. Problem Complexity	3.8	7. Additional Effort under Time-Sharing	4.1
8. Waiting for Results	3.4	8. Problem Complexity	3.9
9. Analysis Time	2.9	9. Problem Formulation Time	3.2
10. Man-Machine Costs	2.6	10. Analysis of Computer Results	2.7

PROBLEM 3— INVENTORY SORTING Factor Names	
1. Batch Halo	12.7
2. Overall Problem Performance	7.2
3. Computer System Service	6.3
4. Frustration with Time-Sharing	4.1
5. Problem-Solving Speed	3.4
6. User Skills	3.4
7. Problem Formulation Time	3.1
8. Problem Warmup Time	2.8
9. Computer Experience	2.7
10. Type of Problem	2.4

PROBLEM 4— SIMPLEX ALGORITHM Factor Names	
1. Batch Halo	11.5
2. Overall Problem Performance	6.2
3. Batch Waiting Time	6.2
4. Computer Service	3.8
5. Problem Warmup Time	3.7
6. Problem-Solving Speed	3.6
7. Open-End Problems	3.6
8. Inefficient Analysis of Results	3.5
9. Computer Experience	3.3
10. Problem Formulation Time	3.2

Table 10.3. SUMMARY OF FACTOR ANALYSES FOR BASIC SCIENCE STUDENTS

PROBLEM 1— EXTENDED EUCLIDEAN ALGORITHM Factor Names	Percent Contributed Variance	PROBLEM 2— STATISTICAL PROCEDURES Factor Names	Percent Contributed Variance
1. Overall Problem Performance	6.5	1. Overall Problem Performance	7.9
2. Computer Experience	6.0	2. Computer Experience	5.7
3. Debugging Skills	5.3	3. Analytic Skills	5.5
4. Waiting for Results	4.9	4. Debugging Skills	4.6
5. Ease of Batch Use	4.9	5. User Skills	4.5
6. User Time and Effort	4.7	6. Computer System Evaluation	4.2
7. User Skills	4.6	7. Batch Waiting Time	4.1
8. General Concept Time	3.1	8. Problem-Solving Speed	3.6
9. Problem Complexity	3.0	9. Problem Warmup Time	3.1
10. Analysis of Results	3.0	10. Problem Formulation Time	2.8

PROBLEM 3—
FILE PROCESSING

Factor Names	
1. Batch Halo	12.1
2. Computer System Service	6.3
3. Overall Problem Performance	6.2
4. Debugging Advantage of Time-Sharing	4.7
5. Problem-Solving Speed	4.4
6. Computer Experience	4.3
7. Perceived Computer System Usefulness	4.2
8. Problem Formulation Time	3.4
9. Problem Warmup Time	3.3
10. User Skills	3.2

PROBLEM 4—
MULTIPLE LINEAR EQUATIONS

Factor Names	
1. Batch Halo	12.9
2. Computer System Service	6.4
3. Overall Problem Performance	5.3
4. Computer Experience	4.2
5. Time-Sharing Enthusiasts	4.2
6. Esoteric Appeal of Time-Sharing	3.7
7. Problem Formulation/Coding Tradeoff	3.3
8. User Skills	3.2
9. Problem Warmup Time	2.6
10. Time Analyzing Results	2.5

10.2 OPEN-END VERBAL RESPONSES

Each cadet answered six open-end questions in the problem questionnaire distributed to him after he completed each of his four class problems. The six questions were:

- What was your biggest difficulty in solving this problem?
- What is your recommendation for reducing or eliminating this difficulty?
- What is the most important insight that you arrived at in solving this problem?
- What information or circumstances were necessary to make this insight possible for you?
- Did this insight occur at your desk (away from the computer), or at the terminal, at some other place, or when you were not working on the problem?
- Name the main stages of problem-solving that you followed in arriving at your program solution.

The problem with which the experimenter was faced was to analyze approximately 1600 open-end verbal responses (approximately 400 subjects multiplied by 4 class problems per subject) for each of 6 questions, a total of approximately 10,000 responses.

The task was too large for a single individual to handle; three programmers, one assigned to each of the three introductory courses, were assigned to collating the responses. These programmers had an average of six years' experience, and one of them had an undergraduate degree in psychology. Their instructions were relatively straightforward: collate the responses into a relatively small number of key headings suggested by the cadet descriptions. The approach was empirical and inductive, based on cadet responses rather than preconceived notions of how they might or ought to respond. The raters worked independently.

This approach yielded roughly 10 categories for each rater for each problem grouping for each course. The categories varied from one rater to the other, and to a certain extent, with different problems. The experimenter then examined these inital categories for common threads. He arrived at a reduced number of general categories into which he fitted most of the raters' items. Each rater's category was assigned to one of the reduced number of general categories to arrive at overall frequency counts.

The general categories are briefly discussed for each of the six questions. The first question was concerned with "your biggest difficulty in solving this problem." After examining the various empirical categories compiled by the raters, it appeared that the responses could be collected under four general heads: Programming Problems, Understanding the Class Problem, Difficulties with Computer System Service, and Personal Problems. This four-way classification provided an empirically-based rational scheme for assigning rater categories according to whether the response emphasized programming skills, the class problem, computer service, or personal problems. Responses that straddled more than one general category, or that did not fit into them at all, were collected under a miscellaneous category (Other). The key point is, as stated above, that the general categories were derived from empirical frequencies rather than being based on preconceived notions on the nature of the question.

The second question was concerned with cadet "recommendations for reducing or eliminating difficulties." For these responses, three broad relatively clear-cut areas emerged for suggested improvements: Improved Instruction in Class, Self-Improvement, and Improved Computer service.

The third question asked cadets to describe the most important insight that they arrived at in solving their class problem. A fourfold classification was suggested by the responses. Two were concerned with a polarization of attitudes toward computers and programming, leading to Appreciation of Computer Techniques and Negative Attitude Toward Computer Programming. The two remaining categories were Understanding Problem Logic (concerned with problem content) and Painstaking, Careful Work (which reflected the exacting personal demands of program coding and debugging).

The fourth question probed into cadet circumstances that made the foregoing insight possible. The four major groupings that emerged from examination of the data were: Studying Alone, Teacher or Class Instruction, Running the Problem, and Technical Documentation.

The fifth question inquired into the place where such insight occurred. The responses fell into five large areas: Alone at the Desk, in Class, at the Instructor's Office, at the Terminal (for time-sharing cadets), or in the Computer Room (for batch students), and More than One Place for some cadets.

The last question asked the cadets to reconstruct their main stages of problem-solving. These responses turned out to be variations of three basic categories: a simple two-step description amounting to Study the Problem—Do It, more elaborate variations specifying Formulate, Code, Debug problem programs, and a third category essentially amounting to Trial and Error.

Tables 10.4 through 10.9 show the results for each of the six open-end questions with respect to the above general categories. These tables show the separate frequencies for each of the three courses, and the totals for all courses combined. In addition to the gross categories mentioned above, two additional categories are found in each table. One is Other for all responses that did not fit into the main categories; and the second is No Response for cases in which the cadet left his questionnaire blank. The Other entry provides some indication of the comprehensiveness of the given classification scheme to incorporate cadet responses; the No Response entry provides an indication of the responsiveness of the subjects for each question and, indirectly, an index of cadet involvement with the given question. Categories are listed in order of observed frequencies, and a percentage score is provided for overall frequencies.

Table 10.4. WHAT WAS YOUR BIGGEST DIFFICULTY IN SOLVING THIS PROBLEM?

	Humanities	Social Sciences	Basic Sciences	Total	Percent
1. Programming Problems	306	249	444	999	62
2. Computer System Service	68	127	129	324	20
3. Understanding the Class Problem	52	59	85	196	12
4. Personal Problems	8	7	28	43	3
5. Other	12	19	1	32	2
6. No Response	0	1	7	8	0
TOTAL	446	462	694	1602	99

Table 10.5. WHAT IS YOUR RECOMMENDATION FOR REDUCING OR ELIMINATING THIS DIFFICULTY?

	Humanities	Social Sciences	Basic Sciences	Total	Percent
1. Improved Instruction	196	146	387	729	46
2. Improved Computer	90	104	120	314	20
3. Self-Improvement	78	101	79	258	16
4. No Response	12	33	108	153	10
5. Other	34	89	0	123	8
TOTAL	410	473	694	1577	100

Table 10.6. WHAT IS THE MOST IMPORTANT INSIGHT THAT YOU ARRIVED AT IN SOLVING THIS PROBLEM?

	Humanities	Social Sciences	Basic Sciences	Total	Percent
1. Appreciation of Computer Techniques	194	164	327	685	47
2. Negative Attitude Toward Computer Programming	31	35	232	298	20
3. Other	68	84	18	170	11
4. Understanding Problem Logic	37	80	15	132	9
5. No Response	24	20	53	97	7
6. Painstaking, Careful Work	13	71	0	84	6
TOTAL	367	454	645	1466	100

Table 10.7. WHAT INFORMATION OR CIRCUMSTANCES WERE NECESSARY TO MAKE THIS INSIGHT POSSIBLE FOR YOU?

	Humanities	Social Sciences	Basic Sciences	Total	Percent
1. Running the Problem	87	203	258	548	35
2. Studying Alone	82	108	125	315	20
3. Teacher/Class Instruction	96	55	117	268	17
4. No Response	39	44	100	183	13
5. Other	72	64	33	169	11
6. Documentation	20	0	50	70	5
TOTAL	396	474	683	1553	100

Table 10.8. DID THIS INSIGHT OCCUR AT YOUR DESK (AWAY FROM THE COMPUTER), OR AT THE TERMINAL, AT SOME OTHER PLACE, OR WHEN YOU WERE NOT WORKING ON THE PROBLEM?

	Humanities	Social Sciences	Basic Sciences	Total	Percent
1. Desk/Alone	129	209	302	640	41
2. Terminal or Computer Room	81	126	160	367	24
3. No Response	42	34	93	169	11
4. Class	45	38	57	140	9
5. Other	64	60	3	127	8
6. More than One Place	0	6	57	63	4
7. Instructor's Office	22	4	22	48	3
TOTAL	383	477	694	1554	100

Table 10.9. NAME THE MAIN STAGES OF PROBLEM-SOLVING THAT YOU FOLLOWED IN ARRIVING AT YOUR PROGRAM SOLUTION

	Humanities	Social Sciences	Basic Sciences	Total	Percent
1. Formulate, Code, Debug	190	221	451	862	56
2. Other	123	123	82	328	21
3. Study the Problem—Do It	47	62	93	202	13
4. No Response	25	32	62	119	8
5. Trial and Error	2	7	6	15	1
TOTAL	387	445	694	1526	99

11

INTERPRETATION OF INDIVIDUAL DIFFERENCES

THE interpretation of individual differences in problem-solving performance, is discussed separately for the factor analyses, related learning effects, and the open-end verbal responses, as was the case in the presentation of results.

11.1 FACTOR ANALYSIS FINDINGS

At the outset, it should be stressed that individual differences in cadet performance were consistently found and were very large. Grades on problems invariably ran from 0 to 100%; man-hours to solve class problems ranged from 1 to almost 50. The man-hour individual differences would have been even larger if all cadets had been required to work up to the same level of performance, such as finding a correct solution for the class problem. Attitudinal differences also ran the gamut from one extreme to the other along the various rating scales and for the open-end responses as well. Accordingly, the factor analyses should be interpreted within the context of these far-ranging individual differences throughout the entire experiment.

The analysis that follows is directed toward answering five questions.

• *Is there a general factor that accounts for a large proportion of the variance of performance and attitude, or is there a plurality of "group" factors that account for the variance in the total data set?*

No general factor emerged that consistently cut across both performance and attitudinal measures for all 12 problems. For example, Tables 10.1, 10.2, and 10.3 show that no factor consistently accounted for more than 10% of the variance.

This generalization also holds for the first unrotated factor, which is another way to test for a general factor. There was a tendency for the first unrotated factor for the 12 problems to cluster around high loadings for the three ratings of time-sharing and batch (value of time-sharing, value of batch, and comparative rating of time-sharing and batch). However, while this factor tended to polarize questionnaire items, it did not cut across the performance nor the experience measures. It is concluded, therefore, that the observed multiple or group factor structure describes the data set for this experiment more effectively than a general factor.

• *Are there systematic group factors that consistently cut across all classes and all problems?*

Within the group factor framework, were there any factors that showed up for all courses and all problems? An inspection of the results shows two such consistent factors, Overall Performance and Computer Experience. The Overall Performance factor appeared in all 12 factor analyses, and it exhibited heaviest loadings in the cadet's problem grade; on this account, it is of special interest. High loadings in this factor were also found with: measures relating to positive satisfaction with problem results; high ratings of usefulness for computer mode; not turning in the problem late; higher grade point averages; and earlier time of insight into the problem. This cluster of measures seems to be psychologically self-consistent. Unfortunately, the only measure that might be used as a valid predictor of problem performance is grade point average, since the other measures have an ex post facto relationship to problem performance. That is, good problem performance leads to subject satisfaction with his own efforts and with the computer system, to earlier insight, and to earlier problem completion. It should also be pointed out that the grade point average only offers a relatively low correlation with problem performance, with a median of .26 for the various samples, a correlation that accounts for only 7% of total class grade variance.

The Computer Experience factor appeared in 11 out of 12 problems. All three experience variables showed high positive loadings: batch experience, time-sharing experience, and general computer experience. For these cadet samples, there was no observable relationship or clustering of experience measures with either problem performance or attitudinal measures. This may be due to the fact that practically all students were computer neophytes with an average computer experience level of less than one month at the beginning of their introductory course. These results should accordingly not be generalized to higher experience levels, since none were tested in this experiment.

There were two group factors that dramatically reflected the changing attitudes of the entire sample between the beginning and the end of the experiment. These were the Batch Halo and Computer System Service factors. In essence, as a result of unfavorable time-sharing system service over the course of the semester, many disenchanted cadet users swung to the rather extreme posture that batch is better than time-sharing in most respects. The Batch Halo factor appears in factor analyses for problems 3 and 4 for all courses as the strongest factor with contributed variance always in excess of 10%. Recall that pretest questionnaire responses were used in factor analyses for problems 1 and 2, and that posttest responses were used for problems 3 and 4. For this factor, heaviest loadings were found for ratings in favor of batch for batch value and for batch vs. time-sharing; batch favoritism was also reflected in substantive factor loadings for ratings of coding, debugging, easier learning, challenge to user, analysis, synthesis, insight, complex problems, creativity, finding and correcting errors, self-teaching, faster solutions, self-organized work, unskilled users, efficient programs, fixed problems, computer service, and less frustration.

Note, in Tables 10.1, 10.2, and 10.3, that the Batch Halo factor captures about twice as much variance as the next strongest factors, ranging from 12% to 17% of total variance. This result illustrates the sensitivity of factor analysis to changing attitudes during the course of the experiment.

The Computer Service factor showed heaviest loadings for favorable ratings of batch on the work log computer service scales, as opposed to less favorable ratings for time-sharing. This factor is obviously linked to the Batch Halo factor, and underscores the strong anti-time-sharing feeling generated by unfavorable computer system service. For obvious proprietary reasons, computer system service has not been extensively researched in the computer user literature. This experiment highlights the value of measuring computer system service in an objective manner to gain insight into fundamental user attitudes and stereotypes toward computers.

• *Are there special factors that distinguish between the three courses (humanities, social science and basic science)?*

The third question was concerned with the possibility of systematic factor differences between classes. The available data do not seem to show any notable distinction in the factor patterns for the three courses, except, perhaps, for one course. The Basic Science group (Course 254) received the hardest class problems and probably had the strongest motivation to master computer techniques, as compared to the Humanities (230) and Social Science (240) groups. The Basic Science group was the only one that consistently showed a User Skill factor for all problems, presumably indicating a greater sensitivity to user sophistication with computers. In their Overall Problem Performance factor for problem 4, the Basic Science group showed the unusual pattern of joint positive loadings for man-hours, problem runs, and class grades. That is, the best students put in the most time and effort. Further, in problem 4, in spite of the negative time-sharing system service experience, they bucked the tide of other cadets and exhibited a Time-Sharing Enthusiasm factor; and they also related time-sharing to challenging, open-end problems in an Esoteric Appeal of Time-Sharing factor. This latter factor showed an interesting positive loading with cadets who had higher grade averages, indicating that time-sharing has a stronger fundamental appeal for the brighter students. The necessary qualification to this suggestive network of related findings is that these patterns did not show up consistently for the Basic Science group, and, as such, the interpretation of greater computer sophistication should be treated as a tentative hypothesis rather than a proved finding.

• *Do each of the 12 problems show a unique factor structure that can be related to class problem characteristics?*

The fourth question relating to unique factor characteristics of problems is difficult to answer. As indicated earlier in the results, and in this section, some factors were common to all problems, others common to some problems, and some unique to particular problems. The conclusion is that there was some communality to skill and attitudinal patterns for performance on all problems, but that much of the factor structure was also relatively unique. Unfortunately, no clues are forthcoming from these results that would suggest an empirical taxonomy for these problems based on factor-related skills. The entire area of computer problem taxonomy remains problematic.

• *In what way do the two basic performance measures—class grade and man-hours—fit into the overall factor pattern?*

The fifth question was concerned with the role of problem grades and man-hours in the total factor structure. We have seen that problem grades showed up consistently as a strong group factor in all analyses. Except for one instance, mentioned above for the Basic Science group, no notable relationship was observed between problem grade and man-hours.

However, a Problem-Solving Speed factor did, in fact, show up at least once for each of the three courses. It was defined by highest loadings in man-hours, with heavy loadings in total problem runs, elapsed time to complete the problem, and time of insight. This cluster makes learning sense in that those who took a longer time to solve problems also arrived later at basic insight into the problem and took more computer runs to complete the problem. But this factor appeared in only 5 out of 12 problems. Slower performers were not necessarily poorer performers, and in one case, as mentioned previously, those who spent more personal and computer time were able to get better grades. There was, however, an unequal level of performance from the cadets. Had all cadets been required to work up to specified levels of problem solution, then evidences of individual differences in man-hours would probably have been less ambiguous. Part of the problem lay in individual differences in subjectively perceived tradeoff between extra effort and expected grades. Another consideration was the differential difficulty level and the open-end nature of the various problems. Taken together, the crosscurrents of these confounding variables tend to blur a clear picture of the dynamics of human time and effort to solve the experimental problems. Factor analysis, in this case, is useful as an exploratory tool but not for fine analysis. A more powerful approach is possible through more detailed analysis of cadet learning performance by work session. Some illustrative examples follow from the pilot study.

11.2 SOME SYSTEMATIC LEARNING EFFECTS

Recall that individual work sessions were separately recorded on the Work Log. An inspection of the average time on the problem spent by the entire pilot sample for each successive work session revealed the trend shown in Figure 11.1. The ordinate is minutes of productive time put into solving the class problem, for the given work session. The abscissa is the serial order of work sessions, up to the first 14 sessions. All 60 subjects in the pilot study are included in the first point, which shows an average of 88 minutes. As the number of work sessions increased, more and more subjects completed or stopped working on the problem, the sample size dropped progressively down to only 5 for the last few data points. Separate analyses of time-sharing and batch groups, of fast vs. slower cadets, showed an essentially similar decreasing trend with successive work sessions. The composite curve in Figure 11.1 is thus reasonably representative of the overall trend even though it is not based on a uniform sample.

The striking result in Figure 11.1 is the emergence of a classic response-time learning curve, varying from an 88 minute average at the beginning to approximately 20 minutes at the end. In this connection, serial work sessions may be viewed as successive learning trials. The pattern suggests that students spent much time formulating the general problem during the early work sessions and then, in later sessions, progressed to the business of trying out specific alternative solutions and debugging them.

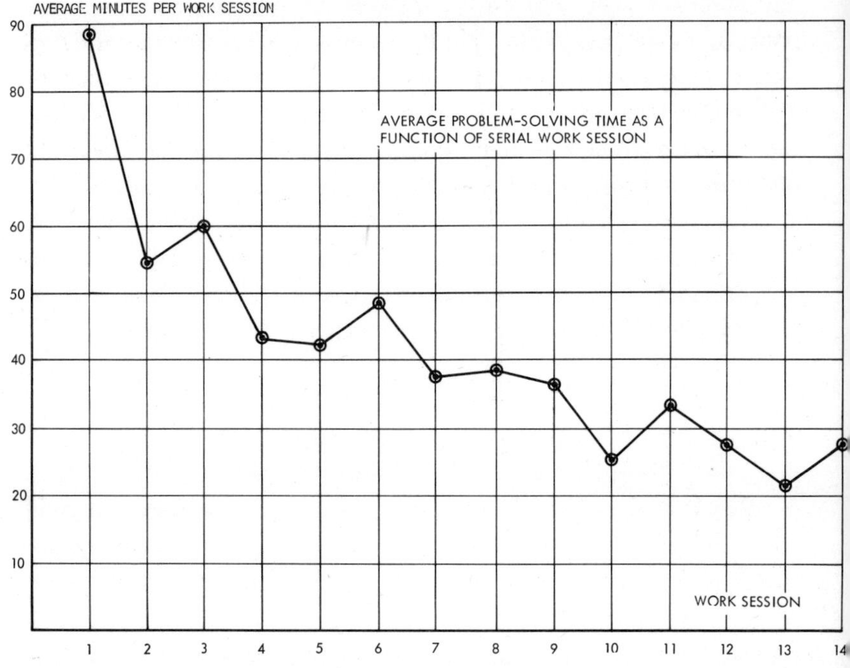

Figure 11.1

An inspection of individual student logs revealed what is probably a more fundamental pattern. Many cadets' logs showed a decreasing sawtooth effect. That is, progressive decrease occurred in serial sessions while a particular logic or solution was being debugged, followed by a sawtooth jump upward for a single session which corresponded to a new problem solution, followed by decreasing work session intervals until a new spike occurred, or until a successful solution terminated the process. In this process, the individual relatively random spikes are smoothed out when the group average is taken, resulting in the relatively smooth decreasing pattern shown in Figure 11.1.

These initial results support the notion of a convergent trial-and-error process in problem solution that becomes increasingly more efficient in terms of user time. They also indicate that the spontaneous individual work session is a valuable unit for operationally defining and measuring problem-solving performance.

Figure 11.2 goes a step further and reveals the group error pattern that accompanied each successive work session for batch users. The ordinate represents average number of syntax errors recorded in the program output for pilot study batch users for the given work session. The abscissa shows successive work sessions, essentially amounting to successive program runs for the batch group.

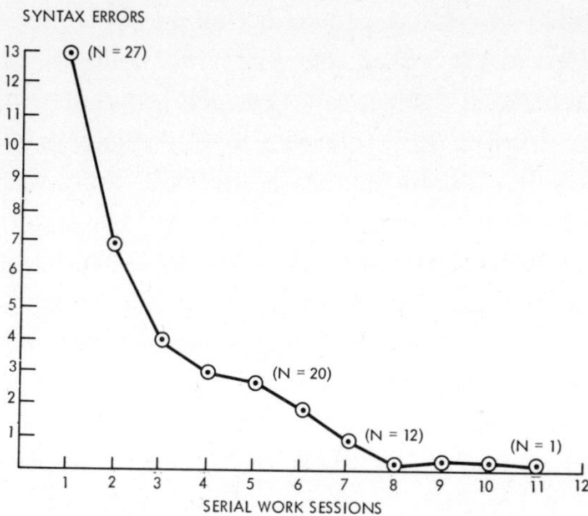

Figure 11.2. BATCH SYNTAX ERRORS VS. SUCCESSIVE WORK SESSIONS

As in Figure 11.1, the entire batch sample is represented in the first data, with sample size decreasing as more and more students completed their problem. Since individuals at skilled and unskilled levels showed similar error-curve patterns, the entire batch sample was pooled for the composite trend. As in the case of Figure 11.1, a sawtooth effect was observed for individuals, essentially reflecting a new logical solution for the class problem with an increase in errors for the new or revised code, which would become progressively debugged until the correct solution was achieved or a new logic was developed. The overall result for the group was the classic error-extinction curve in Figure 11.2.

These two curves suggest a fundamental spontaneous learning pattern for the computer programming process. Initial spontaneous work sessions were longest to formulate and frame the problem. These were followed by successively shorter work sessions to code and debug tentative solutions. Upward sawtooth effects occurred when new solution logic was tried out, and syntax error extinction occurred as the logic was progressively debugged. Throughout the process, however, an overall adaptation occurred in the form of decreasing sawtooth effects such that the time spent in successive sessions and the syntax errors incurred in successive sessions tended to converge toward a minimum. It seems that the subject tended to get locked into his "best" solution for which he strove to achieve a syntactically correct program. This solution could range from a fully correct, to a partially correct, to an incorrect solution, contingent upon the skill, time, and resources that the subject was willing or able to apply to the problem.

These clues suggest that a fertile area for the psychology of programmer learning lies in seizing upon the spontaneous work session and linking it to performance measurement of successive computer runs for the demonstration of systematic learning effects converging toward "locked-in," incorrect solutions, partially acceptable, or "correct" solutions. Such efforts are bound to be marked by a cross-fertilization with the large body of learning theory at hand for understanding the behavioral dynamics of computer programming.

11.3 ANALYSIS OF OPEN-END RESPONSES

Before analyzing the results of the open-end verbal responses, it is desirable to discuss methodology in order to develop a critical framework for the advantages, disadvantages, and limitations of this technique. The open-end technique has obvious advantages for case-history studies in which subjective self-analyses are essential. Unfortunately, the time and resources available for this study precluded deep investigation of individual protocols. Perhaps follow-on studies may capitalize upon such clinical approaches. The primary emphasis here is on group tendencies and trends in spontaneous verbalization for the problem-solving experience.

To arrive at group trends, it was necessary to ask direct questions and request short, simple answers that would lend themselves to unambiguous empirical classification. Hence, the questions were single sentences and responses were requested to be simple phrases or single sentences. The measurement technique is direct tabulation of empirically derived response classes. As discussed under methodology, each of the three raters arrived at his own classification categories independently, and the author collated these independent categories into second-order classifications reported in the results. This procedure resulted in three to five second-order categories for the six questions, as listed in Tables 10.4 through 10.9.

Other approaches could have been used; for example, a standardized classification procedure could have been constructed with many more categories for each question, with rules for deciding ambiguous cases, based on some theory of response classes. Each response could have been classified with respect to multiple scales. An example of a highly elaborate scheme of this sort is the Rorschach inkblot test used in clinical psychology; each open-end response to the inkblot patterns is classified with respect to content, action seen, level of detail, and originality of response against established norms based on large subject samples. However, since the investigation of man-computer problem-solving is so new and rudimentary at this point, it seemed more prudent to work inductively with the raw data to arrive at empirical categories, rather than impose a preconceived structure on the cadet responses. Accordingly, the present method and interpretation should be viewed as an exploratory probe into new terrain, to be superseded, it is hoped, by further study leading to more formalized techniques with quantitative empirical norms for well-defined populations

The procedure followed in interpreting the results of the open-end responses is to look for suggestive patterns in the overall frequency tabulation, and to discuss individual categories in detail if they are of special interest for gaining insight into cadet problem-solving. The first question (Table 10.4), concerned with the greatest difficulty encountered in solving the class problem, provided useful perspective into the cadets' perception of their assigned task. Note that Programming Problems encompassed 62% of all responses, with Computer System Service second highest at 20%. This comparison shows that mastering the programming process was the overwhelming concern of most cadets, and that difficulties with computer service were relatively secondary. The 12% tabulation for Understanding the Class Problems indicates that the content of the class problems was probably well understood by most cadets, and it further underscores the central finding that learning how to write computer programs was the foremost difficulty facing the students. The responses that fell under Programming Problems included: coding, debugging, logical errors, syntax errors, design problems, ALGOL difficulties, formatting.

The second question (Table 10.5) asked for recommendations for dealing with the above difficulties. Improved Instruction received the plurality of responses at 46%; Improved Computer Service was second at 20%, with Self-Improvement third at 16%. Here the focus was primarily on the teaching process and only secondarily on computer service. Although reference to computer service kept coming up, it was not the dominant theme in the cadets' overview of his task. Typical responses for Improved Instructions included: more class instruction, more personal contact with the instructor, more effective mastery of ALGOL, better program design procedures, more team (rather than individual) problem solving, better technical documentation, easier introductory problems, more effective debugging techniques, improved math background, more class examples, more time for problems, and clearer statement of class problem, among others.

The third question inquired into the Most Important Insight achieved by the cadet working on his problem. The results (Table 10.6) reveal a remarkable polarization of opinion among the cadets, with 47% showing an Appreciation of Computer Techniques, and 20% showing a Negative Attitude toward Computer Programming. The remarkable outcome is that this neutrally-worded question effectively triggered most cadets into taking sides for and against computers and computer programming. It is apparent that the widespread problems with computer service, as well as difficulties encountered in mastering the art of computer programming, led a 20% minority to claim that the most important insight they gained was a negative orientation toward computer programming. Note that in the previous two questions, a 20% tally consistently appears for cadets focusing on computer service as their main difficulty, and on improved computer service as their main recommendation. We might be tempted to add the related 6% tally for Painstaking, Careful Work to this dissident minority for a 26% total. Because of the growing public interest in computers, and the heightened concern of the computer world over the public image of computers and computer services, and because this is one of the rare opportunities to look at a large-sample data base gathered under controlled experimental conditions, it is worth taking a closer look at these contrasting responses.

Table 11.1 lists some of the typical positive responses and some of the typical negative responses of the cadets toward computers and computer programming. The entries are essentially self-explanatory. There is no simple way to categorize the positive responses except to point out that they range over the spectrum of skills and attitudes that make up successful computer programming —problem formulation, flow charting, coding, debugging, testing, computer languages, a sensitivity to the power of computers, a feeling of mastery over computers, and an appreciation for the complexities and challenge of computer science. The negative responses are easier to characterize: the hardware is too often unreliable and untrustworthy; the software is unnaturally difficult and requires too much time and painstaking attention; and consistently abortive results are not worth the large personal effort put into the problem.

These results pose a significant challenge for computer education. Introductory computer programming courses are not only concerned with teaching computer programming, they are also deeply involved with the formation of basic attitudes toward computers and computer services. Since such attitudes may be more important for the individual and society over the long run than the immediate skills that are taught, we should inquire into conditions that will generate favorable attitudes and minimize avoidance reactions. We should strive for a more favorable ratio of computer appreciation among students in introducing them to the world of computers.

The next question inquired into circumstances that led to individual insight. The results in Table 10.7 show that basic insight occurred more frequently when running the problem or trying the

Table 11.1. POSITIVE AND NEGATIVE ATTITUDES TOWARD COMPUTERS AND COMPUTER PROGRAMMING

Positive Attitudes

• Understanding program concepts.	• Learning how a computer works.
• Understanding the speed and power of computers.	• Appreciation of computer language.
• Insight into the structure of syntax.	• Batch and/or time-sharing is easy.
• Learning how to debug and test programs.	• Successful communication with computers.
• Appreciation and respect for computers and computer science.	• Sense of triumph over computers.
• Programming is logical.	• Understanding flow charts.

Negative Attitudes

• Inadequate access to computer facilities.	• Batch and/or time-sharing are poor ways to use computers.
• Unreliability of hardware.	• Painstaking care and attention.
• Programming is too complicated.	• Computer is an antagonist.
• Poor support services.	• Batch and/or time-sharing are unreliable.
• Computers are wasteful for many types of easy problems.	• Disappointment in not solving a well-understood problem after great effort.
• Too much work, too time-consuming.	• Antagonism toward computer language.

solution out than under any other circumstances. Here is additional proof that computer programming primarily involves learning by doing (35%), as opposed to studying (20%) and receiving instruction (17%), even though these are also indispensable.

Documentation (5%) is noteworthy for its relatively poor showing in this tabulation, which tends to reinforce the dominance of learning by doing for introductory computer programming. Some of the examples of Running the Problem are: feedback of computer results, experimenting with the logic and the code, finding and chasing down errors, working at the terminal, running in the batch mode, testing the program, and experience working with the computer.

The next question was concerned with the place where insight actually occurred. Table 10.8 shows that insight occurred more often when the cadet was working alone at his problem (41%) than at any other place. This finding suggests that subjective insight tends to occur more frequently under the stimulus of private, concentrated attention and work on a problem, than under other circumstances. The 24% showing for Terminal or Computer Room tends to support this interpretation. Most entries in this category are for insight at time-shared terminals. The case can be made that interactive terminals are one form of private concentrated work on computer problems, in which case the combined percentage is quite high (65%). As a matter of fact, when we look at time-sharing and batch groups separately, reported insight consistently occurs more frequently at the terminal for time-sharing users than at the desk. We might hypothesize from this finding that the experience at the terminal is more conducive for arriving at problem insight because the time-sharing user not only has the advantage of individualized concentration on his problem (which he has at his desk), but also the advantage of interactive reinforcement from computer response to his efforts. Against this hypothesis we should balance a counter-hypothesis: at his desk the user has the advantage of free leisure with a minimum of external pressures and constraints, conditions that do not usually exist at a busy time-shared terminal. The important result to stress is not the competition between batch and time-sharing for enhancing insight, but the necessity for individualized concentration on the problem, and the associated interpretation that insight is fundamentally a human-directed phenomenon flowing from intensive personal effort.

It should not be overlooked, however, that insight can occur anywhere, as shown in Table 10.8. It can occur with others (up to 20%) as well as alone; multiple insight can occur (4%); and for many there will be no particular insight gained. The literature on creativity and insight is complex and hotly disputed, and no attempt is made to enter into it at this point. The main contribution of this study lies in the relative empirical frequencies of occurrence of insight and their implications for mastering computer programming.

The last question inquires into problem-solving stages experienced by the cadets. Table 10.9 shows a fundamental three-step pattern as the top contender (56%): formulation, coding, and debugging the problem. Trial and error is conspicuous by its absence (1%). The only other serious contender is Study the Problem—Do It (13%). This response category is interesting for its emphasis on doing the problem to solve it, which we noted previously as a key circumstance for achieving insight. The rather large percentage of Other responses (21%) reveals how diverse and personalized problem-solving was for many in this sample.

11.4 CONCLUSIONS FOR INDIVIDUAL DIFFERENCES IN PROBLEM-SOLVING

Extent of Individual Differences. Very large individual differences were found in virtually all performance and attitudinal measures used in this study. For example, grades frequently ranged from 0% to 100% for class problems, man-hours varied from as low as 1 hour up to almost 50 hours to solve standard problems, and there were strong time-sharing and strong batch advocates, and equally strong attitudes generated against each or both of these types of computer systems.

General vs. Group Factor Structure. Factor analyses were conducted for each of the 12 problem-course groupings for 49 performance, experiential, and attitudinal measures. One of the key hypotheses was to test for the presence of a substantive general factor cutting across all classes and all problems for performance and attitudinal measures. No such general factor was found; a multiple group factor structure was found to provide a better fit for these data.

Systematic vs. Unique Factors. Another key hypothesis was to test for group factors common to all courses, as opposed to unique group factors specific to particular class problems. Two factors consistently appeared in practically all factor analyses—Overall Performance, which had highest factor loadings in problem grade, and Computer Experience. The Batch Halo factor appeared in all factor analyses using posttest questionnaire results; this factor reflected a striking polarization of cadet attitudes toward batch, in which batch was interpreted to be better than time-sharing in most respects. The positive Batch Halo factor was apparently related to the relatively poor computer system service associated with time-sharing throughout the experiment.

All the other factors, however, appeared in only several of the factor analyses, and in some cases, in just one factor analysis. The upshot is a spectrum of some common and some relatively unique group factors for each experimental problem, indicating that they were associated with both common and unique problem-solving patterns.

Performance Factor Structure. The Overall Performance factor, as mentioned above, appeared as a group factor in all 12 experimental problems, with highest loadings for problem grade. Associated with problem grade in this factor were favorable attitudes toward both computer modes, earlier insight into the class problem, and higher grade point averages. However, the second key performance measure, man-hours, did not show up in a consistent factor concerned with problem-solving speed. Analysis of problem-solving time revealed that cadet effort was a complex function of numerous influences which, in this experiment, precluded simple positive correlation with problem grades. For example, the fact that many students could not complete their problems meant that higher problems grades could be traded off, to some extent, by more man-hours. On the other hand, skilled students often completed their problems earlier and received top grades; the correlation of problem grades and man-hours may operate in opposite directions under different conditions.

Systematic Learning Effects. Analysis of work log data for individual work sessions disclosed systematic learning trends. Classical learning curves were observed for group trends with respect to progressive changes in man-hours per work session and for syntax errors. That is, early work sessions showed longest average man-hours per session, tapering off to shortest man-hours per session for the last work sessions. Also, for batch subjects, earliest computer runs showed the largest number of program syntax errors, tapering off to near-zero errors in the last computer runs during the last work sessions.

Analysis of individual student logs showed a decreasing sawtooth learning pattern for time and errors per work session. That is, both time and errors for a work session tended to show sharp increases when a new solution logic was tried out which progressively decreased as the new solution was debugged, and these sawtooth effects became less pronounced as the cadet converged toward his final or "best" solution. This decreasing sawtooth pattern provides evidence for the joint operation of insight learning (sawtooth), and trial-and-error learning (increasing efficiency with fewer errors and less time per work session).

Problem-Solving Difficulties. The great majority of cadets (62%) reported that programming problems constituted their greatest difficulty. Only 20% reported that computer system service was their main problem, and only 12% indicated that understanding the class problem was their greatest difficulty. Computer programming was viewed by most as a rather difficult set of skills to master.

Cadet Recommendations. Student recommendations were directed primarily at improved instructional techniques (46%) and only secondarily at improved computer system service (20%), or at self-improvement (16%). These results again stressed the need for more powerful and more satisfactory techniques to teach computer programming.

Insight Achieved. A seemingly neutrally-worded question asking the cadets what insight they achieved working with their class problem, resulted in a polarization of attitudes toward computers and computer programming. Approximately half of the cadets were favorably impressed by the power and versatility of computers, whereas roughly one-quarter were disenchanted with the time and effort required to master computer programming. These results indicate that when programming skills are taught in introductory computer science courses, significant attitudes and stereotypes toward computers and computer programming are also developed. These results also suggest that introductory courses should be deliberately designed to foster more constructive and positive attitudes toward the potential of computers, so that a significant segment of the students are not inadvertently turned off by computers.

Circumstances of Insight. The mastery of computer programming, according to the open-end testimony of cadets, primarily involves learning by doing—constructing solutions and trying them out on the computer—as opposed to studying and receiving instruction, even though these are indispensable. This finding reinforces the common-sense dictum that students should have easy, fast, and ample access to computers, whether time-sharing or batch, for effective mastery of computer skills.

Place of Occurrence of Insight. The moment of insight, at least as reconstructed by cadets, seemed to occur at a time and place in which there was intense personal involvement with work on the problem. For batch students insight occurred alone, at the desk; for time-sharing students insight occurred more often at the terminal and, almost as often, alone at the desk. The pattern of insight followed other paths as well—some reported insight at other places, multiple insight at different places, and no notable insight at all. The key finding for this data is that insight and creativity tend to occur where there is concentrated effort and intense individual involvement in the problem; as such, insight in computer programming seems to be primarily a function of personal organization of individual work effort and only secondarily a function of the design and organization of computer services.

Stages of Problem-Solving. The most frequent categorization of problem-solving stages was variations of a fundamental three-step process: formulating, coding, and debugging program solutions (56%). This finding supports a pervasive stereotype of the computer programming process by practitioners. However, analyses of work-session learning curves also showed that these stages were overlapping, iterative, and convergent toward a "best" solution.

The emphasis on debugging in cadet responses suggests the possibility of a built-in bias to teach students correct computer language syntax at the expense of good or useful solutions. Syntax errors are usually visible; logical errors are often invisible, and this fact may lead to selective reinforcement of syntactically correct code at the expense of more effective solutions.

PART IV

EPILOGUE

12

RETROSPECT, PROSPECT, AND SOCIAL IMPLICATIONS

In this chapter the main threads are woven together for the various online/offline studies and related areas reviewed in this book, and projections are made for social and behavioral research in man-computer problem-solving. Accordingly, the first part of this chapter is dedicated to a composite portrait of time-sharing and batch effectiveness; the second part pulls together leading issues in the dynamics of online/offline problem-solving with implications for the problem-solving literature broadly considered; and the final section relates research needs in man-computer problem-solving to the broader context of the computer-serviced society.

12.1 PORTRAIT OF ONLINE/OFFLINE COMPARISONS

Table 12.1 provides a composite overview of key studies and main results in the online/offline literature. It contains comparative experimental findings for the six exploratory studies reviewed in Part I of this book, the Gold study described in Part II, the Air Force Academy pilot study and main study from Part III, plus a recently published study by Frye and Pack (1969).

Table 12.1 shows the results of these ten studies for man-hours, computer time, costs, and user preference. Three of these studies

Table 12.1. COMPOSITE RESULTS: ONLINE VS. OFFLINE PERFORMANCE FOR TEN STUDIES

	Man-Hours	Computer Time	Costs	User Preference
Air Force Academy (1968 Pilot Study)	Time-Sharing * 1.2:1	Batch 1.7:1	Approx. Same	Approx. Same
Air Force Academy (1969 Pilot Study)	Batch 1.2:1	Batch 1.8:1	Batch	Approx. Same
Air Force Academy (Main Study, 1969)	Batch 1.1:1	Batch 1.9:1	Batch	Time-Sharing
Adams and Cohen (1969)	Approx. Same (1:1)	Batch 3.8:1	Batch 6.7:1	Batch
Erikson (1966)	Time-Sharing 1.9:1	Time-Sharing 3.4:1	Time-Sharing	Time-Sharing
Frye and Pack (1969)	Not Reported	Batch 3.8:1	Batch 3.3:1	Time-Sharing
Gold (1967)	Time-Sharing 1.2:1	Batch 5.7:1	Approx. Same	Time-Sharing
Grant and Sackman (1967)	Time-Sharing 1.6:1	Batch 1.4:1	Approx. Same	Time-Sharing
Schatzoff, Tsao, and Wiig (1967)	Batch 2.1:1	Time-Sharing 1.1:1	Batch 1.5:1	Not Reported
Smith (1967)	Instant ** 1.2:1	Batch 1.5:1	Approx. Same	Instant
Median for All Studies	Time-Sharing 1.2:1	Batch 1.8:1	Batch	Time-Sharing Preferred

* The mode showing a reported *advantage* appears in each box together with its favorable ratio; e g, this entry shows less man-hours for time-sharing at a 1.2:1 ratio.

** "Instant" batch is treated in this table as a simulated version of time-sharing.

are Air Force Academy investigations: the informal 1968 comparison of time-sharing and batch, the 1969 pilot study, and the main experiment. In Table 12.1 are listed the direction of the results, the corresponding ratio of time-sharing and batch performance, and the median result for all studies combined. Each study is treated equally as a relatively independent attempt in arriving at median values, which provides some indication, admittely crude, of the composite outcome of independent investigations. The median values, while indicative, should not obscure the great variability of the empirical results under differing experimental conditions.

A fundamental point illustrated by Table 12.1 is that the findings of the main Air Force Academy study are essentially consistent with the general trend of the online/offline literature to date. The median result for man-hours in Table 12.1 is 1.2:1 in favor of time-sharing. This composite result is in the neighborhood of the Academy result of 1.1:1 in favor of batch, particularly when system service is taken into account. The other studies tend toward guaranteed and dedicated computer service under time-sharing as part of experimental design; whereas the main Academy study was performed with less reliable service under time-sharing because of the newness of the system and related constraints on time-sharing availability. These contrasting results are quite close to the break-even point, and the message that emerges is that fundamental man-hour differences between time-sharing and batch do not seem to be substantially different for a wide variety of user tasks.

The results of the main Academy study reinforce previous findings on computer time to solve standard problems. The median for all studies is 1.8:1 in favor of batch, in contrast to 1.9:1 in favor of batch for the large-scale Academy study. The trend is fairly consistent in showing substantially less computer time to solve problems offline.

Immediate man-computer costs tend to average out as slightly higher for time-sharing than for batch, as shown in Table 12.1. The median value shows lower costs under batch. This conclusion applies only to immediate costs in solving standard problems as defined by direct computer time and direct man-hours spent on the problem. The main Academy study indicates moderately lower immediate costs under batch, primarily attributable to savings in computer time. Many other factors enter into total, long-range costs for time-sharing and batch that were not considered in these studies.

A notable case in point is the experience of the United States Department of Commerce Environmental Science Services Administration (ESSA) research laboratories. The report on long-range computer requirements (Slutz, et al., 1968) for the ESSA experience over a three-year period with time-sharing services represents a more comprehensive approach to total costs. This report estimated that the diverse research and engineering population in ESSA facilities effected a 40% savings in total problem-solving costs (man, machine, and organizational costs) compared to problem-solving via batch. Such estimates require comprehensive surveys in depth of the organizational problem-solving environment over extended periods, which may be quite different from isolated experimental results. It should also be emphasized that such results from an applied research environment may not hold for a business or academic environment. The ESSA study is valuable in pointing up the need for a combination of organizational case history techniques together with experimental studies in credible working environments to achieve a balanced assessment of individual and organizational cost-effectiveness.

The findings for user attitudes show two-thirds of all studies reporting preference for time-sharing. Batch was preferred by users over time-sharing in only one study. The remaining studies show no definite preference for either mode. These trends are consonant with the small but consistent edge for time-sharing in cadet ratings for the main Academy study.

There are numerous limitations to the total set of ten studies. Online/offline conditions were often not directly comparable in regard to system service, computers and languages used. Although the more recent investigations extended the range and variety of problems studies, it is still not known how representative the total set of experimental tasks are for data-processing users broadly considered. For example, some might argue that the various experimental problems are academically oriented and are probably too well structured compared to real-worth problems, and that perhaps there should have been more open-end problems in the sample such as the task used by Gold. There are other methodological problems and many of these have been cited throughout the book; the above should suffice to reveal the general limitations of the available studies.

The swift evolutionary changes in online and offline systems complicate the issues further. The appearance of faster batch systems, including instant remote batch, seems likely to reduce the savings in computer time under conventional batch, as shown in Smith's study (1967). Faster batch is also likely to cut back the favorable edge enjoyed by time-sharing in regard to user preference. The appearance of hybrid systems, offering the user the option of time-sharing or batch, may eventually make these comparisons obsolete. Perhaps the central result from these studies is that no really substantive case can be made for the overwhelming, general-purpose advantage of one mode over the other. As in all studies, without exception, individual differences in performance overshadow computer system differences. The key to major breakthroughs in improved man-computer effectiveness seems to lie in the nature and structure of individual differences and in human problem-solving styles. Whether the object of an institution is to teach computer science effectively or to produce cost-effective computer programs, the path to effective achievement of system and institutional goals is fundamental knowledge of human problem-solving in man-computer communication.

12.2 THE DYNAMICS OF MAN-COMPUTER PROBLEM-SOLVING

In this section an attempt is made to characterize man-computer problem solving from the available evidence within the broader context of the behavioral literature on problem-solving. Similarities and differences between online and offline problem solving are noted, gaps and problematic areas are pointed out, new behavioral hypotheses are formulated, and the role of methodology is stressed.

A large and diverse literature already exists in the general field of problem-solving in suggestive areas that overlap with theoretical and practical issues in online/offline problem-solving. Unfortunately, computer science investigators in online/offline work have tended to neglect the mainstream of relevant behavioral literature for useful leads; and for the most part, social science investigators have been slow in making experimental headway in the computer milieu. In this section, some of the well-established areas in the problem-solving literature (such as massed vs. spaced learning, whole vs. part learning, insight vs. trial and error) are used to construct a framework for the available data on online/offline problem-solving. In the behavioral literature, the findings stem from experimental studies on human and animal subjects, with tasks including puzzles, memorization of verbal material, nonsense syllables, various motor problems, and reaction-time studies. The transfer of principles and findings from these to online/offline studies is obviously problematic but nevertheless valuable in suggesting fruitful hypotheses and new leads.

12.2.1 Massed vs. Spaced Learning

The findings in problem-solving are drawn primarily from various compendia of experimental psychology (Stevens, 1951, Woodworth and Schlosberg, 1954, Berelson and Steiner, 1964). The data on massed vs. spaced (or distributed) learning suggests a useful and fundamental analogy to distinguish between online and offline learning. The analogy is suggestive insofar as massed learning, as in time-sharing, represents more intensive and continuous problem-solving over longer blocks of time, in contrast to distributed learning, which, as in batch, represents shorter sessions with longer intervals between sessions. From another point of view, the contrast is between interrupted (batch) learning vs. noninterrupted (time-sharing) learning. The analogy breaks down with respect to subject feedback in that feedback is almost always immediate or soon after each trial in the problem-solving literature, whereas feedback is delayed by machine turnaround time in batch problem-solving. With these and related provisos in mind, consider the comparative advantages of massed vs. spaced problem-solving in Table 12.2.

Table 12.2. MASSED VS. SPACED PROBLEM-SOLVING

Advantages of Massed Effort	*Advantages of Spaced Effort*
Less warmup required.	Less fatigue and boredom.
Better for short tasks directly learned to completion.	Better for longer, but routine tasks.
Less forgetting between sessions.	Fewer interference effects and "mental ruts."
Better for tasks requiring much exploration.	Usually fewer trials to reach performance criterion.
Better for very complex tasks.	Less dependence on immediate memory, and more on long-term memory.

Under the Massed Effort column is an initial suggestive profile of time-sharing advantages. Four out of five of these advantages were demonstrated directly or indirectly in the online/offline literature—less warmup, less forgetting between sessions, and a tendency toward better performance for highly exploratory and complex tasks. The analogy for the remaining item, short tasks, is equivalent to the easy problem that can be solved at one sitting at the time-shared terminal.

The items in the Spaced Effort column are somewhat more problematic for batch problem-solving. Table 12.2 suggests that routine but time-consuming tasks might be solved more effectively under batch (second entry). Type of problem has been repeatedly shown to be a critical and enigmatic factor in the online/offline literature. Intermittent problem-solving might create fewer effects of interference, fatigue, and boredom, particularly for routine problems. The key entry is the advantage of fewer trials in distributed runs to reach the performance criterion. The consistent showing of less computer time and fewer program runs under batch in online/offline studies may be reasonably interpreted as greater problem-solving efficiency in the form of fewer trials to reach the criterion, thus confirming a major expectation from the behavioral problem-solving literature.

The last item in Table 12.2 suggests an interesting additional interpretation for this fundamental batch advantage. Since spaced learning requires more long-time retention to bridge the interpolated intervals spent in other activities, perhaps batch facilitates long-term memory of problem-solving techniques more effectively than time-sharing. However, this hypothesis runs counter to some of Gold's results, which indicated better learning of the Dynamo language, and better verbal conceptualization of the problem with time-sharing. Here again, the batch burden of delayed reinforcement might be invoked as neutralizing some of this advantage.

Another way of approaching this analogy is to consider massed vs. spaced console sessions within time-sharing, and massed vs. spaced runs within batch. The online/offline evidence to date favors relative massing for both computer modes. Better performers in both modes in the Gold study started earlier and kept working steadily at their task, minimizing other interpolated activities. Thus the Gold study indicates that when the subject has the option to work at his own pace, the better performer tends to mass his effort. In contrast, in the Academy study, cadets were compelled to work in short console shifts of 15 minutes, based on prior signup for time-sharing use. This constraint tended to inhibit time-sharing user effectiveness, particularly when computer troubles occurred in this short time period. In the offline setting, the Smith study (1967) clearly demonstrated better human performance under fast batch as compared to conventional batch. The results indicated twice as long an interval between successive computer runs in conventional as opposed to "instant" batch; that is, users spontaneously tended to mass their computer runs more closely together to arrive at problem solutions.

12.2.2 Part vs. Whole Learning

The literature on part-whole learning has already been anticipated in the Gold study in connection with student dropouts. This aspect of the problem-solving literature shows less sophisticated subjects doing better (fewer total trials) when long experimental tasks are broken down into small, manageable pieces. More sophisticated subjects tend to tackle larger parts or even the entire task at one time and tend to require fewer trials and less time to reach criterion performance. The trend is toward larger parts and more "gestalt" conceptualization with increasing learning, skill, and experience. The rule of thumb that emerges from the part-whole studies is that each individual should try to start with the largest unit of the task that he can handle effectively in terms of his skill and experience, and that this optimal unit grows in response to task feedback and progressive learning, generally increasing with successful experience.

In the Gold study, the online mode made it easier for the user to proceed in relatively small steps, which enabled the individual to bite off only what he could chew; relatively speaking, the offline mode forced the user to gamble all on one throw of the dice with each computer run of his entire program or program module. Thus, the marginal performer had the option to cut the problem down to size in the online mode; whereas in the offline mode he was virtually compelled to handle the problem in one fell swoop in order to complete his task within an acceptable time period. Marginal performers fared better under time-sharing, with fewer dropouts than batch. Apparently, in the Gold study, the online mode provided a more favorable and nonpunitive setting for smaller pieces of the problem, gave immediate feedback, and was more permissive with respect to human failure. This online performance advantage for whole vs. part learning was clearly demonstrated only in the Gold study, however; the Academy results were neutral on this point, since problem grades were equivalent under both modes.

12.2.3 Insight vs. Trial-and-Error

Another issue that has been extensively investigated is insight vs. trial-and-error learning. Insightful problem-solving is held to be a kind of sudden learning with marked improvement in performance, a higher-order grasping of problem relationships, an internal rehearsal of a successful solution—the "aha" experience immortalized by Archimedes discovering the buoyancy principle while taking a bath. Trial-and-error problem-solving is held to be a more gradual type of learning, marked by quasi-random exploratory behavior, many empirical trials, and by progressive reinforcement of the more successful responses until the criterion is reached.

Gestalt psychologists (e g, Kohler, 1947) stress insightful problem-solving; behavioral learning theorists lean toward the more systematic, molecular interpretations offered by trial-and-error concepts.

As in the other "dichotomies" (massed vs. spaced, and part vs. whole learning), neither alternative necessarily rules the other out, and the effectiveness of each varies with the task and the experimental setting. To the extent that any trend is discernible in the behavioral literature, trial-and-error seems to be more fruitfully applied to tasks that cannot be conceived as a whole without extensive piecemeal feedback from the environment; in contrast, insightful learning seems to occur when a sufficiently large data base or "apperceptive mass" has been established for a given problem or part of a problem so that a significantly improved solution may be conceptualized and internally rehearsed. The online/offline literature supports both types of problem-solving.

In his original study, Gold (1967) demonstrated a kind of cyclical equilibrium between insightful and trial-and-error problem-solving. The central finding was that the first trial run in a time-sharing session resulted in an improvement that averaged three times the profit score of succeeding interactions during the same console session. In addition, on their questionnaire, the subjects described their main reasons for the first interaction as "trying a new decision rule" or "introducing other factors into the existing decision rule"; for subsequent interactions, the main reasons recorded were "a rerun to try different constants" and "correction of previously undetected program errors."

The difference between the first and subsequent interactions under time-sharing in Gold's experiment suggests the contrast between insightful learning based on a new or modified approach and trial-and-error learning based on parametric variations on the same theme, or on error corrections. This evidence suggests that intervals between console sessions (time away from the computer) were used to arrive at strategic or insightful changes in problem-solving; whereas time spent at the console after the new strategy was first tried was devoted mainly to tactical or trial-and-error problem-solving.

While the console session provided the acid test of reality against proffered solutions, apparently the most creative insights occurred during the time away from the computer. This finding underscores the primacy of human-directed problem solving in man-computer communication, and the need to study total user problem-solving behavior rather than merely a fragment of the user's behavior at the console. Even in a computerized milieu, a look at Rodin's "Thinker" should correct a long-standing error in the computer science literature: human problem-solving is cranial, not manual—the action is in the head, not in the hands.

The increased number of computer trials in the online mode apparently permitted more exploratory trial-and-error learning and provided a richer data base for reflective thinking away from the terminal, leading to more effective insight for the subsequent session. The experimental support for this assertion was pointed out by Gold in his original study: the online group averaged $110 extra profit in the first interaction in a computer session as compared to $90 for the average increase per batch run; the online group, in subsequent interactions during the same session, was able to add an average of about $30 to the initial increment of $110. Thus, the original interaction, resembling strategic or "insightful" modifications was better than the batch counterpart, and the follow-on trial-and-error modifications in the online session widened the difference even further. Apparently, both kinds of problem-solving were aided and abetted by the online condition.

It is of special interest in this connection to note that both groups paced themselves almost exactly the same with regard to number of computer sessions (4.8 mean sessions for batch and 4.7 for time-sharing). When it is considered that the two groups showed equal average elapsed time (slightly over four days) it becomes apparent that the fundamental cycle for "thinking" and computer testing is typically the single work day. This conclusion is supported by the Air Force Academy studies where number of computer runs was consistently close to number of elapsed days to complete the problem (see Table 9.2). Those who performed better, in both groups in Gold's study, tended to use more computer time either by running more than one computer session a day or by starting earlier and finishing later. In this case, the open-end problem was conducive to higher profit scores for more man-machine effort.

An early variant of the "insight" approach to human problem-solving is the theory proposed by Wallas (1926) based in large part on the accounts of scientists and artists describing their own creative experiences. The theory proposes four distinguishable stages in problem-solving—preparation, incubation, illumination, and verification. The "illumination" stage is the insightful stage. The four stages of problem solving proposed by Wallas are representative of various schemes proposed by investigators, as shown in historical order in Table 12.3, adapted from Haefele (1962). Subsequent work has shown these stages to be iterative and overlapping. The Gold study may be interpreted as essentially supporting this description of the problem-solving process, if preparation, incubation, and illumination are construed as occurring away from the computer, with verification interpreted as computer feedback coupled with human evaluation of results. The iteration occurs with successive cycles punctuated by computer runs, and the overlapping occurs with reversals of this order or with parallel activities of more than one process at a time.

Table 12.3. STAGES IN CREATIVITY AND PROBLEM-SOLVING

HELMHOLTZ (1896)

- Preparation
- Incubation
- Illumination

WALLAS (1926)

- Preparation
- Incubation
- Illumination
- Verification

ROSSMAN (1931)

- Observation of a need or difficulty
- Analysis of the need
- Survey of the available information
- Critical analysis of the proposed solutions for advantages and disadvantages
- Birth of the new idea, the invention

- Experimentation to test out the most promising solution; perfection of the final embodiment by repeating some or all of the previous steps

DEWEY (1938)

- Disturbed equilibrium, initiation of inquiry
- Problem formulation
- Hypothesis formulation
- Experimental testing
- Settled outcome, termination of inquiry

YOUNG (1940)

- Assembly of material
- Assimilation of material in our mind
- Incubation
- Birth of the idea
- Development to practical usefulness

OSBORN (1957)

- Orientation: pointing up the problem
- Preparation: gathering pertinent data
- Analysis: breaking down the relevant material
- Hypothesis: piling up alternatives by way of ideas
- Incubation: letting up, to invite illumination
- Synthesis: putting the pieces together
- Verification: judging the resultant ideas

(Adapted from Haefele, 1962)

The Academy studies provide extensive additional evidence for insight and trial-and-error types of learning at individual and group levels. First, we note that problem-solving, in computer programming, essentially follows a three-step process—problem formulation, coding, and debugging. At the group level, we found classical learning curves supporting convergent trial-and-error behavior toward problem solution; that is, with increasing work sessions (or trials), elapsed time per work session steadily decreased, and the number of syntax errors also decreased. Further, a special relationship between insight and trial-and-error learning was observed at the individual level in the form of a "decreasing sawtooth" effect. The sawtooth has two elements in it, the upward spike improvement in problem logic, which corresponds to insight, and progressive improvements in debugging, which correspond more closely to trial-and-error. Within the framework of a tentative logical solution for a problem, the subject tends to improve the syntax of his code until syntactical errors disappear. But his syntactically correct code may not yield a correct logical solution. He then formulates a new and what he hopes is an improved logical solution for his problem, and the new or modified code generates another debugging cycle, with a decreasing level of syntactical errors as the final solution is iteratively approached. Thus the individual spikes correspond to progressive solution by insight, whereas the decreasing error levels between spikes correspond to progressive solution by trial-and-error in debugging.

The Academy data on the nature of insight tends to refute Wallas' (1926) theory, in the sense that insight was reported to occur most frequently during intensive personal work on the problem (at the desk or at the time-shared terminal) rather than during a relatively quiescent period of "incubation." It was also apparent that interaction with the time-sharing terminal was conducive to eliciting such insight during working sessions. Within this context, it is tempting to suggest the hypothesis that a leading advantage of the time-sharing terminal for human creativity is that it tends to reinforce more extensive and more intensive human concentration on the problem.

In view of the elapsed time required to solve Academy class problems (averages running between one to two weeks), it might be argued that intermittent incubation preceded insight. However, our best guide, in terms of available objective evidence, is the subject's description of what he was doing at the time of insight, and this was predominantly some form of intensive, individual work on the problem. When we consider these two views of the preconditions for insight and creativity in man-computer problem-solving, they appear to be contradictory. To reconcile them we must develop real-time problem-solving dynamics which will capitalize on the potential of computers to tap human behavior. The questionnaires and work logs used in the Gold and Academy studies are crude steps in this direction; supplementation of manual procedures by more advanced real-time computerized techniques could lead to a quantum leap in scientific insight into human problem-solving.

Another notable methodological implication lies in the potential for real-world experimentation. A case in point is the systematic learning behavior extracted from the spontaneous work sessions of the cadets. In traditional behavioral experimentation, learning in the laboratory is deliberately set up under highly controlled conditions with an explicit sequence of learning trials, each of which measures quantitative performance toward an operational criterion. In the Academy context, the spontaneous work session in the real world of the cadet was seen to exhibit systematic learning trends in terms of decreasing time and decreasing errors per session. Whereas laboratory experiments may be criticized for being products of the experimenter's imagination, the real-world behavior of subjects exerts more compelling credibility for the generalized validity of test findings. There is no loss of scientific rigor if the reliability and validity of real-world experiments can be systematically tested and replicated, and there is a great potential for massive behavioral breakthroughs once we allow ourselves to think freely of the possibility of systematically tapping real-world human experience, particularly with the aid of computers.

A key conceptual problem in the general area of human creativity with computers lies in the distinction between the formulation of problems and their solution. The online/offline literature and most of the behavioral literature is primarily concerned with solutions to well-defined problems. We have not yet made much experimental headway into the analysis of creativity in the formulation of significant problems, except in case histories and biographical studies. Mackworth (1965) has stated the general case for problem-finding as opposed to problem-solving. In the computer milieu, except for sporadic anecdotal reports, we have not yet accomplished major work on the potential impact of computers in furthering the kind of exploratory behavior that leads to the creation of significant new problems.

12.2.4 The Structure of Human Skills in Man-Computer Problem-Solving

In this section, the intent is to portray the available evidence on individual differences in man-computer problem-solving in a coherent conceptual framework. Major controversies have developed in the last few decades over competing theories of intelligence, personality, and occupational skill and trait structures. Computers are now entering the scene in force and they are bound to reorient and transform such theories.

I have been developing a hypothesis, a Progressive Differentiation Hypothesis, which offers certain advantages in explaining available results on individual differences in man-computer problem-solving. This hypothesis was motivated by several considerations. First, when computers are viewed as an expansion of the human intellect or as an aid to effective human intelligence, they seem to magnify individual differences. There is no need to enlarge upon the ubiquitous presence of very large individual differences in man-computer effectiveness; they are everywhere in the online/offline studies in this book. The proposed hypothesis, as we shall see, goes a step further and asserts that computer developments are likely to continue to enhance effective human intelligence, and that these advances will probably continue to expand individual differences over a growing spectrum of man-computer capabilities.

A second consideration is the apparently limitless number and diversity of problems to which computers can be applied in a man-computer context. This virtually unlimited diversity requires a pluralistic conceptual framework to allow elbow room for new, and perhaps radically different, man-computer applications that could arise in the future.

A third consideration is the need to chart systematically the genesis of computer knowledge and skills in individuals from their first encounter with computers through the most advanced stages of computer skill and expertise.

A fourth consideration is the need for more effective teaching of computer knowledge and skills, and in systematic test and measurement of such attributes in a practical and useful manner.

A fifth consideration is the desirability of studying computer-related skills in conjunction with behavioral experimentation into the skills and traits in intellectual, personality, and occupational areas of inquiry.

With these various considerations in mind, the Progressive Differentiation Hypothesis is defined in two parts, as follows:

- Advancing computer tools and information services tend to expand the range of individual differences in man-computer performance, and such advances will continue to expand effective human differences in a freely competitive and open environment. As astronomy has led to us to an awareness of the expanding physical universe, so will computer science and technology lead us to an awareness of the exploding social universe of effective human intelligence.
- The pattern of expanding individual differences assumes the following general form: when individuals are first exposed to and indoctrinated in the use of computers, either a general factor, or a small number of well-defined group factors, or a combination of both, are held to account for a substantial portion of observed individual differences in man-computer proficiency; however, with the advent of diversified tasks and increasing experience, this relatively small set of general proficiency factors for beginners tends to differentiate progressively into numerous separate and independent factors associated with the user's increasing specialized experience.

The pattern of progressive differentiation of man-computer skills was suggested to the author from the factor findings in the literature on intelligence testing. In essence, at early ages a general verbal factor was found in the scores of children on various tests, whereas at later ages, particularly at the college level, the factor structure progressively changed to differential, specialized skills that were relatively independent of each other, such as numerical, spatial, and logical skills. The analogy in the computer milieu is that computers are rapidly becoming a powerful force in helping to shape effective human intelligence, and that computer skills and services tend to accelerate the pluralistic differentiation of human skills and traits in man-computer tasks.

Additional precedent for progressive differentiation of skills may be found in the validity of occupational tests. Ghiselli (1966) has compiled thousands of published validity coefficients in occupational aptitude testing. Validity correlation coefficients of paper-and-pencil tests average out at approximately .30 against training performance, and at about .20 for job proficiency criteria. These gross averages are consistent, for example, with the median correlation of .26 found in the main Academy study between the various problem grades and cadet grade average. These summary results are also consistent with Mayer and Stalnaker's review of testing techniques for the selection and evaluation of computer personnel (1968). The corroborative point in these examples is that specialized occupational tasks show relatively low correlations against measures of general skills such as intellectual abilities, arithmetic, perceptual, and motor skills. Assuming that computer skills fall into a similar correlational pattern, or that they accelerate the differentiation pattern, as the proposed hypothesis asserts, we may expect equally low correlations linked with the emergence of specialized skills.

An additional corroborative case in point is the experience with the Basic Programming Knowledge Test developed by Berger, et al (1966). Highest correlations with this paper-and-pencil test occurred with the experience level of beginners, tapering off to nonsignificant correlations with several years of computer experience in the normative population. That is, general computer literacy, as measured by the BPKT, was correlated with initial computer experience but not with increasing experience in computer work. The inference, according to the proposed hypothesis, is that generalized initial skills progressively differentiate into more specialized skills with increasing experience.

To what extent does the available online/offline evidence confirm or refute the proposed hypothesis? A substantive and well-defined general problem-solving factor was found in the Gold study with student trainees, but was not found in the exploratory Grant-Sackman (1967) study with highly experienced programmers. The general factor in the Gold study incorporated problem speed, accuracy in man-computer communication, effectiveness of the solution, exploitation of the computer system, attitudinal, experiential, and verbal measures. These findings tend to support this hypothesis.

The main Academy study, which had a trainee population, would be expected, in accordance with the Progressive Differentiation Hypothesis, to come up with a substantive general factor, or a small set of group factors. Although the first part of this expectation did not materialize in the form of a general factor, there was a persistent group factor "Overall Problem Performance" that consistently appeared in all class problems, with characteristics roughly analogous to the general factor found in the Gold study. In all three studies using factor analysis (the main Academy study, Gold's investigation, and the Grant-Sackman study) a variant of a Problem-Solving Speed factor appeared, indicating one form of a generalized man-computer skill. A Computer Experience group factor appeared in the Gold and Academy studies, which is consistent with the proposed hypothesis for trainee populations.

Differences in factor structures appeared between the Gold and Academy studies and within the Academy study which probably reflected the influence of differential problem tasks. Personality-oriented factors such as Hustler and Nit-Picker appeared only in the Gold study. Exploitation of the Computer System also appeared only in the Gold study. Both of these unique factor results may be related to the open-end nature of Gold's profit-making task. The early-bird syndrome of the Hustler and the more extensive use of computer time in Exploitation of the Computer System were both conducive to more thorough exploration of profit alternatives and higher scores in this open-end problem. The Nit-Picker suggests over-cautious behavior that tends to discourage new insight. The Academy problems, in contrast, had fixed, correct solutions, for which extra effort often did not pay off, at least for students who quickly achieved correct solutions. Thus, factor structure is shaped by differential problem skills and problem payoff requirements. This general point, which is consistent with the proposed hypothesis, was further borne out in the mixed, differential pattern of factors for the 12 problems in the main Academy study. Even with a trainee population, differential problem requirements lead to differential factor patterns.

The available evidence is still too meager to draw definitive conclusions with respect to the Progressive Differentiation Hypothesis. This hypothesis offers one interpretation to draw together initial findings, suggest new leads, and recognize the continuing challenge of large and growing individual differences in man-computer performance.

The preceding whirlwind tour of the problem-solving literature has served its purpose if it has demonstrated that man-computer communication can profitably flow into the mainstream of behavioral science, that it could benefit substantively from the work already done, and in turn, that it could strongly influence the methods and findings of these disciplines. It is beyond the scope of this review to enter into the problems, pitfalls, and requisites of a science of real-time man-computer communication; this has been done elsewhere by the author (1967). Unfortunately, the dearth of experimental evidence and the great gaps in present knowledge preclude formulation of comprehensive theories of human problem-solving in man-computer settings.

12.3 PROSPECTS FOR SCIENTIFIC STUDY OF MAN-COMPUTER PROBLEM-SOLVING

This concluding section pulls together various recommendations for needed research in man-computer problem-solving, and explores the role of new evolutionary forms of research in the computer-serviced society of the future. The following recommendations stem from the work reported in this book; the long-range role of man-computer research that is subsequently developed derives from broader social considerations related to the imminent emergence of mass information utilities.

12.3.1 Research Recommendations

Individual Differences. The available online/offline literature highlights the existence of large individual differences in man-computer problem-solving, even with stratified samples of experienced subjects. The greatest economic payoff is in this area, since human performance differences are consistently larger than computer system differences, often by an order of magnitude. An empirical taxonomy of computer users is needed. Special attention should be devoted to the difficulties of marginal performers and to the analysis of man-computer errors. Performance norms need to be developed for representative users against standardized tasks. Motivational and attitudinal differences need to be systematically explored to understand the long-range development of programmer and user skills. This work should investigate team as well as individual performance. These research needs are especially urgent since the analysis of human differences in man-computer computer communication is still in its infancy.

Computer Language and User Terminal Effectiveness. Comparative investigations need to be conducted measuring the performance effectiveness of competing computer languages and alternative user terminals. Applied research in these areas is virtually nonexistent. Learning time, differential human error rates, skill requirements of users, and user attitudes toward computer languages and console configurations should be included as measures of effectiveness in addition to standard measures such as computer time and man-hours to solve standard tasks.

Fast Batch Versus Interactive Time-Sharing. The online/offline contest is narrowing down to time-sharing versus fast batch. The data is still inconclusive as to the performance differential between new and existing forms of time-sharing and improved versions of fast batch. Critical experiments are needed.

Human-Engineered Scheduling Algorithms. Current time-sharing executive systems are optimized for machine throughput, and for "fast" response time to users, but not necessarily for human effectiveness. There is increasing evidence that rapid-fire, conversationally-paced interaction between the user and the computer is fine for routine problem steps, for verification of preconceived and well-understood ideas, and for tactical problem-solving; but strategic or insightful problem-solving, like good wine, may require longer periods for maturation. New human-engineered scheduling algorithms, with responsive options for longer and variable time intervals to service users, may be more conducive for insight at the terminal than the present pattern in which most creative work is done away from the computer. If this suggestion proves useful, effective capacity of time-sharing systems to service many users simultaneously may be substantially increased.

Computer System Service. There is growing evidence that the reliability of computer system service—including the central computer, user tools, and information services—may be more critical from a cost-effective viewpoint than the traditional emphasis on other factors such as the type of computer system, or the type of language or terminal used. Proprietary wraps make objective studies on computer system reliability difficult to achieve. But if experimental results in man-computer problem-solving are to be interpreted in a meaningful manner, they need to be qualified by empirically verified quantitative measures of computer system service. In particular, with the rise of mass information utilities, objective standards for reliable computer system service may become a dominant issue in regulatory and licensing policy.

Real-Time Case Histories. The field of man-computer communication is ripe for a concentrated experimental attack on real-time problem-solving behavior, with detailed case histories tracing empirical behavior of individuals. As Freud made a breakthrough in intensive analysis of clinical behavior of individuals, so should we make a breakthrough in tracking down problem-solving behavior of individuals throughout the complete life-cycle of real-world problems, using all available techniques, manual and computerized. Complete capture of the real-time interchange between man and the computer, as done by regenerative recording (Sackman, 1967), would be invaluable in reconstruction and analysis of real-time behavior in case histories.

Task Taxonomy. The Gold study, in contrast to other online/offline studies, showed many systematic differences in man-machine performance in solving an open-end problem as compared to a fixed problem. There are probably other major classes of problems that will show equally striking differences in problem-solving patterns. An empirically derived taxonomy of man-computer tasks should be developed based on demonstrated differences in human problem-solving style rather than on a confusing welter of strictly descriptive characteristics. For example, Gold's study demonstrated that better performers tend to use more computer time for open-end tasks, whereas other studies on fixed problems tended to show the reverse. The behavioral literature shows major breakthroughs occurring with the formulation of new and different problem situations, as, for example, the Gestalt breakthrough with "insightful" tasks. Similar breakthroughs may occur with investigation of real-world problems in man-computer communication.

Time-Sharing vs. Small Computers. No experimental studies have been conducted comparing the cost-effectiveness of time-sharing against small, "free-standing" computers for standardized problems. Proponents of small computers argue that lower operating costs and the virtual elimination of turnaround time make personally-operated small computers the method of choice. Time-sharing advocates claim that the interactive features of time-sharing make for more effective problem-solving, that more versatile services are available with a more powerful computer, and that time-sharing costs are becoming competitive with small computer costs. As in the online/offline controversy, predisciplinary bickering should be replaced by serious scientific work.

Paper and Pencil Tests. Two general types of paper-and-pencil tests need to be developed more fully for theoretical and applied payoffs—user questionnaires, and standardized tests for selecting, training, and evaluating effectiveness in man-computer communication. Questionnaires were quite effective in the reported online/offline studies, performing a great variety of useful functions quickly and at low cost. The pitfalls and problems of questionnaires are well known. But the fact remains that man-computer problem-solving is first and foremost a human-directed process, and we would be foolish to neglect direct questioning and introspective techniques. In this connection, online questionnaire techniques, still in their infancy, would be a logical and powerful extension of experimental methodology, not only for the investigation of problem-solving, but for the study of online polling in its own right.

Standardized paper-and-pencil tests of user skills in man-computer communication should be pursued more vigorously than at present, in view of the large individual differences that exist in performance and the larger differences that are yet to come as computerized information services become widespread. Although the correlational validity of analogous tests in academic and occupational areas has traditionally been relatively low, or marginally low to moderate, the proper application of such tests to selection, training, and placement of individuals would probably turn out to be cost-effective.

Development of Cost-Effectiveness Models. Simulation models comparing the cost-effectiveness of competitive computing configurations need to be developed. Such models should incorporate human as well as machine and task elements, with emphasis on empirically validated measures of effectiveness and less emphasis on abstract and oversimplified models than has been the case in the past.

Organizational Case Histories. Many large organizations and institutions have accumulated up to two decades of experience in their use of computers. Professional case histories and sociological analyses of such extended computer experience is likely to uncover a mine of invaluable knowledge on the use and misuse of computers for the benefit of all organizations. Educational institutions are in sore need of such guidance for computer science courses and computer center services. The historians of science and technology have virtually no detailed data on the vicissitudes of organizational use of computers. The ESSA study mentioned earlier in this chapter (Slutz, 1968) is a provisional attempt in this direction, and so is the author's historical account of the SAGE air defense system (1967). Experimental analysis of man-computer problem solving is sterile if it is divorced from the broader framework of social and institutional trends in the human use of computers.

Cross-Fertilization with Behavioral Sciences. This book has attempted to demonstrate some of the mutual benefits for man-computer communication and the behavioral sciences in an exchange and interfusion of ideas, methods, and findings. The computer sciences have much to offer in advanced computerized techniques for the study of real-time human behavior, and concepts stemming from the behavioral sciences may conceivably revolutionize man-computer communication as we know it today. More cooperative research is needed from both disciplines.

Social Effectiveness. The study of optimal conditions and approaches to human learning and problem-solving in a computer-aided environment has direct bearing on the enhancement of individual performance, and ultimately on social effectiveness. The findings for dropouts and marginal performers may have social generality beyond the immediate experimental setting; these findings may aid in educating individuals who need extra help and attention to reach desired levels of proficiency. The extension of mass computer utilities could result in chaos if information services are not socially engineered to accommodate the vast range of individual differences and diverse information needs in the general population.

12.3.2 Cooperative Research in Man-Computer Communication for Mass Information Utilities

Concern over social effectiveness in man-computer problem-solving leads us directly to a consideration of research prospects for mass computer utilities. The advent of mass information utilities is a new and complex field in its own right, which has been treated elsewhere (see for example, Sprague, 1969, and Sackman and Nie, 1970); only a highly abbreviated overview is presented in this concluding section to serve as prologue for future social research in man-computer communication.

First, recent Federal rulings on the computer communications scene are making it increasingly apparent that CATV (Community Antenna Television) will probably be the basic broadband communications highway into the American home. The Federal Communications Commission ruling in December 1968 enabled CATV operators to originate programming services in the public interest, which paves the way for transmission of computerized information services into the home via coaxial cable and the home TV screen. There are now more than 3 million viewing families subscribing to over 2000 operative CATV systems in the United States, and approximately half of the viewing public is expected to be "hooked on" to CATV by about 1975.

Second, technological computer communications developments are being designed and tested by leading firms to make it possible to use the home TV, with appropriate modifications, as the basic display device for receiving information services. New electronic addressing techniques allow central computers to receive user requests and send out the desired information from large files to the individual consumer. The central computer can act as a giant digital switch, routing information traffic to appropriate points, serving thousands of users simultaneously. Feasibility is no longer questioned; all the fundamental technological elements are available for mass information utilities. The race is on for the most cost-effective package.

Third, by seizing upon economies of scale, leading computer communications firms, in conjunction with CATV operators, will be able to offer the public a wide variety of information services at low monthly rates, perhaps approaching telephone rates, providing entertainment, educational, shopping, and homekeeping services.

Fourth, and most significant, no one appears concerned with the need for social excellence in the introduction of the mass information utility. Effective guidance in this direction for all involved is totally lacking. The FCC and other cognizant government agencies follow rather than lead technology, and they have virtually no experience in this area. No one has faced up to the problem of social information as a regulated public utility. The computer manufacturers, software houses, and the communications industry have virtually no guidance as to what the public wants or what the public needs. If immediate profits reign triumphant as the supreme end of all social planning because no other serious contenders arise, then the information utility could end up as the most barren wasteland of them all.

Compounding these problems is the unenviable tradition of the computer world, as evident in this book, of having consistently neglected serious study of the human use of computers. With these bleak possibilities looming large, the public's long-range needs are bound to be forgotten. And the socio-economic, political, and educational implications of information utilities can easily stagger the imagination. In particular, new democratic forms may emerge, creating a new configuration between the citizen and the state. It may already be too late to provide early warning toward cooperative, open development of the information utility on behalf of democratic excellence.

The time for vigorous open dialogue on the public stakes of the information utility is long overdue. The development of the information utility is proceeding rapidly along closed lines by privileged groups. The information utility is too important to be left to the FCC and the computer communications industry. It is everyone's concern and we should orient our efforts to airing some of the leading issues, to opening up vigorous debate over key social options, to exploring the public interest in some depth for all levels of society, and to helping introduce the public to the momentous socio-technological changes taking place.

The scope, range, and variety of needed research and development on the human use of computer utilities is staggering. Research needs run the gamut from online voting, to arbitration of consumer complaints, to the detection, diagnosis and correction of error-prone users, to an empirical census of user tasks and data needs, to the development of a doctrine of privacy, and to analyses of the impact of computers on human creativity. Numerous areas of inquiry may be delineated under the general headings of social effectiveness, scientific methodology, normative problems, and behavioral hypotheses. An increase in the tempo of user research is essential, a sizable increase to meet the massive experimental challenge of public information services. The following provisional research recommendations are offered.

The above summary represents an initial assessment of the problem of user research for the information utility. These conclusions converge into a single, fundamental recommendation—the need for cooperative, experimental computer utility prototypes to formulate the problems and gain the experience necessary for intelligent regulation and growth of this new social force. The cooperative interests require a sufficiently diversified consumer community, local government, federal, and local regulatory agencies, computer communications representatives, software and information service suppliers, CATV operators, and a scientific-administrative organization to manage the joint enterprise in accordance with chartered objectives. It is further recommended that more than one such experimental prototype be implemented so that competitive alternatives may be pursued, openly evaluated, and pluralistically resolved in a democratic manner in the public domain as the information utility evolves.

Failure to follow the above general recommendation could result in an extension of the inadequacies and the apparent bankruptcy of current practice to meet the vast needs of mass computer utilities. The current trickle of user research, as manifest in this book, is too little and flows too late to exercise a significant impact on public information services. If we cling anachronistically to the doctrine of maximum effective laissez-faire (the least possible regulation is the best possible regulation), the result may be the same kind of ugly conflicts between public and private interests that have punctuated the history of earlier public utilities. The pulsating information arteries of the country embodied in emerging computer utilities may conceivably become the most vital arteries of all, and they will increasingly be affected by a growing public interest. Industrial leaders should help pioneer the way into this new utility, in the name of and for the sake of the public interest, rather than be dragged into it, kicking and screaming, by an irate public after irretrievable investments had been made in the largest information market of them all. The social problems of the information utility are so vast that no one agency, industry, or interest group can span them without the continued cooperation of the other interests. And new problems are likely to arise so rapidly that only the most powerful method available—scientific method on a broad social scale—can develop the social knowledge and techniques necessary to solve these problems in real time.

Assuming that the proposal for prototype experimental information utilities is desirable, there are several immediate steps that could be pursued. Three are singled out below.

One is to perform systems analyses of proposed computer utility prototypes in sufficient detail that the basic working structure of such prototypes would be spelled out, leading to working estimates of system cost-effectiveness. This type of analysis requires an appropriate interdisciplinary team to mesh all the parts together.

A second step is to try out leading concepts for experimental computer utilities on a small and easily manageable scale in a live setting. One approach is to use a laboratory to test information users in an online setting. Another approach is to instrument a working time-sharing system, with appropriate recording, reduction, and analysis tools superimposed on normal operations, in order to tap user behavior along lines most relevant to computer utility problems. Many of the hypotheses and questions raised in this book could be systematically examined in either of these settings. Such experience would be invaluable in developing pilot methodology and supportive findings to be applied on a larger scale in the recommended cooperative social prototype.

A third and crucial step is to cultivate the interest and cooperation of other parties essential for large-scale social experimentation, using prototype information utilities for one or more specific communities of users. Such efforts would be greatly facilitated by timely guidance from new commissions on information policy at national and state levels. This is an educational and motivational effort to effect the necessary social cooperation required to start working on feasible community prototypes. The goal of this step is to arrive at an authorized charter agreed upon by cognizant interests to initiate the design and development of initial experimental prototypes. This would lead in turn to techniques for open social evaluation of prototype results. Demonstrated initiative in this area could act as a pacesetter for communities throughout the country. Such initiative would go a long way toward making the information utility the hallmark of enlightened public service for the computer-catalyzed society of tomorrow.

APPENDIX: CADET QUESTIONNAIRES AND DATA FORMS

A. PRETEST/POSTTEST QUESTIONNAIRE

Instructions

Please fill out the attached questionnaire as completely and accurately as you can. Your full cooperation is essential for the success of this study. The information gathered in this experiment will contribute toward long-range planning at the Air Force Academy for the future configuration of computer facilities and for more effective methods of teaching computer science courses.

You will not be graded on your responses to this and the other questionnaires and forms that you will fill out in connection with this study. Neither will any student be listed or mentioned by name in the report describing the results. However, since filling out these questionnaires is a requirement of this course, your instructor will notify you if you fail to complete them.

The forms have been designed for rapid and easy completion, with most items self-explanatory.

1. Every questionnaire page requires your name, in case it gets separated from the other pages. Fill in your name for every sheet.

2. For rating scales varying from zero to nine, circle the number that best represents your evaluation.

3. For completion items, make sure that you are using the correct units when filling in the data. Write clearly so that transcription errors will be minimized when the data are keypunched for analysis.

4. Fill the forms out in *pencil* so that you will be able to correct errors more easily.

5. If you have any questions concerning any items, check with your instructor.

PRETEST/POSTTEST QUESTIONNAIRE

Student Name________________ Instructor________________
Course/Section________________ Date________________

Do not write in this space		
(1-13)	14	15

Do not write in this space

1. How many months experience have you had using batch processing systems? ____ ____ (16-17)

2. How many months experience have you had using time-sharing systems? ____ ____ (18-19)

3. How many months experience have you had working with computer languages and computer systems? ____ ____ (20-21)

4. What is the value of the batch processing system in helping you to analyze and solve computer-related problems?

   0 1 2 3 4 5 6 7 8 9

   No Value ... Great Value ____ (22-23)

5. What is the value of the time-sharing system in helping you to analyze and solve computer-related problems?

   0 1 2 3 4 5 6 7 8 9

   No Value ... Great Value ____ (24-25)

6. What is your estimate of the long-term value of batch vs. time-sharing for analyzing and solving data processing problems that you are likely to encounter over the course of your career?

   0 1 2 3 4 5 6 7 8 9

   Batch Superior ... The Same ... Time-Sharing Superior ____ (26-27)

Student Name________________________________

Answer each of the following questions with *T* for time-sharing, *B* for batch, or *U* for undecided—whichever best represents your opinion—in the blank space next to each item. Since we are interested in your attitudes toward these two computing systems, try to minimize the number of undecided responses.

Question	Answer	Do not write in this space
7. Which mode is more effective for coding and assembling your program?	____	____ (28)
8. Which mode is more effective for debugging your program?	____	____ (29)
9. Which mode provides more reliable and dependable service?	____	____ (30)
10. Which mode results in a faster solution of your problem?	____	____ (31)
11. Which mode results in a more efficient (shorter and faster-running) program?	____	____ (32)
12. Which mode makes it easier for you to organize your work in your own way and to proceed at your own pace?	____	____ (33)
13. Which mode is easier to learn and understand?	____	____ (34)
14. Which mode is more challenging and interesting?	____	____ (35)
15. Which mode makes it easier for you to break your problem up into small, manageable pieces for stepwise solution?	____	____ (36)
16. Which mode is more effective in helping you to see your problem as a whole, in its entirety?	____	____ (37)
17. Which mode allows you to exploit available computer system facilities more fully?	____	____ (38)

18. Which mode leads to greater insight in problem-solving?	____	____ (39)
19. Which mode leads to greater creativity in arriving at new and unusual solutions?	____	____ (40)

Student Name______________________________

		Do not write in this space
20. Which mode is more helpful in detecting and understanding errors?	____	____ (41)
21. Which mode is more helpful in correcting errors?	____	____ (42)
22. Which mode is more effective for self-teaching?	____	____ (43)
23. Which mode permits you to explore and try out more alternative solutions?	____	____ (44)
24. Which mode is more effective for short, simple problems?	____	____ (45)
25. Which mode is more effective for long, complex problems?	____	____ (46)
26. Which mode is more useful for well-structured problems with fixed solutions?	____	____ (47)
27. Which mode is more useful for open-end problems with many possible solutions?	____	____ (48)
28. Which mode is more effective for unskilled users?	____	____ (49)
29. Which mode is more effective for skilled users?	____	____ (50)
30. Which mode is more frustrating to work with?	____	____ (51)

31. What is your opinion of the value of these questionnaires? (Check one alternative) ____ ____ (52)

0	An annoying imposition, valueless	____
1	Time-consuming, marginal value	____
2	Moderate value	____
3	Well worth the time	____

B. WORK LOG

Instructions

The attached work log should be filled out accurately and completely. It contains key cost-effectiveness measures for comparative evaluation and time-sharing and batch processing. You will not be graded on these forms, nor will your name be used in any reports on this study. This data are a requirement for your course. All items on the Work Log are objective, fill-in questions, requiring a minimum of your time and effort to provide us with the desired information.

Fill all items in with *pencil* for easy correction of errors. Enter your data at the time you do your work—do not fill it in at a later time when the details have been forgotten.

The items are filled out as follows. Enter appropriate identification information at the top of the Work Log (student name, course and section, problem number, instructor, and computer mode).

1. *Work Session:* this is the fundamental unit of work. It refers to each integral block of time that you devoted to work on your problem. Each work session is numbered in order, starting with one.

2. *Date:* month, day, and year; e g, 11/25/68.

3. *Location:* D = at your desk, away from the computer.
   C = computer room, but not at the time-sharing terminal.
   T = time-sharing terminal.

   Combination responses may be listed. For combination entries, indicate the category where you spent most of your time for the given work session. For example, an entry of D, C means that most of the time was spent at your desk, with less time in the computer room.

4. *Start Time:* hours and minutes, e g, 14:35.

5. *Completion Time:* same.

6. *Elapsed Productive Time:* minutes, e g, 73: normally this entry should be the difference between items 4 and 5, but if you had a significant interruption during this period with no productive work (e g, waiting for the equipment, a long coffee break, some other school activity) subtract out the nonproductive time.

7. *Activity:* list any combination of the three following activities for this entry, in order of time spent on each.

   PF: Problem familiarization; familiarization with instruction manuals, console, or programming language; studying the problem, organizing the work, flow charting, etc., but before coding a possible solution.

   C: Coding possible program solutions, includes initial run preparation.

   D: Debugging, both syntax and logic, after an initial program has been assembled.

   (e g, a response of C, D means coding and debugging were done with more time spent in coding.)

Items 8 through 12 are for work sessions involving work at time-sharing consoles.

8. *Waiting Time for Terminal:* in minutes, how long you had to "hang around" and wait for an available terminal before you could log in.

9. *Productive Console Time:* productive time at the terminal, total useful working time in minutes between logging in and logging off at the console over the complete work session. If you logged in more than once, enter total useful time, excluding waiting time, system down time, or other nonproductive interruptions.

10. *Program Runs:* number of attempted runs for the problem program, whether or not the runs were successful; this is equivalent to the number of times the RUN command was executed for time-sharing, or the number of times the card deck was submitted for batch processing.

11. *System Failures:* number of times the central system or input/output equipment went down or would not work while you were logged in at the console. Enter 0 if no failures occurred.

12. *Response Time Rating:* from your point of view with respect to your own natural pace at the terminal, the computer response time to your commands during this console session was:

0	Very Poor	3	Good
1	Poor	4	Very Good
2	Fair		

    Enter the number that best describes your evaluation.

Items 13 through 18 are for batch runs only.

13. *Key Punch Waiting Time:* in minutes, how long you had to "hang around" and wait for the key punch equipment.

14. *Type of Submission:* deck or coding form, enter D or C.

15. *Submission Time:* date, hours and minutes, e g, 11/25/68; 15:09.

16. *Job Time:* clock time at which job was run, in date, hours, and minutes, listed on printout.

17. *Pickup Time:* time when you picked up your results, date, hours, and minutes.

18. *Syntax Errors:* number of computer detected syntax errors, as listed on output.

The remaining items are filled out after the problem has been completed.

19. *Total Man-Hours:* the sum of "Elapsed Productive Time" (item 6) over all work sessions. This item represents the total time that you put into this problem. Hours and minutes.

20. *Elapsed Time:* the difference between actual start date and actual completion date for this problem, in days, rounded off to the nearest whole day.

21. *Total Program Runs:* the sum of all program runs for this problem (item 10 for time-sharing users, machine runs for batch users).

If these work logs are filled out before you complete your problem, use additional forms as necessary. Each data sheet has room for "comments." Fill in any information that you believe significant for evaluating your data.

Student Name________________ Instructor________________

Course/Section__________ Problem__________ Time-Sharing__________ or Batch_____

Do not write in this space	
(1-13)	14

WORK LOG: both modes

(15-16) Work Session	(17-20) Date (day mo., yr.)	(21-23) Location (D: desk C: computer room T: t/s terminal)	(24-27) Start Time (hrs., min.)	(28-31) Completion Time (hrs., min.)	(32-34) Elapsed Productive Time (min.)	(35-37) Activity (PF: prob. formulat. C: coding D: debugging)
1						
2						
3						
4						
5						
6						
7						
8						
9						
10						

Comments:

Student Name__________ Instructor__________

Course/Section__________ Problem__________ Time-Sharing__________ or Batch__________

Do not write in this space	
	0
(1-13)	14

WORK LOG: time-sharing runs only

	(15-16) Work Session	(17-19) Waiting Time for Terminal (min.)	(20-22) Productive Console Time (min.)	(23-25) Program Runs	(26-28) System Failures	(29) Response Time Rating (0, very poor; 4, very good)
1						
2						
3						
4						
5						
6						
7						
8						
9						
10						

Comments:

Student Name________________ Instructor________________

Course/Section________ Problem________ Time-Sharing________ or Batch________

Do not write in this space	
	1
(1-13)	14

WORK LOG: batch runs only

(15-16) Work Session	(17-19) Key Punch Waiting Time (min.)	(20) Type of Submission (D: deck C: coding form)	(21-24) (25-28) Submission Time (date, hrs., min.)	(29-32) (33-36) Job Time (date, hrs., min.)	(37-40) (41-44) Pickup Time (date, hrs., min.)	(45-46) Syntax Errors (listed on (output)
1						
2						
3						
4						
5						
6						
7						
8						
9						
10						

Comments:

Student Name__________ Instructor__________
Course/Section______ Problem______ Time-Sharing____ or Batch____

Do not write in this space

(1-14)

WORK LOG: summary form

		Do not write in this space
19. Total Man-Hours (hours and minutes)	______	______ (15-18)
20. Elapsed Time (days and hours)	______	______ (19-22)
21. Total Program Runs	______	______ (23-25)

22. (Time-sharing cadets only)
In meeting my class problem needs for machine availability when I wanted it, and in getting dependable service while working with it, I found the time-sharing system to be:

Very Poor 0 1 2 3 4 5 6 7 8 9 Excellent ______ (26)

23. (Batch cadets only)
In meeting my individual needs for this class problem, I found the turn around time and the dependability of batch service to be:

Very Poor 0 1 2 3 4 5 6 7 8 9 Excellent ______ (27)

What was your greatest difficulty with computer system service?

What is your recommendation for reducing or eliminating this difficulty?

C. PROBLEM QUESTIONNAIRE

Instructions

This questionnaire is to be filled in by each student after he completes each class problem and turns it in to his instructor. You will not be graded on your responses to these items, nor will any student be mentioned by name in reports concerning this research. However, since these questionnaires are a course requirement, your instructor will notify you if you fail to furnish the requested information.

The attached questionnaire consists of two parts. The first consists of objective items and the second has open-ended questions. The objective portion is largely self-explanatory. Rating scale questions should be answered by circling the value of the integer (ranging from zero to nine) that best fits your personal evaluation. The other objective items are completion questions—make sure you understand the measurement unit specified in such questions. The last item asks you to estimate proportions of your total time spent in various problem-solving activities. Your entries should add up to 100% for more useful comparability of results. Answer your questionnaire in *pencil* so that errors may be more easily corrected.

The second part requires short, verbal responses. In most cases, a single sentence or part of a sentence should be sufficient. Explain your ideas in your own words, but take care that the ideas are clear and communicable. This part of the questionnaire is exploratory, and, among other objectives, we are looking for useful new leads from your comments. If you have any questions, check with your instructor.

Student Name______________________ Instructor______________________

Course/Section______________ Problem______________ Time-Sharing__________ or Batch__________

Do not write in this space

(1-13) 14

PROBLEM QUESTIONNAIRE

Do not write in this space

1. How useful was the computer system you worked with (batch or time-sharing) in helping you solve your class problem?

   0 1 2 3 4 5 6 7 8 9

   Useless ... Very Useful

   ______ (15-16)

2. How satisfied are you with your final program solution?

   0 1 2 3 4 5 6 7 8 9

   Not at All ... Completely Satisfied

   ______ (17-18)

3. How useful would the other computer system have been in helping you solve your class problem?

   0 1 2 3 4 5 6 7 8 9

   Useless ... Very Useful

   ______ (19-20)

4. How much effort and attention did you divert from your other courses because of this problem?

   0 1 2 3 4 5 6 7 8 9

   None ... A Great Deal

   ______ (21-22)

5. When did you develop the basic concept or insight that led to your successful solution of this problem? After ________ hours of work.

   ______ (23-25)

6. Approximately what percentage of your total time on this problem was spent on the following?

   a. General Concept Time ________% ______ (26-27)
   b. Program Coding and Debugging Time ________% ______ (28-29)
   c. Time Waiting for Computer Results ________% ______ (30-31)
   d. Time Analyzing Computer Results ________% ______ (32-33)
   e. Reacquaintance Time ________% ______ (34-35)
   f. Total ________%

PROBLEM QUESTIONNAIRE

Student Name____

7. What was your greatest difficulty in solving this problem?

8. What is your recommendation for reducing or eliminating this difficulty?

9. What is the most important insight that you arrived at in solving this problem?

PROBLEM QUESTIONNAIRE

Student Name____

10. What information or circumstances were necessary to make this insight possible for you?

11. Did this insight occur at your desk (away from the computer), or at the terminal, at some other place, or when you were not working on the problem?

12. Name the main stages of problem-solving that you followed in arriving at your program solution.

REFERENCES

CHAPTER 1

Barmack, Joseph E., and Sinaiko, H. Wallace. 1966. Human factors problems in computer-generated graphic displays. Arlington, Va.: Institute for Defense Analyses, Study S-234.

Biluzer, D., and Easley, P. 1962. Description and use of a computer-controlled teaching system. *In Proceedings of the National Electronics Conference,* pp. 787-92.

Cohen, A.M. 1964. Changing small-group communications networks. In *Readings in managerial psychology.* Edited by H.J. Leavitt and L.R. Pondy, pp. 391-405. Chicago: University of Chicago Press.

Corbató, F.J.; Merwin-Daggett, M.; and Daley, R.C. 1962. An experimental time-sharing system. In *Proceedings of the Spring Joint Computer Conference,* pp. 335-44.

Davis, Ruth M. 1966. Man-machine communication. In *Annual review of information science and technology.* Edited by Carlos A. Cuadra, pp. 221-54. New York: Wiley.

Emerson, Marvin. 1965. The "small" computer versus time-shared systems. *Computers and automation.* September: 18-20.

Fano, R.M., and Corbató, F.J. 1966. Time-sharing on computers. *Scientific American* 215: 128-40.

Festinger, L.; Schachter, S.; and Back, K. 1950. *Social pressures in informal groups.* New York: Harper and Row.

Gold, Michael. 1967. Methodology for evaluating time-shared computer usage. Ph.D. dissertation, Massachusetts Institute of Technology, Alfred P. Sloan School of Management.

Holland, James C. 1960. Teaching psychology by a teaching machine program (unpublished). Harvard University Psychology Department, Cambridge, Mass.

Leavitt, H.J. 1958. *Managerial psychology.* Chicago: University of Chicago Press.

Lynch, W.C. 1967. Description of a high-capacity, fast turnaround university computer center. In *Proceedings of the 22nd National Conference Association for Computing Machinery,* pp. 273-88. Washington, D.C.: Thompson Book Company.

Macdonald, Neil. 1965. A time-shared computer system—the disadvantages. *Computer and automation.* September: 21-22.

Mitnick, L. 1966. Man-machine interface: Implications for time-shared systems from human interactions. Schenectady, N. Y.: General Electric Company, Technical Information Series No. 65DSD 200.

Patrick, R.L. 1963. So you want to go on-line? *Datamation* 9:25-27.

Pollock, William T., and Gildner, Gilbert G.G. 1963. Study of computer manual input devices project 9678, Task 967801, Technical Documentary Report No. ESD-TDR-63-545, L.G. Hanscom Field, Bedford, Mass.

Porter, D. 1959. Some effects of year-long teaching machine instruction. In *Automatic teaching: the state of the art,* edited by E. Galanter, pp. 85-90. New York: Wiley.

Roethlisberger, F. J., and Dickson, W.J. 1939. Management and the worker. Cambridge, Mass: Harvard University Press.

Sackman, H. 1967. *Computers, system science, and evolving society.* New York: Wiley.

Schwartz, Jules I.; Coffman, Edward G.; and Weissman, Clark. 1964. A general purpose time-sharing system. In *American Federation of Information Processing Societies Conference Proceedings, Spring Joint Computer Conference* 25:397-411.

Shaw, C.J. 1964. The JOSS system. *Datamation* 10: 32-36.

Weinwurm, George F. 1965. Research in the management of computer programming. Santa Monica, Calif.: System Development Corporation, SP-2059.

Wiener, Norbert. 1954. *The human use of human beings.* New York: Doubleday.

———1964. God and Golem Inc. Cambridge, Mass.: The M.I.T. Press.

CHAPTER 2

Bryan, D.G. 1967. JOSS: 20,000 hours at a console—a statistical summary. In *AFIPS Conference Proceedings Fall Joint Computer Conference* 31: 769-77.

Erikson, W.J. 1966. A pilot study of interactive versus noninteractive debugging. Santa Monica, Calif.: System Development Corporation, TM-3296.

———1967. An analytical cost comparison of computer operating systems. Santa Monica, Calif.: System Development Corporation, TM-3525.

Gold, Michael M. 1967. Methodology for evaluating time-shared computer usage. Ph.D. dissertation, Massachusetts Institute of Technology, Alfred P. Sloan School of Management.

Grant, E.E., and Sackman, H. 1967. An exploratory investigation of programmer performance under on-line and off-line conditions. *IEEE transactions on human factors in electronics* HFE-8: 33-48.

McIssaac, Paul V. 1966. Job descriptions and scheduling in the SDC Q-32 time sharing system. Santa Monica, Calif., System Development Corporation, TM-2996.

Parkhill, D.F. 1966. *The challenge of the computer utility.* Reading, Mass.: Addison-Wesley.

Popell, S.D., et al. 1966. *Computer time-sharing.* Englewood Cliffs, N.J.: Prentice-Hall.

Raynaud, Thierry G. 1967. Operational analysis of a computer center. Operations Research Center Technical Report No. 32. Massachusetts Institute of Technology, Cambridge, Mass.

Scherr, Allan L. 1967. *Analysis of time-shared computer systems.* Research Monograph No. 36. Cambridge, Mass.: The M.I.T. Press.

Shaw, J.W. 1965. JOSS: Experience with an experimental computing service for user at remote typewriter consoles. Santa Monica, Calif.: The RAND Corporation, P-3149.

Totschek, Robert A. 1966. An empirical investigation into the behavior of the SDC time-sharing system. Santa Monica, Calif.: System Development Corporation, SP-2191.

CHAPTER 3

Adams, Jeanne, and Cohen, Leonard. 1969. Time-sharing vs. instant batch processing. *Computers and Automation* March: 30-34.

Berger, Raymond M.; Rigney, Joseph W.; Wilson, Robert C.; and Teplitzky, Frank. 1966. Computer personnel selection and criterion development: III. The basic programming knowledge test. University of Southern California, Los Angeles, Calif.

Erikson, W.J. 1966. A pilot study of interactive versus noninteractive debugging. Santa Monica, Calif.: System Development Corporation, TM-3296.

Gold, M. 1967. Methodology for evaluating time-shared computer usage. Ph.D. dissertation, Massachusetts Institute of Technology, Alfred P. Sloan School of Management.

Grant, E.E., and Sackman, H. 1967. An exploratory investigation of programer performance under on-line and off-line conditions. *IEEE transactions on human factors in electronics* HFE-8: 33-48.

Kennedy, Phyllis R. 1965. The TINT users' guide. Santa Monica, Calif.: System Development Corporation, TM-1933/000/03.

Sackman, H. 1969. Experimental evaluation of time-sharing and batch processing in teaching computer science. Santa Monica, Calif.: System Development Corporation, SP-3411.

Sackman, H., and Gold, Michael M. 1968. Time-sharing versus batch processings: an experimental inquiry into human problem-solving. Joint Study by System Development Corporation and Carnegie-Mellon University, SP-3110.

Samelson, K., and Bauer, F. 1960. Sequential Formula Translation. *Communications of the ACM* 3: 76-83.

Schatzoff, M.; Tsao, R.; and Wiig, R. 1967. An experimental comparison of time-sharing and batch processing. *Communications of the ACM* 10: 261-65.

Schwartz, Jules I. 1965. Observations on time-shared systems. *20th National ACM Conference,* Cleveland, Ohio, August 24-26, pp. 525-542.

Schwartz, Jules I.; Coffman, Edward G.; and Weissman, Clark. 1964. A general purpose time-sharing system. In *American Federation of Information Processing Societies Conference Proceedings, Spring Joint Computer Conference* 25: 397-411.

Smith, Lyle B. 1967. A comparison of batch processing and instant turnaround. *Communications of the ACM* 10: 495-500.

CHAPTER 4

Adams, Jeanne, and Cohen, Leonard. 1969. Time-sharing vs. instant batch processing. *Computers and Automation* March 30-34.

Erikson, W.J. 1966. A pilot study of interactive versus noninteractive debugging. Santa Monica, Calif.: System Development, TM-3296.

Grant, E.E., and Sackman, H. 1967. An exploratory investigation of programmer performance under on-line and off-line conditions. *IEEE transactions on human factors in electronics* HFE-8:33-48.

Sackman, H. 1967. *Computers, system science, and evolving society.* New York: Wiley.

Schatzoff, M.; Tsao, R.; and Wiig, R. 1967. An experimental comparison of time sharing and batch processing. *Communications of the ACM* 10: 261-65.

Smith, Lyle B. 1967. A comparison of batch processing and instant turnaround. *Communications of the ACM* 10: 495-500.

———1967. A survey of most frequent syntax and execution-time errors. Stanford Computation Center, Stanford University.

CHAPTER 5

Gold, Michael M. 1967. Methodology for evaluating time-shared computer usage. Ph.D. dissertation, Massachusetts Institute of Technology, Alfred P. Sloan School of Management.

McCormack, R.L. 1968. Statistical programs and services. Santa Monica, Calif.: System Development Corporation, N-23959.

Sackman, H., and Gold, Michael M. 1968. Time-sharing versus batch processing: an experimental inquiry into human problem-solving. Santa Monica Calif.: System Development Corporation, SP-3110.

CHAPTER 6

Harman, Harry H. 1967. *Modern factor analysis.* 2nd ed. Chicago: University of Chicago Press.

CHAPTER 7

Adams, Jeanne, and Cohen, Leonard. 1969. Time-sharing vs. instant batch processing. *Computers and Automation* March 30-34.

Schatzoff, M.; Tsao, R.; and Wiig, R. 1967. An experimental comparison of time sharing and batch processing. *Communications tions of the ACM* 10: 261-65.

CHAPTER 8

Sackman, H., and Gold, Michael M. 1968. Time-sharing versus batch processing: an experimental inquiry into human problem-solving. Santa Monica, Calif.: System Development Corporation, SP-3110.

Schatzoff, M.; Tsao, R.; and Wiig, R. 1967. An experimental comparison of time-sharing and batch processing. *Communications of the ACM* 10: 261-65.

United States Air Force Academy. 1967. Digital computers and selected applications. Computer Science 240, Colorado Springs, Colo.

Walker, Robert K. 1967. Preliminary reference manual for the RADC-GE 635/645 on-line computer system. Rome Air Development Center, EMI-TM-67-3. Grifiss Air Force Base, N. Y.

CHAPTER 9

Edwards, Allen L. 1946. *Statistical analysis.* New York: Rinehart.

Ezekiel, Mordecai, and Fox, Karl A. 1959. *Methods of correlation and regression analysis.* New York: Wiley.

CHAPTER 10

Harman, Harry H. 1967. *Modern factor analysis.* 2nd ed. Chicago: University of Chicago Press.

McCormack, R.L. 1968. Statistical programs and services. Santa Monica, Calif.: System Development Corporation, N-23959.

CHAPTER 12

Adams, Jeanne, and Cohen, Leonard. 1969. Time-sharing vs. instant batch processing. *Computers and automation* March: 30-34.

Berelson, Bernard, and Steiner, Gary A. 1964. *Human behavior*. New York: Harcourt, Brace & World.

Berger, Raymond M.; Rigney, Joseph W.; Wilson, Robert C.; and Teplitzky, Frank. 1966. Computer personnel selection and criterion development: III. The basic programming knowledge test. University of Southern California, Los Angeles, Calif.

Erikson, W.J. 1966. A pilot study of interactive versus noninteractive debugging. Santa Monica, Calif.: System Development Corporation, TM-3296.

Frye, Charles H., and Pack, Elbert C. 1969. A comparison of three computer operating modes for high school problem-solving. Santa Monica, Calif. System Development Corporation, TM-4356/001/00.

Ghiselli, Edwin E. 1966. *The validity of occupational aptitude tests.* New York: Wiley.

Gold, M. 1967. Methodology for evaluating time-shared computer usage. Ph.D. dissertation, Massachusetts Institute of Technology, Alfred P. Sloan School of Management.

Grant, E.E., and Sackman, H. 1967. An exploratory investigation of programmer performance under on-line and off-line conditions. *IEEE transactions on human factors in electronics* HFE-8: 33-48.

Haefele, John W. 1962. Creativity and innovation. New York: Reinhold.

Helmholtz, H. 1926. *The art of thought.* Edited by G. Wallas. New York: Harcourt, Brace & World.

Kohler, Wolfgang. 1947. *Gestalt psychology.* New York: Liveright.

Mackworth, Norman H. 1965. Originality. *American psychologist* 20: 51-66.

Mayer, David B., and Stalnaker, Ashford W. 1968. Selection and evaluation of computer personnel—the research history of Sig/CPR. In *Proceedings of 23rd National Conference, Association for Computing Machinery,* pp. 657-70. Princeton, N.J.: Brandon/Systems Press, Inc.

Osborn, Alex. 1957. *Applied imagination.* New York: Scribner's.

Rossman, Joseph. 1931. *The psychology of the inventor.* Washington, D.C.: Inventor's Publishing Company.

Sackman, H. 1967. *Computers, system science, and evolving society.* New York: Wiley.

Sackman, H., and Nie, Norman, eds. 1970. *The information utility and social choice.* Montvale, N.J.: AFIPS Press.

Schatzoff, M.; Tsao, R.; and Wiig, R. 1967. An experimental comparison of time sharing and batch processing. *Communications of the ACM* 10: 261-65.

Slutz, Ralph J., et al. 1968. Longe-range computer requirements for ESSA Boulder. ESSA Research Laboratories, Boulder, Colo.

Smith, Lyle B. 1967. A comparison of batch processing and instant turnaround. *Communications of the ACM* 10: 495-500.

Sprague, Richard O. 1969. *Information utilities.* Englewood Cliffs, N.J.: Prentice-Hall.

Stevens, S.S. 1951. *Handbook of experimental psychology* New York: Wiley.

Wallas, G., ed. 1926. *The art of thought.* New York: Harcourt, Brace.

Woodworth, Robert S., and Scholsberg, Harold. 1954. *Experimental psychology.* New York: Holt, Rinehart & Winston.

Young, J.W. 1940. *Technique for producing ideas.* Chicago: Advertising Publications, Inc.

INDEX